Praise for *Essential PHP Tools: Modules, Extensions, and Accelerators*:

"Sklar's writing is clear, concise, and accurate . . . The book is a definite recommendation for intermediate to advanced programmers both as a text and as a reference. It certainly has earned itself a spot on my frequently used bookshelf!"

—Timothy Boronczyk, Codewalkers (www.codewalkers.com)

"The tools are easy to find and useful, the documentation excellent, and the writing style easy to follow. All this makes Essential PHP Tools *a highly recommended book for anyone using PHP on their web server."*

—Harold McFarland, Midwest Book Review (www.midwestbookreview.com)

"From Pear packages to parsing XML files, this book is a huge time-saver to developing your own solutions."

—Richard Testani, AppleTalk weblog (www.apple-sauce.com/blogger/blogger.html)

Essential PHP Tools: Modules, Extensions, and Accelerators

DAVID SKLAR

APress Media, LLC

Essential PHP Tools: Modules, Extensions, and Accelerators

Originally published by Apress in 2004

ISBN 978-1-59059-280-9 ISBN 978-1-4302-0714-6 (eBook)
DOI 10.1007/978-1-4302-0714-6

Technical Reviewer: Adam Trachtenberg

Editorial Board: Steve Anglin, Dan Appleman, Gary Cornell, James Cox, Tony Davis, John Franklin, Chris Mills, Steve Rycroft, Dominic Shakeshaft, Julian Skinner, Jim Sumser, Karen Watterson, Gavin Wray, John Zukowski

Assistant Publisher: Grace Wong

Project Manager: Kylie Johnston

Copy Editor: Kim Wimpsett

Production Manager: Kari Brooks

Production Editor: Noemi Hollander

Proofreader: Thistle Hill Publishing Services, LLC

Compositor: Kinetic Publishing Services, LLC

Indexer: Valerie Perry

Artist: Kinetic Publishing Services, LLC

Cover Designer: Kurt Krames

Manufacturing Manager: Tom Debolski

Contents at a Glance

Contents

About the Author

David Sklar is an independent software development and strategic technology consultant. He was a cofounder and the Chief Technology Officer of Student.com and TVGrid.com. At both companies, David oversaw the development of varied systems that delivered personalized dynamic content to users around the world.

He created the PX (`http://px.sklar.com/`), which enables PHP users to exchange programs, after discovering PHP as a solution to his Web programming needs in 1996. Since then, David continues to rely on PHP for personal and professional projects. He is also the coauthor of *PHP Cookbook* (O'Reilly, 2002).

When away from the computer, David eats mini-donuts, plays records, and likes to cook. He is a principal of The Transparency Project, a nonprofit organization that coordinates data markup standards and builds tools that analyze publicly available political and campaign finance information. David lives in New York City and has a degree in Computer Science from Yale University.

Acknowledgments

Most important, a tremendous thanks to the authors of the software that this book is about: Dietrich Ayala, Stig Bakken, Marcus Boerger, Shane Caraveo, Daniel Cowgill, Tomas V.V. Cox, Adam Daniel, Edd Dumbill, James E. Flemer, Chuck Hagenbuch, Richard Heyes, Sterling Hughes, Martin Jansen, Dan Libby, John Lim, Arnaud Limbourg, Nick Lindridge, Bertrand Mansion, Monte Ohrt, Jon Parise, Derick Rethans, Rob Richards, George Schlossnagle, Yavor Shahpasov, Dmitry Stogov, Andrei Zmievski, and many other contributors.

Thanks also to the numerous coders, architects, bug-fixers, and other maintainers who have made PHP the powerful, popular language it is today.

Many people at Apress worked hard to make this book a reality: Martin Streicher (whose idea this book was in the first place), Kylie Johnson (who keeps the trains running on time), Kim Wimpsett (whose copyediting caught plenty of errors), and Doris Wong (who made sure the book is one people want to buy). Without Valerie Perry there would be no index, and without Kurt Krames there would be no cover. Thanks also to Christine Calderwood and John Ferguson. The feedback, discipline, and professionalism of everyone involved with this book is much appreciated.

Many people who don't work for Apress also made essential contributions to this book's completion: Stewart Ugelow and Max Goldberg provided server resources that allowed me to test and benchmark software in different environments, Adam Trachtenberg diligently reviewed the entire book, and Bertrand Mansion and George Schlossnagle each reviewed individual chapters.

And, in an entirely separate category, thanks to Susannah for encouragement and her eyelids' flutter.

Introduction

This introduction lays out who the book is written for, provides an overview of what is covered, and gives some background details on a package management utility you'll use to install many of the add-ons covered in the book.

Who This Book Is For

Although PHP has a lot of built-in functionality, many common Web programming tasks are simpler with add-on modules and packages. This book is for you if you are looking for an easier way to do these kinds of tasks with PHP:

- Access a database.
- Generate robust Web forms.
- Use a page templating system.
- Create or parse XML documents.
- Request or serve XML-RPC or SOAP methods.
- Send HTML or multipart e-mail messages.
- Authenticate users.
- Inspect your scripts with a debugger.
- Boost server performance without rewriting any code.

This book assumes you have a basic knowledge of PHP programming: You know how to perform tasks such as include files, write functions, create objects, and look in `$_REQUEST`, `$_GET`, or `$_POST` to find submitted form data.

However, to take advantage of the tips and explanations in this book, you definitely don't have to be an advanced PHP programmer. Each chapter covers the complete details of installing and using one or two modules, complete with plenty of examples. So if you've never heard of any of the packages discussed here, this book is perfect for you. You'll be exposed to a lot of high-quality PHP code that you can use, for free, to make your own programs better.

How This Book Is Organized

The book has five parts, and each chapter discusses one or more modules or add-ons that extend PHP's capabilities:

Part One, "Databases," discusses two database abstraction layers: PEAR DB in Chapter 1 and ADODB in Chapter 2. These packages each supply a standard set of functions for talking to many different kinds of databases. This is in contrast to PHP's native database access functions where, for example, you would use the `mysql_query()` function to send a query to a MySQL database but the `ociparse()` and `ociexecute()` functions to send a query to an Oracle database. The ADODB package provides an interface similar to the Microsoft ADO data access standard.

Part Two, "HTML," details two packages that assist you with common HTML generation tasks: HTML_QuickForm in Chapter 3 and Smarty in Chapter 4. HTML_QuickForm manages forms for you, taking care of details such as ensuring a standard layout for forms and preserving default values when a page is reloaded. Smarty is a comprehensive and powerful templating system, which helps you separate your application code from your page design. It also includes caching features that make your pages more efficient.

Part Three, "XML," explores parsing and using XML in PHP. Chapter 5 talks about the XML_Parser module, which provides an event-based parsing infrastructure. Chapters 6 and 7 deal with XML-RPC and SOAP, the two most popular XML-based remote procedure calling formats. These protocols let you call functions that run on remote servers and instantly use the results in your PHP programs. Chapter 8 introduces SimpleXML, an exciting PHP 5–only extension that is the most straightforward way to process small, uncomplicated XML documents in PHP.

Part Four, "Networking," focuses on two tasks: sending e-mail and authenticating users. Chapter 9 discusses how the Mail and Mail_mime modules make it easy to send e-mail messages with HTML, embedded images, and other advanced features. Chapter 10 shows you how to use the Auth and Auth_HTTP modules to implement flexible access control for your Web site.

Part Five, "Debugging, Caching, and Optimizing," goes behind the PHP scenes. Chapter 11 is an overview of PHP internals: the steps that PHP takes to parse and execute one of your scripts in response to a Web request. Chapter 12 shows you Xdebug, a debugger that helps you diagnose problems in your programs. With Xdebug, you can even pause a PHP script while it is running to examine variables and see what functions have been called. Chapter 13 analyzes three code cache modules. Also known as *accelerators*, these extensions enhance your server's speed without requiring you to rewrite any of your scripts.

About PEAR

PEAR, the PHP Extension and Application Repository, is a collection of PHP classes that perform various useful tasks such as talking to a SOAP server or creating an e-mail message with embedded images. You can browse the many classes that are part of PEAR at the PEAR Web site: `http://pear.php.net/`. Many of the classes and add-ons discussed in this book are from PEAR.

The PEAR package manager, a command line program named `pear`, helps you install, upgrade, and remove PEAR packages. This tool and some core PEAR classes are installed with new installations of PHP. You can also install them separately. The rest of this introduction shows you how to work with the `pear` command line tool.

Installing PEAR

The PEAR package manager is installed by default with PHP version 4.3.0 and later. If you're running an earlier version of PHP or you didn't install the package manager with PHP, then you need to follow a few steps to install it. The specific steps to take to install the package manager vary based on your operating system.

On Unix, the easiest way to install `pear` is by executing the following command:

```
# lynx -source http://go-pear.org/ | php
```

This downloads the content of the URL `http://go-pear.org/` and feeds that content, which is a PHP script, to your local PHP binary. The downloaded PHP script retrieves the `pear` program and associated support files from the PEAR Web site, configures them, and installs them.

If you don't have the text-based browser lynx installed, you can install `pear` by viewing `http://go-pear.org/` in a regular Web browser, saving the source code of the page to a file and then running the saved file through PHP. If you've saved the source of `http://go-pear.org` to `/tmp/go-pear.php`, for example, then run this:

```
# php /tmp/go-pear.php
```

On Windows, run the `go-pear.bat` batch file installed in your PHP directory. For example:

```
C:\> c:\php\go-pear.bat
```

The installation method of saving the contents of `http://go-pear.org/` and then running that saved file through PHP also works on Windows.

On both Unix and Windows, this installation process installs the `pear` package management program and some core PEAR packages that the package management program needs to function.

Using the Package Manager

The pear package manager accepts a number of commands that perform different package management operations. Because pear needs to be able to write to the directories that it installs modules into, you often need to run it as root. In this book, commands that should be run as root, such as pear shown next, are shown with a # prompt. The $ prompt is for commands you can run as a regular user. To get a list of the commands, run pear with no arguments:

```
# pear
Usage: pearcmd.php [options] command [command-options] <parameters>
Type "pearcmd.php help options" to list all options.
Type "pearcmd.php help <command>" to get the help for the specified command.
Commands:
build                   Build an Extension From C Source
bundle                  Unpacks a Pecl Package
clear-cache             Clear XML-RPC Cache
config-get              Show One Setting
config-help             Show Information About Setting
config-set              Change Setting
config-show             Show All Settings
cvsdiff                 Run a "cvs diff" for all files in a package
cvstag                  Set CVS Release Tag
download                Download Package
download-all            Downloads each available Package from master_server
info                    Display information about a package
install                 Install Package
list                    List Installed Packages
list-all                List All Packages
list-upgrades           List Available Upgrades
login                   Connects and authenticates to remote server
logout                  Logs out from the remote server
makerpm                 Builds an RPM spec file from a PEAR package
package                 Build Package
package-dependencies    Show package dependencies
package-validate        Validate Package Consistency
remote-info             Information About Remote Packages
remote-list             List Remote Packages
run-tests               Run Regression Tests
search                  Search remote package database
shell-test              Shell Script Test
sign                    Sign a package distribution file
uninstall               Un-install Package
upgrade                 Upgrade Package
upgrade-all             Upgrade All Packages
```

Many of the commands that pear supports are useful only to people producing packages. This introduction covers the five commands most useful for downloading and installing packages: list, install, upgrade, uninstall, and help.

To see what packages are installed, run pear list:

```
# pear list
Installed packages:
===================
Package         Version  State
Archive_Tar     1.1      stable
Console_Getopt  1.0      stable
DB              1.5.0RC1 stable
HTTP            1.2.1    stable
Mail            1.1.0    stable
Net_SMTP        1.2.3    stable
Net_Socket      1.0.1    stable
PEAR            1.3b3    beta
XML_Parser      1.0.1    stable
XML_RPC         1.0.4    stable
```

For each PEAR package that's installed on your machine, the pear list command shows you the name of the package, the version of the package that's installed, and the state of the installed version; packages are generally in the stable state, but sometimes you'll want to have an alpha or beta package installed.

To add a package to your setup, use pear install. For example, to install the Mail_mime package, which is discussed in Chapter 9, use this:

```
# pear install Mail_mime
downloading Mail_Mime-1.2.1.tar ...
Starting to download Mail_Mime-1.2.1.tar (-1 bytes)
.................done: 77,312 bytes
install ok: Mail_Mime 1.2.1
```

When you tell it to install something, the package manager downloads the code archive for the package from http://pear.php.net, unpacks the individual files from the archive, and copies them to the right place in your PHP include path. To see what directory the files end up in, use the pear config-get command to look at the php_dir package manager configuration variable:

```
# pear config-get php_dir
php_dir=/usr/local/lib/php
```

This means that new PEAR modules are installed under /usr/local/lib/php.

To work properly, some packages require that other packages be installed. To install a package and all of its dependencies, pass the -a flag to pear install. For example, the XML_Beautifier package depends on the XML_Util package. Installing XML_Beautifier without the -a flag produces an error:

```
# pear install XML_Beautifier
downloading XML_Beautifier-1.0.1.tgz ...
Starting to download XML_Beautifier-1.0.1.tgz (9,837 bytes)
.....done: 9,837 bytes
requires package 'XML_Util' >= 0.5
XML_Beautifier: Dependencies failed
```

With the -a flag, pear downloads and installs XML_Util as well:

```
# pear install -a XML_Beautifier
downloading XML_Beautifier-1.0.1.tgz ...
Starting to download XML_Beautifier-1.0.1.tgz (9,837 bytes)
.....done: 9,837 bytes
downloading XML_Util-0.5.2.tgz ...
Starting to download XML_Util-0.5.2.tgz (6,540 bytes)
...done: 6,540 bytes
install ok: XML_Util 0.5.2
install ok: XML_Beautifier 1.0.1
```

Use the upgrade command when there is a newer version of a package than the one you have installed. This command downloads the most recent version of the package, removes the installed version, and installs the newer version. To use upgrade, pass it the name of the package to upgrade. For example, if Mail_mime 1.2 is installed, this is how to upgrade to version 1.2.1:

```
# pear upgrade Mail_mime
downloading Mail_Mime-1.2.1.tgz ...
Starting to download Mail_Mime-1.2.1.tgz (15,268 bytes)
.....done: 15,268 bytes
upgrade ok: Mail_Mime 1.2.1
```

If you already have the most recent version of a package installed, upgrade prints a message telling you so:

```
# pear upgrade Mail_mime
Package 'Mail_Mime-1.2.1' already installed, skipping
```

When you want to remove a package, use `uninstall`. This deletes a package and its files from your system. For example, to uninstall the Mail_mime package, use this:

```
# pear uninstall Mail_mime
uninstall ok: Mail_Mime
```

By default, the package manager won't uninstall a package on which another installed package depends. The SOAP package depends on the Mail_mime package, so if SOAP is installed, the package manager reports an error if you attempt to uninstall Mail_mime:

```
# pear uninstall Mail_Mime
Package 'soap' depends on 'Mail_Mime'
uninstall failed
```

Tell `pear` to ignore package dependencies and force uninstallation by passing the `-n` flag after the `uninstall` command:

```
# pear uninstall -n Mail_mime
uninstall ok: Mail_Mime
```

To learn more about each `pear` command, use the `help` command. Pass a command name to `pear help` to get more information about it. For example:

```
# pear help uninstall
pearcmd.php uninstall [options] <package> ...
Uninstalls one or more PEAR packages.  More than one package may be
specified at once.

Options:
  -n, --nodeps
        ignore dependencies, uninstall anyway
  -r, --register-only
        do not remove files, only register the packages as not installed
  -R DIR, --installroot=DIR
        root directory used when installing files (ala PHP's INSTALL_ROOT)
  --ignore-errors
        force install even if there were errors
```

The `help` command is especially useful for listing all the options that each `pear` command accepts. These options let you perform tasks such as ignoring package dependencies and changing the directory that `pear` stores its packages.

Downloading the Code

To follow along with the examples, you can download all the code used in this book. Go to the Downloads section of the Apress Web site (`http://www.apress.com/`). All the code from this book is packaged into one zip file. Inside the zip file is a directory for each chapter in the book. Inside each directory is a plain-text file for each code snippet or example from that chapter.

Part One

Databases

CHAPTER 1

Accessing Databases with DB

PEAR DB PROVIDES a consistent set of methods for using a relational database no matter what database you're using. It supports the following PHP database extensions: FrontBase, Informix, InterBase, Microsoft SQL Server, mSQL, ODBC, MySQL, Sybase, OCI8, and PostgreSQL. A driver that supports new features in version 4 of MySQL is also in the works. This chapter covers DB version 1.4.

Exploring a Simple DB Example

Retrieving a result and displaying it in a table with DB looks like this:

```
// Load the DB code
require 'DB.php';

// Connect to the database
$dbh = DB::connect('mysql://user:password@host/database');

// Send a SELECT query to the database
$sth = $dbh->query('SELECT flavor, price, calories FROM ice_cream');

// Check if any rows were returned
if ($sth->numRows()) {
    print "<table>";
    print "<tr><th>Ice Cream Flavor</th><th>Price per Serving</th><th>Calories➥
 per Serving</th></tr>";
    // Retrieve each row
    while ($row = $sth->fetchRow()) {
        // And print out the elements in the row
        print "<tr><td>$row[0]</td><td>$row[1]</td><td>$row[2]</td></tr>\n";
    }
    print "</table>";
} else {
     print "No results";
}
```

DB::connect() is a static class method that returns an object. You interact with the database by calling methods on this object. In this example, the object is assigned to the variable $dbh, which stands for *database handle*. The argument to DB::connect() is a Data Source Name (DSN). DSNs are explained in the next section.

Next, you send a query to the database server with the $dbh->query() method. This method returns a statement handle that is assigned to $sth. This variable is a DB_Result object with methods that return information about the retrieved rows. The $sth->numRows() method returns the number of retrieved rows. In this example, it's used to determine whether to print the retrieved data or just a message saying that no data was retrieved. The "Query Information" section explains methods such as numRows() that provide information about a query.

The $sth->fetchRow() method returns an array that contains one row of data retrieved from the database. The statement handle maintains an internal counter of what the "next" row to return is, so the first time you call fetchRow(), you get the first row retrieved from the database; the second time you call fetchRow(), you get the second row, and so on. After all retrieved rows have been returned, fetchRow() returns NULL instead of a result array. This makes it easy to use in a while() loop as the example does.

The fetchRow() method returns an indexed array with retrieved data. The first field requested by the SELECT query is in element 0 of the array, the second field in element 1, and so on. In this example, $row[0] is the value of the flavor column in each row, $row[1] is the price column, and $row[2] is the calories column. You can also retrieve rows as associative arrays or objects. The "Sending Queries and Retrieving Results" section discusses fetchRow() in more detail.

Introducing DSNs

As shown in the previous example, the argument to DB::connect() tells DB about the database to which you want to connect. This argument is a DSN, which has the following form:

```
databasetype://username:password@hostname/databasename
```

databasetype is the type of database you're connecting to: MySQL, Oracle, ODBC, Sybase, and so on. Table 1-1 shows the acceptable databasetype values.

Table 1-1. The `databasetype` *Values in DSNs*

databasetype	Database
fbsql	FrontBase
ibase	InterBase
ifx	Informix
mssql	Microsoft SQL Server
msql	mSQL
mysql	MySQL
oci8	Oracle 7, Oracle 8, Oracle 8*i*
odbc	ODBC
pgsql	PostgreSQL
sybase	Sybase

The `username` and `password` components of a DSN are the username and password necessary for connecting to the database server, and the `hostname` component is the IP address or host name of the machine on which the database server is running. The `databasename` component is the name of the individual database to access.

If the database server is running on the same machine as your Web server, you can connect to it by specifying `localhost` as the host name or by using a slightly different syntax to specify a Unix socket to connect to instead:

```
$dbh = DB::connect('mysql://user:password@unix(socketpath)/database');
```

For example, if the filename of the Unix socket you want to use is `/tmp/mysql.sock`, your DSN would look like this:

```
$dbh = DB::connect('mysql://user:password@unix(/tmp/mysql.sock)/database');
```

Sending Queries and Retrieving Results

As you saw in the "Exploring a Simple DB Example" section, the `DB::query()` method sends queries to the database. These can be `SELECT` queries that retrieve data from the database:

```
$sth = $dbh->query('SELECT * FROM ice_cream');
```

They can be INSERT, UPDATE, or DELETE queries that alter data in the database:

```
$res = $dbh->query("INSERT INTO ice_cream (flavor, price)
                    VALUES ('Chocolate',4.50)");
$res = $dbh->query("UPDATE ice_cream SET price = 5.95
                     WHERE flavor LIKE 'Vanilla'");
$res = $dbh->query("DELETE FROM ice_cream WHERE price < 2.00");
```

They can be queries that create, alter, or drop tables:

```
$res = $dbh->query('CREATE TABLE ice_cream (flavor VARCHAR(255),
                     price DECIMAL(6,2), calories INT)');
$res = $dbh->query('ALTER TABLE ice_cream ADD flavor_id INT UNSIGNED NOT NULL');
$res = $dbh->query('DROP TABLE ice_cream');
```

The query() method sends to the database whatever SQL you specify. If you specify an SQL query, then query() returns a DB_Result object that provides access to the returned data. The DB_Result::fetchRow() method returns one row from the retrieved data:

```
$sth = $dbh->query('SELECT flavor,price FROM ice_cream');
$row = $sth->fetchRow();
// Prints out the first retrieved row
print "Flavor: $row[0], Price: $row[1]\n";
// Prints out the second retrieved row
$row = $sth->fetchRow();
print "Flavor: $row[0], Price: $row[1]\n";
```

Each time you call fetchRow(), you get the next retrieved row. The fetchRow() method returns NULL when there are no more rows available. The fetchInto() method is similar to fetchRow(), but it puts the row of data directly into a variable instead of returning it:

```
$sth = $dbh->query('SELECT flavor,price FROM ice_cream');
$sth->fetchInto($row);
// Prints out the first retrieved row
print "Flavor: $row[0], Price: $row[1]\n";
```

By default, fetchRow() and fetchInto() arrange data retrieved from the database in an indexed array. You can pass either of them an additional argument to change that. The constant DB_FETCHMODE_ASSOC causes the data to be put in an associative array, and DB_FETCHMODE_OBJECT causes the data to be returned as properties of an object. Pass one of these constants as the only argument to fetchRow():

```
$sth = $dbh->query('SELECT flavor,price FROM ice_cream');
$row = $sth->fetchRow(DB_FETCHMODE_ASSOC);
// Prints out the first retrieved row
print "Flavor: $row[flavor], Price: $row[price]\n";
// Prints out the second retrieved row
$row = $sth->fetchRow(DB_FETCHMODE_OBJECT);
print "Flavor: $row->flavor, Price: $row->price\n";
```

Or, pass it as the second argument to fetchInto():

```
$sth = $dbh->query('SELECT flavor,price FROM ice_cream');
$sth->fetchInto($row,DB_FETCHMODE_ASSOC);
// Prints out the first retrieved row
print "Flavor: $row[flavor], Price: $row[price]\n";
// Prints out the second retrieved row
$sth->fetchInto($row,DB_FETCHMODE_OBJECT);
print "Flavor: $row->flavor, Price: $row->price\n";
```

The DB::setFetchMode() method sets a default fetch mode that is used on all subsequent calls to fetchRow() or fetchInto(). Pass setFetchMode() the constant that corresponds to the default fetch mode you want:

```
$dbh->setFetchMode(DB_FETCHMODE_ASSOC);
$sth = $dbh->query('SELECT flavor,price FROM ice_cream');
$row = $sth->fetchRow();
// Prints out the first retrieved row
print "Flavor: $row[flavor], Price: $row[price]\n";
// Prints out the second retrieved row
$row = $sth->fetchRow();
print "Flavor: $row[flavor], Price: $row[price]\n";
```

Aside from DB_FETCHMODE_ASSOC and DB_FETCHMODE_OBJECT, you can also use DB_FETCHMODE_ORDERED to specify the default behavior of an indexed array. For example, with DB_FETCHMODE_ORDERED, the first two columns are accessed as $row[0] and $row[1]:

```
$dbh->setFetchMode(DB_FETCHMODE_ORDERED);
$sth = $dbh->query('SELECT flavor,price FROM ice_cream');
$row = $sth->fetchRow();
// Prints out the first retrieved row
print "Flavor: $row[0], Price: $row[1]\n";
$row = $sth->fetchRow();
```

```
// Prints out the second retrieved row
print "Flavor: $row[0], Price: $row[1]\n";
```

With DB_FETCHMODE_OBJECT, the columns are accessed as $row->flavor and $row->price:

```
$dbh->setFetchMode(DB_FETCHMODE_OBJECT);
$sth = $dbh->query('SELECT flavor,price FROM ice_cream');
$row = $sth->fetchRow();
// Prints out the first retrieved row
print "Flavor: $row->flavor, Price: $row->price\n";
$row = $sth->fetchRow();
// Prints out the second retrieved row
print "Flavor: $row->flavor, Price: $row->price\n";
```

The query() method only returns a DB_Result object when it successfully executes a SELECT query. If it successfully executes another kind of query that doesn't return any rows, it returns the constant DB_OK. This is what happens for INSERT, DELETE, and UPDATE queries as well as for queries that change the structure of the database with CREATE TABLE, ALTER TABLE, or DROP TABLE.

If the query() method doesn't successfully execute any kind of query, it returns a DB_Error object. A query may fail because of a syntax error, missing data, or larger problems with the database server. Use the DB::isError() static method to check that a query has executed successfully:

```
$sth = $dbh->query('SELECT flavor,price FROM ice_cream');
if (DB::isError($sth)) {
    print "Error!";
} else {
    // display results
}
```

The DB_Error object has some methods that return information about the error. The two most useful of these are getMessage() and getUserInfo(). The getMessage() method returns a broadly descriptive error message, and the getUserInfo() returns more specific error information. For example, this query tries to retrieve records from a table that doesn't exist:

```
$sth = $dbh->query('SELECT * FROM frozen_yogurt');
if (DB::isError($sth)) {
    print $sth->getMessage() . "\nDetails: " . $sth->getUserInfo();
} else {
    // display results
}
```

The error is displayed like this:

```
DB Error: no such table
Details: SELECT * FROM frozen_yogurt [nativecode=1146 ** Table➥
'test.frozen_yogurt' doesn't exist]
```

The "Introducing Error Handling" section discusses how to handle errors.

Understanding Quoting and Placeholders

Frequently, database queries contain user input and other dynamic values. Before putting these data into queries, however, you need to escape any characters that have special meaning to your database. These characters are as follows:

- `'`: The single quote character delimits string literals in queries. This helps the database tell the difference between string values and field and table names.
- `%`: The percent character is an SQL wildcard that means "match any number of characters," like `*` in the shell or in a regular expression.
- `_`: The underscore character is an SQL wildcard that means "match one character," like `?` in the shell or `.` in a regular expression.
- `\`: The backslash character is used by some databases as an escape character, so it itself has to be escaped.

The proper way to escape these characters in many databases is to put a backslash before them: `SELECT * FROM songs WHERE title LIKE 'Don't Be Cruel'` becomes `SELECT * FROM songs WHERE title LIKE 'Don\'t Be Cruel'`. The single quote in `Don't` is escaped to tell the database the song title is the entire string `Don't Be Cruel`, not just `Don`. Some databases escape the single quote character by turning it into two single quote characters: `SELECT * FROM songs WHERE title LIKE 'Don''t Be Cruel'`.

Placeholders

PEAR DB makes it easy for you to escape single quotes by providing query placeholders. These are special characters in the query that are replaced by actual data when the query is sent to the database. When the data replaces the placeholder in the query, it is appropriately quoted. To use a placeholder, put a `?` character where you want the data to end up and pass a second argument to `query()` that contains an array holding the data:

```
$sth = $dbh->query('SELECT * FROM ice_cream WHERE flavor LIKE ?',
     array($_REQUEST['flavor']));
```

The query method replaces the ? with the value of `$_REQUEST['flavor']`, surrounded by single quotes. Any single quotes in `$_REQUEST['flavor']` are escaped in a method appropriate for the database you're using. For example, if the value of `$_REQUEST['flavor']` is `Straw's Berry`, then the query that's sent to MySQL is this:

```
SELECT * FROM ice_cream WHERE flavor LIKE 'Straw\'s Berry'
```

The query that's sent to PostgreSQL is this:

```
SELECT * FROM ice_cream WHERE flavor LIKE 'Straw''s Berry'
```

The ? placeholder only quotes strings. Integers and doubles are put into the query as is, and nulls are replaced with NULL (without quotes).

The ! placeholder is replaced by a value without any quoting or modification. This is useful for interpolating table names or column names. In this example, the table name to work with comes from `$_REQUEST['dessert']`, and the value to insert comes from `$_REQUEST['flavor']`:

```
$desserts = array('ice_cream' => 1, 'frozen_yogurt' => 1, 'sorbet' => 1);
if ($desserts[$_REQUEST['dessert']]) {
    $dbh->query('INSERT INTO ! (flavor) VALUES (?)',
              array($_REQUEST['dessert'], $_REQUEST['flavor']));
} else {
    print "No such dessert.";
}
```

Checking to see whether the specified table is defined in the `$desserts` array is necessary to prevent a malicious user from inserting data into an arbitrary table in your database. If you use the ! placeholder to specify table or field names, always check to see whether the value that is going to be substituted for the placeholder is an acceptable one before running the query.

In addition to ? and !, there is a third placeholder: &. This is replaced with the contents of a file. Include the name of the file in the array of values passed to `query()` as a second argument:

```
$dbh->query("INSERT INTO dessert_pictures (flavor,image) VALUES (?,&)",
                    array('Rum Raisin','rum-raisin.jpeg'));
```

The DB::quote() Method

To quote values outside of query(), use the DB::quote() method. When passed a string, it returns the string quoted with single quotes escaped. It returns integers and doubles unmodified and returns the string NULL when passed a null value. For example:

```
$flavor = $dbh->quote($_REQUEST['flavor']);
$dbh->query("SELECT * FROM ice_cream WHERE flavor LIKE $flavor");
```

SQL Wildcards

Placeholder quoting and the quote() method make strings safe for inclusion in queries. They don't escape the SQL wildcard characters % and _. You have to escape those characters yourself with str_replace():

```
$safe_for_select = str_replace(array('%','_'),array('\%','\_'),
                               $_REQUEST['flavor']);
```

Replacing % with \% and _ with _ tells the database to treat those characters as a literal percent sign and underscore and not as SQL wildcards. If the value of $_REQUEST['flavor'] is Chocolate%, $dbh->query("SELECT * FROM ice_cream WHERE flavor LIKE '$safe_for_select'") only finds rows where flavor exactly matches the string Chocolate%, not all rows where flavor begins with Chocolate.

Using str_replace() to escape SQL wildcards can present a problem when used with query placeholders. The string quoting must happen before the wildcard escaping. Otherwise, the backslashes that the wildcard escaping inserts are themselves escaped by the string quoting. A single % character becomes \% by the wildcard escaping. The \% is turned into '\\%' by string quoting. The expression '\\%' matches any string that begins with a literal backslash character because \\ is interpreted by the database as a literal backslash and then % is interpreted as "match any number of characters." If the string quoting happens first, % is turned into '%', and then the wildcard escaping makes it '\%'. This matches only a one-character string containing a percent sign.

What does all this mean in practice? If you want to protect against errant SQL wildcards in user input, use quote() to quote strings before escaping wildcards. Put these quoted and escaped values into queries explicitly instead of using placeholders:

```
$flavor = str_replace(array('%','_'),array('\%','\_'),
          $dbh->quote($_REQUEST['flavor']));
$sth = $dbh->query("SELECT * FROM ice_cream WHERE flavor LIKE $flavor");
```

Magic Quotes

PHP has some configuration settings that affect string quoting. These settings don't change PEAR DB's behavior, so improper configuration may result in values getting quoted twice.

If the `magic_quotes_gpc` configuration setting is on, single quotes and backslashes in incoming GET, POST, and cookie data are automatically backslash-escaped. If the `magic_quotes_runtime` configuration setting is on, the same quoting happens automatically for data read from a file or database. If `magic_quotes_sybase` is on, then `magic_quotes_gpc` and `magic_quotes_runtime` escape a single quote with another single quote and don't escape backslashes at all.

Using query placeholder quoting with GET, POST, or cookie data when `magic quotes_gpc` is on or with data read from a file or database when `magic_quotes runtime` is on results in data being quoted twice. If the submitted POST form variable `flavor` contains `Straw's Berry` and `magic_quotes_gpc` is on, then the value of `$_REQUEST['flavor']` is `Straw\'s Berry`. A problem results if that value is substituted for the placeholder in this query:

```
$sth = $dbh->query('SELECT * FROM ice_cream WHERE flavor LIKE ?',
        array($_REQUEST['flavor']));
```

The query sent to the database is `SELECT * FROM ice_cream WHERE flavor LIKE 'Straw\\\'s Berry'`. Because the backslash inserted by `magic_quotes_gpc` is itself escaped by the placeholder substitution, this query doesn't find the appropriate rows.

The easiest way to avoid this double escaping is to turn off `magic_quotes_gpc` and `magic_quotes_runtime` in your `php.ini` or Web server configuration file. If you can't do that, use `stripslashes()` to remove the escaping that was added:

```
$_REQUEST['flavor'] = stripslashes($_REQUEST['flavor']);
$sth = $dbh->query('SELECT * FROM ice_cream WHERE flavor LIKE ?',
array($_REQUEST['flavor']));
```

To make your code more portable, call `stripslashes()` only when necessary. The `get_magic_quotes_gpc()` function returns `1` if `magic_quotes_gpc` is on. Use `get magic_quotes_gpc()` to determine whether to call `stripslashes()`:

```
if (get_magic_quotes_gpc()) {
    $_REQUEST['flavor'] = stripslashes($_REQUEST['flavor']);
}
$sth = $dbh->query('SELECT * FROM ice_cream WHERE flavor LIKE ?',
array($_REQUEST['flavor']));
```

> **NOTE** *The* stripslashes() *function turns* \\ *into* \ *and* \' *into* '. *It doesn't unquote Sybase-style quoted strings. To do that, use* str_replace(): $str = str_replace("''","'",$str);.

Examining Data Retrieval Convenience Methods

PEAR DB provides methods that make common data retrieval operations easier. These methods combine query() and fetchRow(), allowing you to send a SELECT query to the database and retrieve its results in one step.

DB::getRow()

Use the getRow() method when you want all values in the first or only row returned from a query. getRow() returns an array or an object, depending on the current fetch mode. The default fetch mode is an indexed array:

```
$row = $dbh->getRow('SELECT flavor,price FROM ice_cream WHERE id = 56');
print "Flavor: $row[0], Price: $row[1]";
```

Placeholders work with getRow() just as they do with query():

```
$row = $dbh->getRow('SELECT flavor,price FROM ice_cream WHERE id = ?',
                    array($id));
```

An alternate fetch mode can be passed as a third argument to getRow():

```
$row = $dbh->getRow('SELECT flavor,price FROM ice_cream WHERE id = ?',
                    array($id),DB_FETCHMODE_OBJECT);
print "Flavor: $row->flavor, Price: $row->price";
```

Placeholders must be passed to getRow() in an array, just as they must be passed to query().

DB::getAll()

Use getAll() when you want all values in all rows returned from a query. Just like getRow(), getAll() accepts an array of placeholder replacements as a second argument and an optional alternate fetch mode as a third argument. The getAll() function always returns an array, but the type of each element in the array is controlled by the fetch mode. Iterate through the array that getAll() returns to display results:

```
$results = $dbh->getAll('SELECT flavor,price FROM ice_cream');
foreach($results as $row) {
    print "Flavor: $row[0], Price: $row[1]<br>";
}
```

DB::getOne()

Use getOne() when you want the first value from the first or only row returned from a query. The getOne() function accepts an array of placeholder replacements as an optional second argument. It returns a string containing the retrieved value or NULL if the query returned no results. It also returns NULL if the first value of the first row of the result is NULL:

```
$flavor = $dbh->getOne('SELECT flavor FROM ice_cream ORDER BY price DESC LIMIT 1');
if (is_null($flavor)) {
    print "We don't have any ice cream!";
} else {
   print "Our most expensive flavor is $flavor.";
}
```

DB::getCol()

Use getCol() when you want the value of a particular column in all the rows returned from a query. The getCol() function accepts a column name or number to return as an optional second argument. If this is not specified, getCol() returns the first column. The function also accepts an array of placeholder replacements as an optional third argument. The retrieved values are returned as an indexed array:

```
$flavors = $dbh->getCol('SELECT flavor FROM ice_cream');
print "Our flavors: <ul> <li> " . join('<li>',$flavors) . "</ul>";
```

DB::getAssoc()

Use getAssoc() when you want an entire result set, such as getAll(), but you want to easily access particular rows of the result. The getAssoc() function returns an associative array whose keys are the values of the first column of the query results. If you select two columns, the associative array values are the values of the second column:

```
$res = $dbh->getAssoc('SELECT flavor,price FROM ice_cream');
print "A serving of Heavenly Hash costs: ".$res['Heavenly Hash']
```

If you select more than two columns, the associative array values are themselves arrays of the remaining column values for each row:

```
$res = $dbh->getAssoc('SELECT id,flavor,price FROM ice_cream');
if ($flavor = $res[$_REQUEST['flavor_id']]) {
    print "Your selected flavor is: $flavor[0] with price $flavor[1].";
} else {
    print "No flavor has ID $_REQUEST[flavor_id].";
}
```

To force getAssoc() to return values as arrays instead of scalars when only one column of values is involved, pass true as a second argument when calling the function:

```
$res = $dbh->getAssoc('SELECT flavor,price FROM ice_cream', true);
print "A serving of Heavenly Hash costs: ".$res['Heavenly Hash'][0];
```

The third argument to getAssoc() is an array of values to replace any placeholders in the query:

```
$res = $dbh->getAssoc('SELECT id,flavor,price FROM ice_cream WHERE price > ?',
true,array($_REQUEST['min_price']));
if ($flavor = $res[$_REQUEST['flavor_id']]) {
    print "Your selected flavor is: $flavor[0] with price $flavor[1].";
} else {
    print "No flavor has ID $_REQUEST[flavor_id].";
}
```

Tell getAssoc() to return each array of values as an associative array instead of an indexed array by passing DB_FETCHMODE_ASSOC as a fourth argument:

```
$res = $dbh->getAssoc('SELECT id,flavor,price FROM ice_cream',
       null, null, DB_FETCHMODE_ASSOC);
if ($flavor = $res[$_REQUEST['flavor_id']]) {
    print "Your selected flavor is: $flavor[flavor] with price $flavor[price].";
} else {
    print "No flavor has ID $_REQUEST[flavor_id].";
}
```

The getAssoc() function returns an array whose values are easy to display as an HTML <select> widget. Select the columns for the value and label of each option and then use foreach to loop through the array:

```
$flavors= $dbh->getAssoc('SELECT id,flavor FROM ice_cream');
print '<select name="flavor">';
foreach ($flavors as $id => $flavor) {
    print "<option value=\"$id\">$flavor</option>";
}
print '</select>';
```

Understanding Query Information

In addition to methods that send queries to the database and return results, DB provides some methods that return information about a query. These methods tell you the size of the result set returned or modified by a query.

DB_Result::numRows()

The `numRows()` method returns the number of rows in a result set. This is useful for checking if any rows were selected before printing them:

```
$res = $dbh->query('SELECT flavor FROM ice_cream WHERE price < 5');
if ($res->numRows() > 0) {
    print "Your choices: <ul>";
    while($row = $res->fetchRow()) { print "<li> $row[0]</li>"; }
    print "</ul>";
} else {
   print "No flavors available for less than five dollars.";
}
```

The `numRows()` method is called on the statement handle, not on the database handle. You can only call `numRows()` after a `SELECT` query.

DB_Result::numCols()

The `numCols()` method returns the number of columns in a result set. You can use `numCols()` to dynamically display information about a table:

```
$res = $dbh->query('SELECT * FROM ice_cream');
print 'There are '.$res->numCols().' columns in the ice_cream table.';
print '<table>';
while($row = $res->fetchRow()) {
    print '<tr>';
    foreach ($row as $val) { print "<td>$val</td>"; }
```

```
    print '</tr>';
}
print '</table>';
```

Like numRows(), the numCols() method is called on the statement handle, not on the database handle. You can only call numCols() after a SELECT query.

DB::affectedRows()

The affectedRows() method returns how many rows were changed by an UPDATE, INSERT, or DELETE query. It is called on the database handle, not the statement handle. This is because the query() method doesn't return a statement handle for these kinds of queries, just a status code or error object:

```
$dbh->query("UPDATE ice_cream SET price = price - 1 WHERE flavor
             LIKE 'Chocolate%'");
print 'Discount applied to ' . $dbh->affectedRows() . ' Chocolate flavors.';
```

Running a Query Multiple Times

Often, a program needs to run a query many times with different values each time. A query that inserts a product into a product catalog is called ten times to insert ten new products into the catalog. Each time, the structure of the query is identical. However, new values such as product name and price must be incorporated into the query on each invocation.

DB::prepare() and DB::execute()

To run a query multiple times with different values each time, use prepare() and execute(). Call prepare() once with placeholders representing the values that change on each query execution. This returns a prepared statement handle. Then, call execute() with the prepared statement handle and each set of values:

```
$prh = $dbh->prepare('INSERT INTO ice_cream (flavor,price) VALUES (?,?)');
$dbh->execute($prh,array('Coffee',1.25));
$dbh->execute($prh,array('Pistachio',2.00));
$dbh->execute($prh,array('Caramel Pecan',1.75));
```

The prepare() method supports the same set of placeholders that query() does, so you can use ! for unquoted values and & for file contents:

```
$prh = $dbh->prepare('INSERT INTO ! (flavor,price,image) VALUES (?,?,&)');
$dbh->execute($prh,array('frozen_yogurt','Tofu Health Crunch',2.50,
                         'yogurt-tofu-crunch.jpg'));
$dbh->execute($prh,array('ice_cream','Vanilla',1.40,'delicious-vanilla.jpg'));
```

These methods can be used for SELECT queries as well. Each successful execute() of a SELECT query returns a statement handle. These are the same statement handles that query() returns:

```
$prh = $dbh->prepare('SELECT flavor FROM !');
$res = $dbh->execute($prh,'frozen_yogurt');
print_flavors('Frozen Yogurt',$res);
$res = $dbh->execute($prh,'ice_cream');
print_flavors('Ice Cream',$res);
```

DB::autoPrepare() and DB::autoExecute()

While prepare() and execute() make it easier to run the same query multiple times, autoPrepare() and autoExecute() make it easier to build queries from arrays of field names and values. The autoPrepare() method returns a prepared statement handle just like prepare(). Instead of passing it an SQL query with placeholders, however, you pass it a table name, an array of field names, and a mode. For example, these calls to autoPrepare() and prepare() return identical statement handles:

```
$dbh->autoPrepare('ice_cream',array('flavor','price'),DB_AUTOQUERY_INSERT);
$dbh->prepare("INSERT INTO ice_cream ('flavor','price') VALUES (?,?)");
```

The first argument to autoPrepare() is the name of the table to use. The second argument is an array of field names. The third argument tells autoPrepare() whether to prepare an INSERT or UPDATE query. To prepare an UPDATE query, use DB_AUTOQUERY_UPDATE:

```
$dbh->autoPrepare('ice_cream',array('flavor','price'),
                  DB_AUTOQUERY_UPDATE);
```

This returns a prepared statement handle as if you had called this:

```
$dbh->prepare('UPDATE ice_cream SET flavor = ?, price = ?');
```

To include a WHERE clause in an UPDATE query generated by autoPrepare(), pass it as a fourth argument to autoPrepare():

```
$dbh->autoPrepare('ice_cream',array('flavor','price'),DB_AUTOQUERY_UPDATE,
                              'price < 10');
```

This returns a prepared statement handle as if you had called this:

```
$dbh->prepare('UPDATE ice cream SET flavor = ?, price = ? WHERE price < 10');
```

The autoExecute() method takes autoPrepare() one step further. It prepares a query but also executes it with an array of values. Instead of an array of field names such as autoPrepare(), autoExecute() takes an associative array of fields and values:

```
$dbh->autoExecute('ice_cream',array('flavor' => 'Blueberry', 'price' => 3.00),
DB_AUTOQUERY_INSERT);
```

This prepares and executes a query as if you had called this:

```
$prh = $dbh->prepare('INSERT INTO ice_cream (flavor,price) VALUES (?,?)');
$dbh->execute($prh, array('Blueberry',3.00));
```

The autoExecute() method runs UPDATE queries just like autoPrepare():

```
$dbh->autoExecute('ice_cream',
                  array('flavor' => 'Blueberry', 'price' => 3.00),
                  DB_AUTOQUERY_UPDATE);
```

This prepares and executes a query as if you had called this:

```
$prh = $dbh->prepare('UPDATE ice_cream SET flavor = ?, price = ?');
$dbh->execute($prh, array('Blueberry',3.00));
```

The autoExecute() method also accepts a WHERE clause just like autoPrepare():

```
$dbh->autoExecute('ice_cream',array('flavor' => 'Blueberry', 'price' => 3.00),
DB_AUTOQUERY_UPDATE,'id = 23');
```

This prepares and executes a query as if you had called this:

```
$prh = $dbh->prepare('UPDATE ice_cream SET flavor = ?, price = ? WHERE id = 23');
$dbh->execute($prh, array('Blueberry',3.00));
```

The autoPrepare() and autoExecute() methods are especially useful for saving information from a Web form that has many fields. Define those fields in an array, and use autoExecute() to save information from the $_REQUEST array into the database. If the fields in the form change, you have to only update the line of code that defines the $fields array, and the query is automatically changed as well:

```
$fields = array('flavor','price','id','rating');
$values = array();
foreach ($fields as $f) { $values[$f] = $_REQUEST[$f]; }
$dbh->autoExecute('ice_cream',$values,DB_AUTOQUERY_INSERT);
```

Introducing Sequences

A *sequence* is a source of unique integer identifiers. When you need an ID for an item in your database, ask a sequence for its next available ID. This ID is guaranteed to be unique within the sequence. If two queries ask the same sequence for an ID at the same time, each query gets a different answer.

The easiest way to use a sequence is just to call the `DB::nextID()` method. This creates the specified sequence if it doesn't already exist and returns the next available ID in the sequence:

```
$flavor_id = $dbh->nextID('flavors');
$dbh->query('INSERT INTO ice_cream (id,flavor) VALUES (?,?)',
            array($flavor_id,'Walnut'));
```

To create sequences explicitly, use `createSequence()`:

```
$dbh->createSequence('flavors');
```

If you are creating your sequences with `createSequence()`, you can tell `nextID()` not to create sequences automatically by passing `false` as a second argument:

```
$flavor_id = $dbh->nextID('flavors',false);
if (DB::isError($flavor_id)) { die("Can't get sequence ID"); }
$dbh->query('INSERT INTO ice_cream (id,flavor) VALUES (?,?)',
            array($flavor_id,'Walnut'));
```

Whether they are created automatically by `nextID()` or explicitly with `createSequence()`, the `dropSequence()` method deletes a sequence:

```
$dbh->dropSequence('flavors');
```

Introducing Error Handling

DB methods return a `DB_Error` object if they fail. The `DB_Error` object contains fields that describe the error condition.

The "Sending Queries and Receiving Results" section describes the basic use of `DB::isError()`. This function returns `true` when the object passed to it is a DB_Error object. To comprehensively catch errors with this test, use it each time you call a DB method that may return an error:

```
$dbh = DB::Connect('mysql://user:pwd@localhost/dbname');
if (DB::isError($dbh)) { die("Can't connect: ".$dbh->getMessage()); }
$sth = $dbh->query('SELECT flavor,price FROM ice_cream');
if (DB::isError($dbh)) { die("Can't SELECT: ".$sth->getMessage()); }
while($res = $sth->fetchRow()) {
    if (DB::isError($res)) { die("Can't get row: ".$res->getMessage()); }
    print "Flavor: $res[0], Price: $res[1]";
}
```

Instead of testing each call to DB::isError() with if(), you can use the and logical operator instead, which is slightly more concise:

```
$dbh = DB::Connect('mysql://test:@localhost/test');
DB::isError($dbh) and die("Can't connect: ".$dbh->getMessage());
$sth = $dbh->query('SELECT flavor,price FROM ice_cream');
DB::isError($sth) and die("Can't SELECT: ".$sth->getMessage());
while($res = $sth->fetchRow()) {
    DB::isError($res) and die("Can't get row: ".$res->getMessage());
    print "Flavor: $res[0], Price: $res[1]\n";
}
```

Still, using DB::isError() after each relevant method call is cumbersome and error prone. If you forget to check the results of one method and it fails, subsequent operations won't work properly. The DB::setErrorHandling() method allows you to tell DB to automatically take an action whenever a DB method call returns an error. To print the error and exit the program immediately, pass the constant PEAR_ERROR_DIE to setErrorHandling():

```
$dbh = DB::Connect('mysql://test:@localhost/test');
DB::isError($dbh) and die($dbh->getMessage());
$dbh->setErrorHandling(PEAR_ERROR_DIE);
$sth = $dbh->query('SELECT flavor,price FROM ice_cream');
while($res = $sth->fetchRow()) {
    print "Flavor: $res[0], Price: $res[1]\n";
}
```

To print the error but continue program execution, use PEAR_ERROR_PRINT instead of PEAR_ERROR_DIE. You can also use setErrorHandling() to have a custom function called each time there's a DB error. Pass PEAR_ERROR_CALLBACK as the first argument to setErrorHandling() and the name of the function to call as the second argument:

```
$dbh = DB::Connect('mysql://test:@localhost/test');
DB::isError($dbh) and die($dbh->getMessage());
$dbh->setErrorHandling(PEAR_ERROR_CALLBACK,'db_error');
$sth = $dbh->query('SELECT flavor_name,price FROM ice_cream');
while($res = $sth->fetchRow()) {
    print "Flavor: $res[0], Price: $res[1]\n";
}
function db_error($err_obj) {
    print "Error! [$err_obj->code] $err_obj->userinfo";
}
```

Because this example has an unknown field in the SQL query (`flavor_name` instead of `flavor`), the `db_error()` error callback is called, and it prints this:

```
Error! [-19] SELECT flavor_name,price FROM ice_cream
[nativecode=1054 ** Unknown column 'flavor_name' in 'field list']
```

Error callbacks are useful for queries inside of a transaction. If there's an error, the callback can automatically roll back the transaction and print a message or return the proper value to indicate that the transaction failed.

CHAPTER 2

Accessing Databases with ADODB

ADODB IS A DATABASE wrapper library that simplifies many database-related tasks in PHP. The ADODB API is based on Microsoft ADO, a data access library used in Visual Basic and other Microsoft products. Although ADODB provides query helper functions such as PEAR DB, it also has functions that automate more complicated database tasks, such as turning a set of database rows into an HTML `<select>` menu or automatically paginating results. PEAR DB has a more rigorously defined object-oriented structure than ADODB. Because it's a core part of the PEAR library, it integrates better with other PEAR modules than ADODB does. However, ADODB offers more advanced functionality than PEAR DB, especially with regard to HTML generation. Choosing ADODB over PEAR DB gives you more features but at the loss of some flexibility.

This chapter describes the behavior of ADODB version 4.03. You can download ADODB from `http://php.weblogs.com/ADODB`. The databases supported by this version of ADODB are Access, ADO, DB2, FrontBase, Informix, InterBase, Microsoft SQL Server, MySQL, Oracle, ODBC, PostgreSQL, SAPDB, SQLAnywhere, SQLite, Sybase, and Visual FoxPro.

Connecting and Simple Queries

This section dissects a complete ADODB example to explain some fundamentals of connecting to a database, sending a query, and retrieving results. The section "Introducing Record Sets" discusses manipulating data returned from a query.

An ADODB Example

Retrieving a result and displaying it in a table with ADODB looks like this:

```
// Load the ADODB code
require 'adodb/adodb.inc.php';

// Connect to the database
$conn = &ADONewConnection('mysql');
$conn->connect('localhost','phpgems','phpgems1','phpgems');
```

```
// Send a SELECT query to the database
$rs = $conn->execute('SELECT flavor, price, calories FROM ice_cream');

// Check if any rows were returned
if ($rs->RecordCount() > 0) {
    print "<table>";
    print "<tr><th>Ice Cream Flavor</th><th>Price per Serving</th><th>Calories p
er Serving</th></tr>";
    // Retrieve each row
    while (! $rs->EOF) {
        print "<tr><td>{$rs->fields[0]}</td><td>{$rs->fields[1]}</td><td>{$rs->f
ields[2]}</td></tr>\n";
        $rs->MoveNext();
    }
    print "</table>";
} else {
    print "No results";
}
```

The connection to the database is established with the `ADONewConnection()` function call and the `Connect()` method call on the returned connection handle. `ADONewConnection()` takes one parameter—the type of database to which to connect. It returns a connection handle object that is not yet connected to a database server. The `Connect()` method establishes the actual database connection. The parameters to `Connect()` are the host to which to connect, the username and password to use for the connection, and the database name to which to connect. After the connection is made, the `Execute()` method sends a query to the database. The return value of `Execute()` is a record set. A *record set* is an object that lets you access the rows returned from a `SELECT` query. This example uses a few properties and methods of the record set to retrieve each row from the query results. The record set holds the rows in the order in which they were returned from the database. The `RecordCount()` method returns the number of rows inside the record set. You use the value returned from `RecordCount()` to make sure there are some rows to print before executing the code to print them.

Inside the record set is a pointer to one of the rows. This pointer starts out at the first row returned from the database. The `MoveNext()` method advances the pointer to the next row in the record set. The `EOF` property of a record set is `true` when the internal pointer has advanced past all of the rows in the record set. `EOF` and `MoveNext()` provide the way you loop through the entire record set in the example. As long as `EOF` isn't `true`, the internal pointer is pointing to a valid row, so you print data from the row and use `MoveNext()` to advance to the next row. If `MoveNext()` moves the internal pointer past the last row in the record set, then `EOF` is `true` and the `while()` loop ends.

The data from the row that the internal pointer is pointing to is accessible through the `fields` property of the record set. This is an array whose first element (index 0) is the first field in the row, whose second element (index 1) is the second field, and so on. You need to surround each array element with curly braces in the example to tell PHP how to interpolate the values properly in the double-quoted string.

Connecting

The `Connect()` method calls the appropriate underlying PHP functions to connect to the appropriate database. ADODB also has a `PConnect()` method to establish a persistent connection to the database. This is supported for Oracle, MySQL, PostgreSQL, Microsoft SQL Server, and ODBC. The `tests/testdatabases.inc.php` file in the ADODB distribution includes lots of example syntax for `Connect()` and `PConnect()` with the different kinds of databases that ADODB supports. Table 2-1 lists the driver strings that can be passed to `ADONewConnection()` and the databases to which they correspond. Because some databases have multiple driver string possibilities, check the online ADODB manual at `http://php.weblogs.com/adodb_manual` for the latest details on a particular driver string.

Table 2-1. ADODB Driver Strings and Databases

Driver String	Database
ado	A generic ADO database
access	Microsoft Access
ado_access	Microsoft Access via ADO
vfp	Visual FoxPro
db2	DB2
fbsql	FrontBase
ibase	InterBase 6 or earlier
firebird	InterBase (Firebird version)
borland_ibase	InterBase 6.5 or later (Borland version)
informix72	Informix 7.2 or earlier
informix	Informix
mysql	MySQL (without transaction support)
mysqlt	MySQL (with transaction support)

Table 2-1. ADODB Driver Strings and Databases

Driver String	Database
maxsql	Same as mysqlt
oci8	Oracle 8 and 9
oci805	Oracle 8.0.5
oci8po	Oracle 8 and 9*
odbc_oracle	Oracle via ODBC
odbc	An ODBC DSN
postgres7	PostgreSQL 7
postgres64	PostgreSQL 6.4 and earlier
postgres	Same as postgres7
sapdb	SAPDB via ODBC
sqlanywhere	SQLAnywhere via ODBC
sqlite	SQLite (only available with PHP 5)
mssql	Microsoft SQL Server 7 or later
mssqlpo	Microsoft SQL Server 7 or later**
ado_mssql	Microsoft SQL Server via ADO
odbc_mssql	Microsft SQL Server via ODBC
sybase	Sybase

* Uses ? for bind variables in `Prepare()` and lowercase for field names

** Converts the `||` concatenation operator to +

Queries and Quoting

The `Execute()` method is the central way in ADODB to send a query to the database server. In its simplest form, as used previously, you pass `Execute()` an SQL query, and it returns a record set that holds the results. You can also use placeholders with `Execute()`. Any question marks in your query are replaced with values from an array passed to `Execute()` as a second argument. The question marks are placeholders for the values that come from the array. This technique is useful if you need to run similar queries repeatedly:

```
$sql = 'SELECT * FROM ice_cream WHERE flavor LIKE ?';
// Get information about Chocolate
$rs = $conn->execute($sql,array('Chocolate'));
// Get information about Vanilla
$rs = $conn->execute($sql,array('Vanilla'));
```

Placeholders also make quoting easier. String values substituted for placeholders are surrounded by single quotes and have single quotes in them escaped in the appropriate manner for the database you're using. If you're not using placeholders, you can quote values with the `qstr()` method:

```
$flavor = $conn->qstr($_REQUEST['flavor']);
$rs = $conn->execute("SELECT * FROM ice_cream WHERE flavor LIKE $flavor");
```

Introducing Record Sets

The fundamental unit of data manipulation in ADODB is the record set. It is the set of rows that results from a database query that retrieves information from the database, such as a `SELECT` query. The record set maintains an internal pointer that starts out pointing at the first row in the record set. A record set object contains methods to move that internal pointer around as well as to retrieve a row or rows based on where the internal pointer is. Rows are usually represented as ordered arrays, but you can also tell ADODB to provide them as associative arrays. The row of data that the internal pointer points to is available in the `fields` property of the record set. When the internal pointer moves, the `fields` property changes to hold the values of the new row that is pointed to.

Moving the Internal Pointer

In the previous section, you used the `MoveNext()` method to move the internal pointer to the next row in the record set. The similarly named methods `MoveFirst()` and `MoveLast()` move the internal pointer to the first and last rows of the record set, respectively:

```
$rs = $conn->execute('SELECT flavor,calories,price FROM ice_cream');
// print last row
$rs->MoveLast();
print "Flavor {$rs->fields[0]} has {$rs->fields[1]} calories and costs
print "\${$rs->fields[2]}.\n";
// print first row
$rs->MoveFirst();
```

```
print "Flavor {$rs->fields[0]} has {$rs->fields[1]} calories and costs
print "\${$rs->fields[2]}.\n";
```

To move the internal pointer of a record set to a specific row, use the Move() method and pass it the row number:

```
$rs = $conn->execute('SELECT flavor,calories,price FROM ice_cream');
// print second row
$rs->Move(2);
print "Flavor {$rs->fields[0]} has {$rs->fields[1]} calories and costs
print "\${$rs->fields[2]}.\n";
```

To find the position of the internal pointer, use the CurrentRow() method. It returns the current row number, starting at 0.

Only some ADODB database drivers support moving the internal pointer backward using Move() or MoveFirst(). These are the mysql driver and the postgres64 driver. The hasMoveFirst property of the ADOConnection object is true if you can move the internal pointer backward in record sets from a given connection.

Row Format

You can change the format of record set rows by setting the global variable $ADODB_FETCH_MODE. The possible values are these four constants:

- ADODB_FETCH_DEFAULT
- ADODB_FETCH_NUM
- ADODB_FETCH_ASSOC
- ADODB_FETCH_BOTH

The default value of $ADODB_FETCH_MODE is ADODB_FETCH_DEFAULT, which means the default fetch mode of the particular database driver you are using. To have record set rows be formatted as ordered numeric arrays, use ADODB_FETCH_NUM. For associative arrays, use ADODB_FETCH_ASSOC. For arrays with both numeric and string keys, use ADODB_FETCH_BOTH. The ADODB_FETCH_BOTH setting creates an array that holds all the keys and values from the numeric array that ADODB_FETCH_NUM creates as well as all the keys and values from the associative array that ADODB_FETCH_ASSOC creates.

To access a row in the record set as an object instead of an array, use the FetchObject() method. It returns an object whose properties correspond to each field in the current record set row. The property names are all uppercase. You can use FetchObject() and the object it returns instead of the fields array of the record set:

```
$rs = $conn->execute('SELECT flavor,calories,price FROM ice_cream');
while (! $rs->EOF) {
    $ob = $rs->FetchObject();
    print "Flavor $ob->FLAVOR has $ob->CALORIES calories and costs
    print "\$$ob->PRICE.\n";
    $rs->MoveNext();
}
```

If you want a record set row as an object whose property names are not changed to uppercase, use FetchObj() instead. It sets the property names to what the database reports the field names are without changing their case.

Retrieving Multiple Rows

The record set object also provides some methods to retrieve many rows at once. The GetArray() method returns an numeric array whose values are the individual rows in the record set. The rows themselves are arrays whose structure depends on the value of $ADODB_FETCH_MODE. The GetArray() method retrieves all of the rows from the position of the record set internal pointer to the end of the record set. To retrieve fewer rows, pass the number of rows you want to GetArray():

```
$rs = $conn->execute('SELECT flavor,calories,price FROM ice_cream');
// Just retrieve three rows
$rows = $rs->GetArray(3);
```

You can also use GetRows() as a synonym for GetArray(). Similar to GetArray() is GetAssoc(), which returns an associative array instead of a numeric array. The keys of this associative array are the values of the first field of each row in the record set. For example, in this query, the keys of $rows are the different values in the flavor column of the table:

```
$rs = $conn->execute('SELECT flavor,calories,price FROM ice_cream');
$rows = $rs->GetAssoc();
```

The keys of $rows are Chocolate, Vanilla, "Heavenly" Hash, and Diet Cardboard. Although the keys in the returned associative array of GetAssoc() are different from the returned numeric array of GetArray(), the values are the same. Each value in the returned array is itself an array containing one row of the record set. Whether that array is numeric or associative depends on $ADODB_FETCH_MODE.

With $ADODB_FETCH_MODE set to ADODB_FETCH_ASSOC, the array returned previously by GetArray() looks like this, when formatted with print_r():

```
Array
(
    [0] => Array
        (
            [flavor] => Chocolate
            [calories] => 10
            [price] => 4.50
        )

    [1] => Array
        (
            [flavor] => Vanilla
            [calories] => 20
            [price] => 4.50
        )

    [2] => Array
        (
            [flavor] => "Heavenly" Hash
            [calories] => 60
            [price] => 5.95
        )

    [3] => Array
        (
            [flavor] => Diet Cardboard
            [calories] => 0
            [price] => 1.15
        )

)
```

In contrast, the array returned by GetAssoc() looks like this:

```
Array
(
    [Chocolate] => Array
        (
            [calories] => 10
            [price] => 4.50
        )
```

```
    [Vanilla] => Array
        (
            [calories] => 20
            [price] => 4.50
        )

    ["Heavenly" Hash] => Array
        (
            [calories] => 60
            [price] => 5.95
        )

    [Diet Cardboard] => Array
        (
            [calories] => 0
            [price] => 1.15
        )

)
```

Both GetArray() and GetAssoc() return rows starting at the current position of the internal pointer. Both return all rows from the internal pointer to the end of the record set, but you can restrict the number of rows that GetArray() returns as discussed previously.

Processing Rows

ADODB also provides a way to process all rows in a record set with its RSFilter() function, which is defined in the adodb/rsfilter.inc.php file. Provided a record set and a callback function, RSFilter() calls the callback function on each row in the record set. This example uses the built-in function money_format() to format the price of each ice cream flavor:

```
require 'adodb/rsfilter.inc.php';
setlocale(LC_MONETARY,'en_US');
$rs = $conn->Execute('SELECT flavor,calories,price FROM ice_cream');
$rs = RSFilter($rs,'fix_price');
function fix_price(&$ar,$rs) { $ar[2] = money_format('%.2n',$ar[2]); }
```

After retrieving a record set with Execute(), you call RSFilter(), passing it the record set and the callback name. The RSFilter() function returns the modified record set, so you have to assign its result back to $rs. The callback function, fix_price(), accepts two arguments. The first, passed by reference, is the array that holds a row of the record set. The second argument is the record set itself. The fix_price() callback doesn't need it, but you could use properties of the record set object to determine how to format data inside your callback. Inside fix_price(), the third element of $ar, corresponding to the price field in the row, is reformatted using money_format(). Because $ar is passed by reference to fix price(), you can just assign it a new value, and you don't need to return anything. After processing all the rows, RSFilter() moves the internal pointer to the beginning of the record set.

Accessing Rows with the Iterator Interface

In PHP 5, ADODB provides Iterator access to a record set. You can call all of the Iterator interface methods on the record set object and loop through the record set with foreach. Using foreach lets you work with each row individually:

```
$rs = $conn->execute('SELECT flavor,calories,price FROM ice_cream');
foreach ($rs as $index => $row) {
    printf("Row %d is %s, calories = %d, price = \$%.02f\n",
           $index, $row['flavor'], $row['calories'], $row['price']);
}
```

This prints the following:

```
Row 0 is Chocolate, calories = 10, price = $4.50
Row 1 is Vanilla, calories = 20, price = $4.50
Row 2 is "Heavenly" Hash, calories = 60, price = $5.95
Row 3 is Diet Cardboard, calories = 0, price = $1.15
```

Each time through the foreach loop, $index is set to the numerical row index, starting at 0, and $row is set to an array of data retrieved from the database. The format of $row respects the $ADODB_FETCH_MODE variable with regard to whether it is an associative array, a numeric array, or a combination of the two.

Understanding Error Handling

There are four ways to handle errors in ADODB. The first is to check the return value from each ADODB function call and explicitly take an appropriate action if there is an error. If you turn on the $conn->debug flag, you can see the error messages:

```
$conn->debug = 1;
$rs = $conn->execute('SELECT flavor,calories,price FROM cookies');
if (! $rs) { print "Query Error"; }
```

Because the cookies table doesn't exist, an error message is printed that includes this text:

```
1146: Table 'phpgems.cookies' doesn't exist
```

Turning on $conn->debug also causes some diagnostic information about queries to be displayed, so this is not something you should do in a production environment. It is helpful for testing and debugging, however.

The second way is to use ADODB's trigger_error() error-handling mode. In this mode, ADODB throws an error with PHP's trigger_error() function whenever Connect(), PConnect(), or a query execution function such as Execute() fails. You don't have to do anything special to check return values because your program exits when there is an error. To turn on this error handling mode, require the file adodb/adodb-errorhandler.inc.php. For example:

```
require 'adodb/adodb-errorhandler.inc.php';
// ... establish connection to the database ...
$rs = $conn->execute('SELECT flavor,calories,price FROM cookies');
```

This exits with the following error message:

```
Fatal error: mysql error: [1146: Table 'phpgems.cookies' doesn't exist] in
EXECUTE("SELECT flavor,calories,price FROM cookies") in
/usr/local/php/lib/adodb/adodb-errorhandler.inc.php on line 75
```

Because ADODB uses trigger_error() to throw these errors, you can catch them by defining your own error handler. Call set_error_handler() with the name of your error-handling function. The error-handling function can do whatever you want with the error. This example just prints the error message to the error log:

```
set_error_handler('check_errors');
$rs = $conn->execute('SELECT flavor,calories,price FROM cookics');
function check_errors($errno, $error, $file, $line) {
    error_log("ADODB Error: $error");
}
```

The check_errors() function writes the following message to the error log:

```
ADODB Error: mysql error: [1146: Table 'phpgems.cookies' doesn't exist] in
EXECUTE("SELECT flavor,calories,price FROM cookies")
```

One benefit of defining your own error handler is that your program doesn't automatically exit when ADODB throws an error. If you want it to exit, you can call exit() or die() inside your error handler, but you don't have to do so.

The third error handling method is to use ADODB's PEAR_Error error-handling mode. Turn on this mode by requiring the file adodb/adodb-errorpear.inc.php. In this mode, ADODB creates a PEAR_Error object when Connect(), PConnect(), or a query execution function fails. You can use the PEAR_Error objects in two ways. First, by testing the return values from the ADODB functions and using the ADODB PEAR_Error() function, you can retrieve the error object when necessary and process it:

```
require 'adodb/adodb-errorpear.inc.php';
// ... establish a connection to the database ...
$rs = $conn->execute('SELECT flavor,calories,price FROM cookies');
if (! $rs) {
    $err = ADODB_PEAR_Error();
    error_log('Query Error: '.$err->getMessage());
}
```

Just like you can take action automatically on errors generated by trigger_error() if you set your own error handler, you can take action automatically when PEAR errors occur by using the PEAR::setErrorHandling() method. Call PEAR::setErrorHandling() with a constant that indicates how you want errors to be handled. The PEAR_ERROR_PRINT constant causes the errors to be printed. The PEAR_ERROR_DIE constant causes errors to be printed, and then the program immediately exits:

```
PEAR::setErrorHandling(PEAR_ERROR_DIE);
$rs = $conn->execute('SELECT flavor,calories,price FROM cookies');
```

PEAR_Error mode also supports custom error handlers. Indicate the custom error handler to be called with the PEAR_ERROR_CALLBACK constant:

```
PEAR::setErrorHandling(PEAR_ERROR_CALLBACK,'check_errors');
$rs = $conn->execute('SELECT flavor,calories,price FROM cookies');
function check_errors($err) {
    error_log('Query Error: '.$err->getMessage());
}
```

When an error occurs, the callback set up by PEAR::setErrorHandling() is called with a PEAR_Error object as its only argument. Inside the callback, you can print error messages, e-mail your database administrator there has been a problem, exit the program, or take any other action that the error warrants.

The fourth error handling method is with exceptions. This is only available if you are using PHP 5. Turn on this mode by requiring the file adodb/adodb-exceptions.inc.php. In this mode, ADODB throws an exception of type ADODB_Exception when an error occurs. Put your code that uses ADODB functions inside a try/catch block to handle an error:

```
require 'adodb/adodb-exceptions.inc.php';
try {
    $conn = &ADONewConnection('mysql');
    $conn->Connect('localhost','phpgems','phpgems1','phpgems');
    $rs = $conn->execute('SELECT flavor,calories,price FROM cookies');
} catch (ADODB_Exception $e) {
    print 'Database Error: '.$e->getMessage();
} catch (Exception $e) {
    print "Something else went wrong: ".$e->getMessage();
}
```

The first catch block in the previous code handles any exceptions generated by ADODB, and the second catch block handles any other exceptions that may have been generated. In a database context, exceptions are useful for cleaning up any unfinished business. When handling an ADODB_Exception, you can roll back a partially completed transaction or close any open connections to a database.

Introducing Sequences

ADODB provides integer sequences for you to use. You can retrieve the next value from a particular sequence by passing the sequence name to the genID() method:

```
$flavor_id = $conn->genID('flavors');
$conn->Execute('INSERT INTO ice_cream (id,flavor) VALUES (?,?)',
 array($flavor_id,'Walnut'));
```

If you call genID() without a sequence name, it retrieves the next value from the default sequence, named adodbseq. The genID() method creates a sequence if it doesn't already exist. You can create a sequence without getting a new value from it with CreateSequence():

```
$conn->CreateSequence('flavors');
```

Whether created automatically by genID() or explicitly by CreateSequence(), sequences start at 1 by default. You can start a sequence by passing a second argument to genID() or CreateSequence():

```
$flavor_id = $conn->genID('flavors',31);
$conn->CreateSequence('flavors',31);
```

The genID() method only uses the second argument to set the start value of the sequence if it is creating the sequence. If the sequence already exists, genID() returns the next value in the sequence.

To delete an existing sequence, use DropSequence():

```
$conn->DropSequence('flavors');
```

Generating HTML

ADODB makes it very easy to perform common HTML generation tasks with information retrieved from a database. These tasks include displaying a record set in an HTML table, printing <select> tags containing data from a record set, and splitting data from a record set across multiple pages.

Displaying a Record Set in an HTML Table

The rs2html() function produces an HTML table of results with just one function call. The function is defined in the adodb/tohtml.inc.php file, so you must include or require that file to use rs2html(). Just pass a record set to rs2html(), and it prints an HTML table:

```
require 'adodb/tohtml.inc.php';
// Assume $conn is a valid database connection
$rs = $conn->execute('SELECT flavor,calories,price FROM ice_cream');
rs2html($rs);
```

This prints the following HTML:

```
<TABLE COLS=3 BORDER='1' WIDTH='98%'>

<TH>flavor</TH><TH>calories</TH><TH>price</TH>

<TR valign=top>
        <TD>Chocolate </TD>
        <TD align=right>10 </TD>
        <TD align=right>4.50 </TD>
</TR>

<TR valign=top>
        <TD>Vanilla </TD>
```

```
        <TD align=right>20 </TD>
        <TD align=right>4.50 </TD>
</TR>

<TR valign=top>
        <TD>&quot;Heavenly&quot; Hash </TD>
        <TD align=right>60 </TD>
        <TD align=right>5.95 </TD>
</TR>

<TR valign=top>
        <TD>Diet Cardboard </TD>
        <TD align=right>0 </TD>
        <TD align=right>1.15 </TD>
</TR>

</TABLE>
```

Figure 2-1 shows a rendered version of the HTML table.

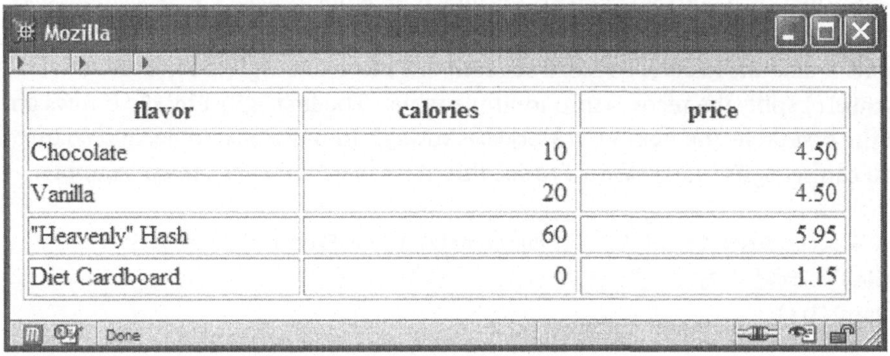

Mozilla

flavor	calories	price
Chocolate	10	4.50
Vanilla	20	4.50
"Heavenly" Hash	60	5.95
Diet Cardboard	0	1.15

Done

Figure 2-1. The rs2html() *function generates an HTML table.*

By default, the table produced by rs2html() has BORDER='1' WIDTH='98%' as the attributes for the <table> tag, but you can override those defaults by passing different attributes as a second argument to rs2html(). Using the record set from the previous example, rs2html($rs,'CLASS="fancytable"') prints a table whose opening tag is as follows:

```
<TABLE COLS=3 CLASS="fancytable">
```

You can also change the text of the table's header row. By default, rs2html() uses the column names in the result set, but if an array of strings is passed as the third argument to rs2html(), it uses the values in that array instead. Using the record set from the previous example, `rs2html($rs,false,array('Ice Cream Flavor','Calorie Count','Cost'))` prints a table whose header row is as follows:

```
<TH>Ice Cream Flavor</TH><TH>Calorie Count</TH><TH>Cost</TH>
```

By passing `false` as a second argument to `rs2html()` in this example, you tell the function to use the defaults for `<table>` tag attributes.

The fourth argument to `rs2html()` is a boolean that controls whether string values in the table have their HTML entities encoded by `htmlentities()`. It defaults to `true`. If you don't want those values to have their entities encoded, pass `false`. This doesn't affect entity encoding of the values in the table header row. When `rs2html()` uses the column names from the result set, it always encodes their HTML entities. When it uses column names passed in as its third argument, it never encodes their HTML entities.

The fifth argument to `rs2html()` is a boolean that controls whether the function prints data or returns data. The default, `true`, means that `rs2html()` prints an HTML table. Passing `false` for this argument tells `rs2html()` to return the HTML table as a string instead.

The behavior of `rs2html()` is also controlled by two global variables: `$gSQLMaxRows` and `$gSQLBlockRows`. The `$gSQLMaxRows` variable controls how many rows from one record set `rs2html()` prints. It defaults to `1000`. The `$gSQLBlockRows` variable controls how many rows from one record set `rs2html()` prints in one table. It defaults to `20`. If a record set contains more than `$gSQLBlockRows` rows, `rs2html()` splits the records into multiple tables. The first `$gSQLBlockRows` rows go in the first table, the next `$gSQLBlockRows` rows go into the next table, and so on. You can set `$gSQLBlockRows` to `2` to see this at work with the ice cream example:

```
$rs = $conn->execute('SELECT flavor,calories,price FROM ice_cream');
$gSQLBlockRows = 2;
rs2html($rs);
```

The following is the HTML output. Figure 2-2 shows what it looks like in a browser:

```
<TABLE COLS=3 BORDER='1' WIDTH='98%'>

<TH>flavor</TH><TH>calories</TH><TH>price</TH>

<TR valign=top>
        <TD>Chocolate </TD>
        <TD align=right>10 </TD>
        <TD align=right>4.50 </TD>
</TR>
```

```
<TR valign=top>
	<TD>Vanilla </TD>
	<TD align=right>20 </TD>
	<TD align=right>4.50 </TD>
</TR>

</TABLE>

<TABLE COLS=3 BORDER='1' WIDTH='98%'>

<TH>flavor</TH><TH>calories</TH><TH>price</TH><TR valign=top>
	<TD>&quot;Heavenly&quot; Hash </TD>
	<TD align=right>60 </TD>
	<TD align=right>5.95 </TD>
</TR

<TR valign=top>
	<TD>Diet Cardboard </TD>
	<TD align=right>0 </TD>
	<TD align=right>1.15 </TD>
</TR>

</TABLE>
```

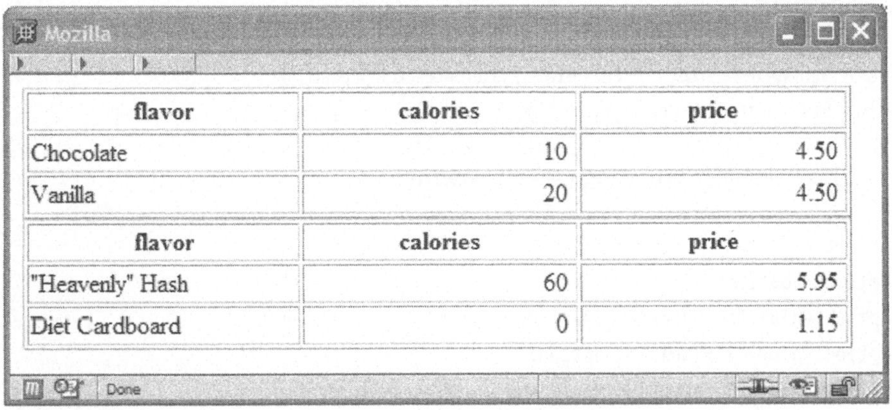

flavor	calories	price
Chocolate	10	4.50
Vanilla	20	4.50

flavor	calories	price
"Heavenly" Hash	60	5.95
Diet Cardboard	0	1.15

Figure 2-2. The `rs2html()` *function can generate multiple tables per page.*

After putting two rows in the first table, `rs2html()` closes the table and starts a new one, complete with header row. The remaining two rows are put in the second table. Splitting large record sets into multiple tables can help browsers render the data quicker because a browser can't render a table until it receives all the data in the table. It can also be helpful for users to see the header row interspersed periodically throughout a large data set so they know what each column means.

The `rs2html()` function prints rows from the record set starting from the current internal pointer position in the record set. If you've moved the internal pointer, by calling `MoveNext()`, for example, you need to move it back to the beginning of the record set with `MoveFirst()` if you want `rs2html()` to print the entire record set. After `rs2html()` runs, it leaves the internal pointer at the end of the record set, so you also need to use `MoveFirst()` if you want to call `rs2html()` twice on the same record set:

```
rs2html($rs);
$rs->MoveFirst();
rs2html($rs);
```

Printing <select> Tags Containing Data from a Record Set

Record set objects have two methods that return `<select>` tags built from the data in the record set: `GetMenu()` and `GetMenu2()`. The functions are identical except for how they handle default values (more about that in a few paragraphs). The functions use the first column in the record set as the labels for each option and the second column as the values. If you have an ID column and a name column in a table, put the name column first and the ID column second in your query:

```
$rs = $conn->execute('SELECT flavor,id FROM ice_cream');
print $rs->GetMenu('which_flavor');
```

This prints the following `<select>` menu:

```
<select name="which_flavor" >
<option></option>
<option value="1">Chocolate</option>
<option value="2">Vanilla</option>
<option value="3">&quot;Heavenly&quot; Hash</option>
<option value="4">Diet Cardboard</option>
</select>
```

The first argument to `GetMenu()` is used as the `name` attribute of the `<select>` tag. The `<option>` tags are printed one per line in the order that their rows appear in the result set. HTML entities, such as the quotation marks in `"Heavenly" Hash`, are encoded.

To have one `<option>` tag marked as `selected` so the browser treats it as the default value, pass the label for that tag as the second argument to `GetMenu()`:

```
$rs = $conn->execute('SELECT flavor,id FROM ice_cream');
print $rs->GetMenu('which_flavor','Vanilla');
```

This produces the following:

```
<select name="which_flavor" >
<option></option>
<option value="1">Chocolate</option>
<option selected value="2">Vanilla</option>
<option value="3">&quot;Heavenly&quot; Hash</option>
<option value="4">Diet Cardboard</option>
</select>
```

Default value handling is where `GetMenu()` and `GetMenu2()` differ. The `GetMenu2()` function marks a choice as `selected` when its value matches the second argument passed in. To make `Vanilla` the default with `GetMenu2()`, pass `2` as a second argument:

```
$rs = $conn->execute('SELECT flavor,id FROM ice_cream');
print $rs->GetMenu2('which_flavor',2);
```

This prints the same menu as in the previous example.

The menus that you've produced with `GetMenu()` and `GetMenu2()` so far all have an initial blank option. This is useful for checking that a user has selected an option in mandatory fields. If you want to turn it off, pass `false` as the third argument to either function:

```
$rs = $conn->execute('SELECT flavor,id FROM ice_cream');
print $rs->GetMenu2('which_flavor',null,false);
```

This produces a menu without an initial blank option:

```
<select name="which_flavor" >
<option value="1">Chocolate</option>
<option value="2">Vanilla</option>
<option value="3">&quot;Heavenly&quot; Hash</option>
<option value="4">Diet Cardboard</option>
</select>
```

By passing `null` as the second argument to `GetMenu2()`, you avoid setting any option to selected while still being able to specify that you don't want an initial blank.

The next two arguments to `GetMenu()` and `GetMenu2()` control whether the user is allowed to select multiple options of the menu and, if so, how many options to display at once. These arguments set the multiple and size attributes of the <select> tag. To set the multiple attribute, pass true as a fourth argument. To set the size attribute, pass the value to set size to as the fifth argument. The size attribute is only relevant if the multiple attribute is set. If multiple is set, then the menu name has square brackets appended to it. This tells PHP to treat the submitted form values as an array. The following is an example:

```
$rs = $conn->execute('SELECT flavor,id FROM ice_cream');
print $rs->GetMenu('which_flavor',null,false,true,3);
```

This produces the following menu:

```
<select name="which_flavor[]" multiple size=3 >
<option value="1">Chocolate</option>
<option value="2">Vanilla</option>
<option value="3">&quot;Heavenly&quot; Hash</option>
<option value="4">Diet Cardboard</option>
</select>
```

The sixth argument to the menu functions is a string containing additional attributes for the <select> tag. You can use this argument to specify values for a style, class, or other attribute. If you want to pass additional attributes in this argument, you need to fill in defaults or appropriate values for all of the preceding arguments:

```
$rs = $conn->execute('SELECT flavor,id FROM ice_cream');
print $rs->GetMenu('which_flavor',null,false,null,null,'class="bigselect"');
```

This adds the class="bigselect" attribute to the <select> tag:

```
<select name="which_flavor" class="bigselect">
<option value="1">Chocolate</option>
<option value="2">Vanilla</option>
<option value="3">&quot;Heavenly&quot; Hash</option>
<option value="4">Diet Cardboard</option>
</select>
```

Splitting Data Across Multiple Pages

The ADODB_Pager class, defined in the adodb-pager.inc.php file, provides a class that formats and displays a certain number of the rows in a record set with appropriate links to display more of the record set on other pages. You provide a database connection and a query when creating an ADODB_Pager object. The Render() method displays the results, shown in Figure 2-3.

```
$pager = new ADODB_Pager($conn,"SELECT id,flavor,calories,price FROM➥
ice_cream_big");
$pager->Render();
```

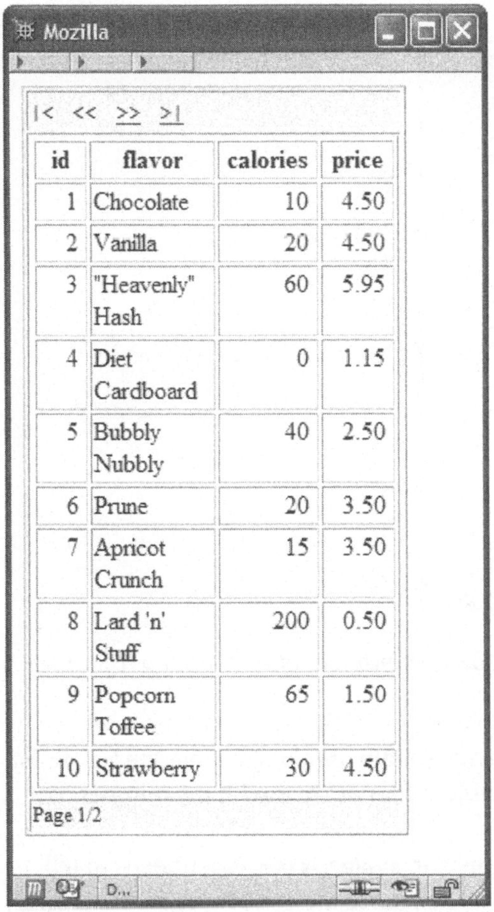

Mozilla

|< << >> >|

id	flavor	calories	price
1	Chocolate	10	4.50
2	Vanilla	20	4.50
3	"Heavenly" Hash	60	5.95
4	Diet Cardboard	0	1.15
5	Bubbly Nubbly	40	2.50
6	Prune	20	3.50
7	Apricot Crunch	15	3.50
8	Lard 'n' Stuff	200	0.50
9	Popcorn Toffee	65	1.50
10	Strawberry	30	4.50

Page 1/2

Figure 2-3. ADODB_Pager *displays a record set with pagination links.*

The data is displayed in a table with formatting and navigation links. The leftmost link in the table goes to the first page, the second link goes to the previous page, the third link goes to the next page, and the rightmost link goes to the last page of data. The links contain a variable that controls what page is displayed, but they don't automatically include other GET or POST variables that may have been set. By default, ADODB_Pager displays ten rows per page. You can override that by passing an argument to `Render()` with the number of rows per page you want. The following code generates a five-row table, shown in Figure 2-4:

```
$pager = new ADODB_Pager($conn,"SELECT id,flavor,calories,price FROM➥
ice_cream_big");
$pager->Render(5);
```

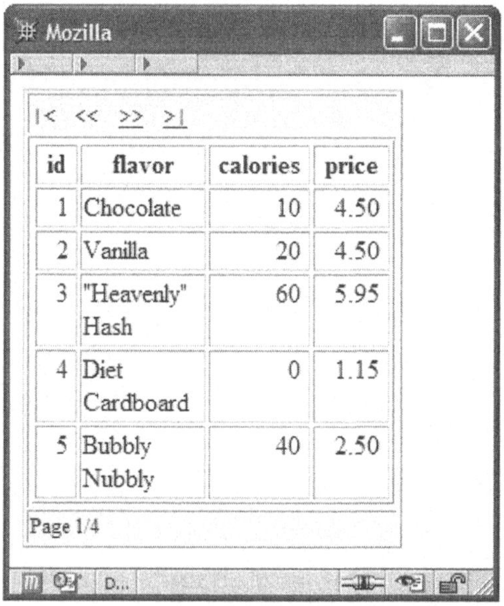

Mozilla

|< << >> >|

id	flavor	calories	price
1	Chocolate	10	4.50
2	Vanilla	20	4.50
3	"Heavenly" Hash	60	5.95
4	Diet Cardboard	0	1.15
5	Bubbly Nubbly	40	2.50

Page 1/4

Figure 2-4. `ADODB_Pager` *can display a specified number of rows from a record set.*

Internally, `ADODB_Pager` uses the `rs2html()` function to generate the HTML for the table. It overwrites the global variable `$gSQLBlockRows` with the number of rows per page it is displaying.

If you put more than one pager object in a page, `ADODB_Pager` needs to tell them apart so the next and previous links advance the correct pager. To accomplish this, each pager object needs a unique ID. The ID is specified as the third argument to the `ADODB_Pager` constructor. The default is `adodb`. To use two pager objects in one page, specify different IDs when you create the objects. The following code creates one pager with five rows and one with two rows:

```
$pager1 = new ADODB_Pager($conn,"SELECT id,flavor,calories,price FROM➥
ice_cream_big",'big');
$pager1->Render(5);
```

```
$pager2 = new ADODB_Pager($conn,"SELECT id,flavor,calories,price FROM➥
ice_cream", 'little');
$pager2->Render(2);
```

Figure 2-5 shows the two pager tables.

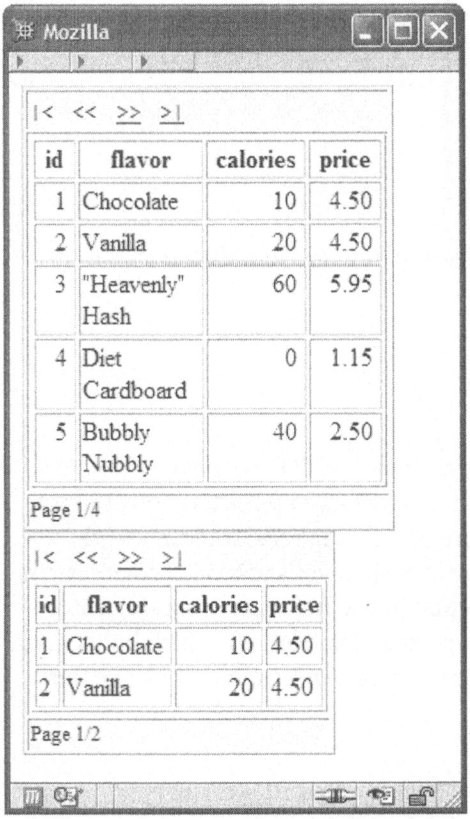

Mozilla

|< << >> >|

id	flavor	calories	price
1	Chocolate	10	4.50
2	Vanilla	20	4.50
3	"Heavenly" Hash	60	5.95
4	Diet Cardboard	0	1.15
5	Bubbly Nubbly	40	2.50

Page 1/4

|< << >> >|

id	flavor	calories	price
1	Chocolate	10	4.50
2	Vanilla	20	4.50

Page 1/2

Figure 2-5. `ADODB_Pager` *can display multiple tables on a page.*

You can also include direct links to individual pages in the navigation by passing `true` as the fourth argument to the `ADODB_Pager` constructor. The following code creates a three-row table with individual page links:

```
$pager = new ADODB_Pager($conn,"SELECT id,flavor,calories,price FROM➥
ice_cream_big",'big',true);
$pager->Render(3);
```

Figure 2-6 shows the table.

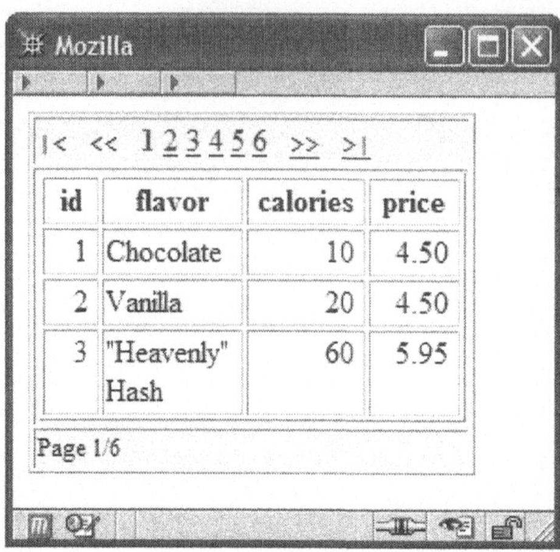

Figure 2-6. `ADODB_Pager` *can display navigation links to individual pages in the record set.*

Pivot Tables

Another handy feature of ADODB is its generation of SQL for pivot tables. Also known as *cross-tabs* (which, in turn, is short for *cross-tabulations*), pivot tables are a way of summarizing totals across multiple categories. You can create a pivot table that summarizes how many of each flavor various ice cream eaters have ordered. This requires the introduction of two new tables: `eaters`, which holds information about people eating ice cream, and `orders`, which holds information about which flavors the eaters order to eat. These tables look like this:

```
CREATE TABLE eaters (
  id int(10) unsigned NOT NULL,
  name varchar(255) default NULL,
  PRIMARY KEY  (id)
);
CREATE TABLE orders (
  eater_id int(11) default NULL,
  ice_cream_id int(11) default NULL
);
```

Both tables need to be populated with some sample data:

```
INSERT INTO eaters VALUES (1,'Ireneo Funes');
INSERT INTO eaters VALUES (2,'Bioy Casares');
INSERT INTO eaters VALUES (3,'John Vincent Moon');
INSERT INTO eaters VALUES (4,'Teodelina Villar');
INSERT INTO orders VALUES (1,2);
```

```
INSERT INTO orders VALUES (1,3);
INSERT INTO orders VALUES (1,4);
INSERT INTO orders VALUES (2,4);
INSERT INTO orders VALUES (2,3);
INSERT INTO orders VALUES (3,1);
INSERT INTO orders VALUES (4,1);
INSERT INTO orders VALUES (4,4);
INSERT INTO orders VALUES (2,4);
INSERT INTO orders VALUES (3,1);
```

The following example generates a pivot table summarizing how many of each flavor each person has ordered. The record set that holds the results has one row for each flavor and one column for each person. It also has a column for the total number of orders per flavor. The `PivotTableSQL()` function generates the SQL query that creates the record set that holds the pivot table results. You need to pass it five arguments. The first is a connection handle. The second is a string containing a comma-separated list of tables from which to retrieve data. The third argument is the name of the database field that should be used for the rows of the table, and the fourth argument is the name of the field that should be used for the columns of the table. The last argument is the appropriate SQL to link together the different tables in the query. In this example, you join `eaters` and `orders` on `eaters.id` and `orders.eater_id`, and you join `ice_cream` and `orders` on `ice_cream.id` and `orders.ice_cream_id`. The `PivotTableSQL()` function is defined in a separate file, `pivottable.inc.php`, so you `require` that at the beginning of the example:

```
// Load the pivot table code
require 'adodb/pivottable.inc.php';
// Load the rs2html code
require 'adodb/tohtml.inc.php';

// Connect to the database
$conn = &ADONewConnection('mysql');
$conn->connect('localhost','phpgems','phpgems1','phpgems');

// Generate the query
$sql = PivotTableSQL($conn,
                     'eaters, ice_cream, orders',
                     'ice_cream.flavor',
                     'name',
                     'eaters.id = orders.eater_id and ' .
                     'ice_cream.id = orders.ice_cream_id');
```

```
// Send the query to the database and get a record set
$rs = $conn->execute($sql);
// Display the results
rs2html($rs);
```

Figure 2-7 shows the pivot table from this example.

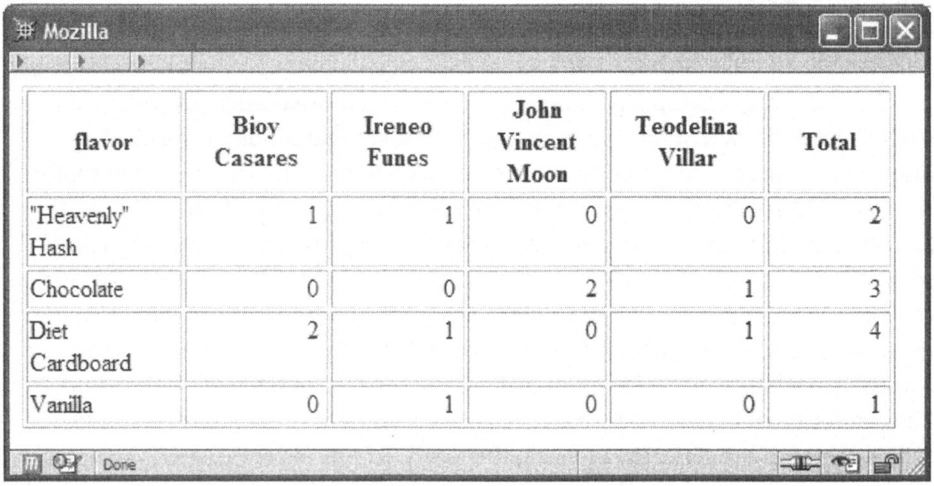

flavor	Bioy Casares	Ireneo Funes	John Vincent Moon	Teodelina Villar	Total
"Heavenly" Hash	1	1	0	0	2
Chocolate	0	0	2	1	3
Diet Cardboard	2	1	0	1	4
Vanilla	0	1	0	0	1

Figure 2-7. A pivot table summarizes totals across categories.

Each row contains the number of orders each person placed for that row's flavor, as well as the total number of orders for that flavor. Each column contains the number of orders that column's person placed for each flavor.

Instead of passing `PivotTableSQL()` a single column name as a fourth argument, you can also pass an array of labels and SQL expressions. `PivotTable()` treats each of the labels as column headers and uses the SQL expressions to determine what values are grouped into each column. For example, the following code summarizes each person's orders grouped into calorie ranges:

```
$sql = PivotTableSQL($conn,
                     'eaters, ice_cream, orders',
                     'name',
                     array('diet' => 'calories > 0 and calories <= 20',
                           'fatty' => 'calories > 30',
                           'bland' => 'calories = 0'),
                     'eaters.id = orders.eater_id and ice_cream.id =
orders.ice_cream_id');

$rs = $conn->execute($sql);
rs2html($rs);
```

Figure 2-8 shows the pivot table this code generates.

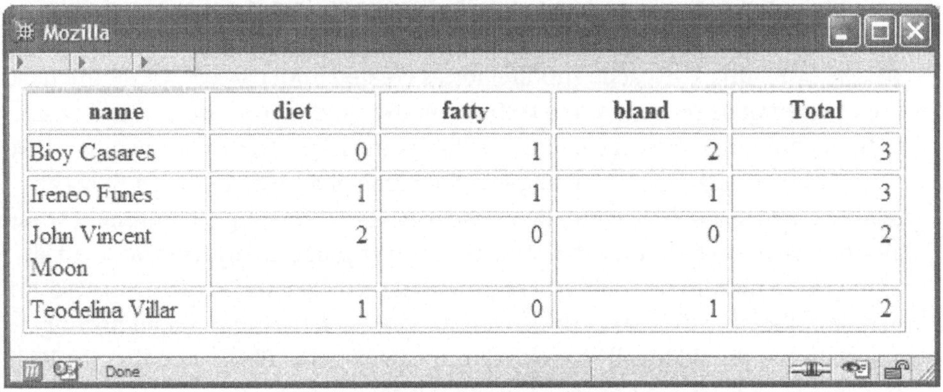

name	diet	fatty	bland	Total
Bioy Casares	0	1	2	3
Ireneo Funes	1	1	1	3
John Vincent Moon	2	0	0	2
Teodelina Villar	1	0	1	2

Figure 2-8. A pivot table can use custom labels for categories.

In this pivot table, each row contains the number of orders placed by that row's person for a flavor whose calories fall into each category: diet for flavors with more than 0 but fewer than or equal to 20 calories, fatty for flavors with more than 30 calories, and bland for flavors with no calories. The total column contains the total number of orders placed by the row's person.

Caching

ADODB has a built-in caching mechanism that you can invoke using a special function to run your queries. Instead of calling `Execute()`, use `CacheExecute()` for a query. The first argument to `CacheExecute()` is how many seconds you want the result of the query cached. The rest of the arguments are the same as `Execute()`:

```
// Cache this recordset for 10 seconds
$rs = $conn->CacheExecute(10,'SELECT flavor, price, calories FROM ice_cream');
```

Record sets are cached in individual files. The filename is calculated from the SQL query passed to `CacheExecute()` and information from the connection handle: the database type, the database name, and the database user. For the purpose of calculating a cache filename, these values are all case-sensitive. If you call `CacheExecute()` twice with two queries that are identical to the database but have different spacing or capitalization, the second call to `CacheExecute()` doesn't retrieve the data from the cache—it sends the query to the database. The query, database type, database name, and database user must be exactly the same for a record set to be retrieved from the cache.

By default, ADODB puts its cache files in subdirectories it creates under the `/tmp` directory. You can change this base cache directory by setting the value of the global variable $ADODB_CACHE_DIR to your chosen directory name. ADODB's caching behavior requires you to consider the permissions on the cache files and directories carefully to make sure that sensitive data is not exposed. First, the user that your Web server is running as must have write permission to $ADODB CACHE_DIR. The cache subdirectories created under $ADODB_CACHE_DIR have their permissions set so that the Web server user and group can read and write to them, but other users have only execute permission. This opens two potential security holes. First, if a user can guess the name of a cache file, then they can read the data inside it. Second, if you are in a shared-hosting environment where all users' sites are served by the same Web server process, any user can read all of the cache files. To deal with these potential security risks, set $ADODB_CACHE_DIR to a new directory that other users can't access. Each user in a shared hosting environment should ideally have their own space in the file system that the Web server serving their site can read but other Web servers can't.

Record sets expire from the cache when their time, as specified to CacheExecute(), expires, but you have two ways to explicitly expire a record set. The first is to call CacheExecute() with a time value of 0. This forces ADODB to send the query to the database and overwrite any possibly cached values with new results. The second way is to call the CacheFlush() method. With no arguments, CacheFlush() removes everything from the cache. If you pass an SQL query to CacheFlush(), it removes from the cache the record set that corresponds to that query.

Both CacheExecute() and CacheFlush() calculate cache filenames based on the SQL query after any placeholders have been replaced. Both the query that contains placeholders and the placeholder array must be identical for two queries to have the same cache file:

```
// Get inexpensive ice cream
$rs = $conn->CacheExecute(10, 'SELECT flavor FROM ice_cream WHERE price < ?',
                          array(4));
// Purge the query from the cache
$conn->CacheFlush('SELECT flavor FROM ice_cream WHERE price < ?',array(4));
```

Exporting Data

The toexport.inc.php file defines some functions that export record sets as tab-delimited or Comma-Separated Value (CSV) data. The rs2csv() function returns a string containing the record set as a series of CSV lines:

```
$rs = $conn->Execute('SELECT * FROM ice_cream');
$csv = rs2csv($rs);
```

The rs2tab() function returns a string containing the record set as a series of lines with tab-delimited values:

```
$rs = $conn->Execute('SELECT * FROM ice_cream');
$csv = rs2tab($rs);
```

Both functions escape double quotes by doubling them. A double quote mark in a value is turned into `""` in the output. Fields with double quotes in them are also surrounded by double quotes. The `rs2csv()` function also surrounds fields that contain commas with double quotes.

There are also versions of these functions that save the CSV or tab-delimited data directly to a file, called `rs2csvfile()` and `rs2tabfile()`. These functions should be passed a file handle as a second argument:

```
if ($fh = fopen('/tmp/ice_cream.csv','w')) {
    $rs = $conn->Execute('SELECT * FROM ice_cream');
    rs2csvfile($rs,$fh);
    fclose($fh);
} else {
    print "Can't open /tmp/ice_cream.csv";
}
```

Additionally, there are versions of `rs2csv()` and `rs2tab()` that print the exported string rather than returning it. They are called `rs2csvout()` and `rs2tabout()`:

```
$rs = $conn->Execute('SELECT * FROM ice_cream');
rs2tabout($rs);
```

Aside from the conversion of double quotes in values, all six export functions convert newlines in values to spaces in output. They also include a title line consisting of the column names in the record set. To suppress the title line, pass `false` as a last argument to any of the functions.

Part Two

HTML

CHAPTER 3

Using HTML_QuickForm for Form Processing

The HTML_QuickForm module makes working with HTML forms easier. Instead of printing form elements one by one, you use its methods to define a form structure that you can print all at once. HTML_QuickForm automatically preserves defaults across form element submission, displays error messages, assures a consistent look to your forms, and simplifies file uploads.

This chapter describes HTML_QuickForm version 3.1. First, the chapter covers the basics of using HTML_QuickForm: the different form elements it supports and how to use them together in a form. It also explains element groups, which are a collection of related elements, such as two radio buttons that offer a Yes/No choice or three text boxes that hold the three parts (area code, exchange, and last four digits) of a phone number. Next, the chapter shows you how to process submitted form data with HTML_QuickForm, including how to handle uploaded files. Finally, the chapter details HTML_QuickForm's validation capabilities. These let you check that the values submitted for specific form elements meet certain requirements, such as exceeding a particular length or matching a specific regular expression. HTML_QuickForm makes it easy to run these validation checks not only on the server once a form has been submitted but via JavaScript in the browser before the fields are submitted.

Creating and Displaying a Form

Usually, displaying a form in PHP is a sequence of `print` statements with logic to handle default values and loops to take care of tedious option lists for giant `<select>` menus that offer choices among all the days in a month or hours in the day. HTML_QuickForm works differently. The elements in a form are specified, in the order they should appear, and then the entire form is displayed at once. The following section details the basics of using HTML_QuickForm.

An HTML_QuickForm Example

This program uses HTML_QuickForm to display, validate, and process a simple form with three elements: a text box, a select box, and a submit button. When the form is submitted, the program checks to make sure that a value was typed in the text box. If so, it prints a message using the submitted data. If not, it redisplays the form with an error message. Figure 3-1 shows the rendered form. Figure 3-2 shows what happens if you submit the form without entering a value in the text box. Figure 3-3 shows what happens when you submit the form with a value in the text box. The following is a simple example:

```
// Load the HTML_QuickForm module
require 'HTML/QuickForm.php';

// Instantiate a new form
$form = new HTML_QuickForm('book');
// Add a text box
$form->addElement('text','title','Book Title:');
// Add a select box
$subjects = array('Math','Ice Fishing','Anatomy');
$form->addElement('select','subject','Subject(s): ',$subjects);
// Add a submit button
$form->addElement('submit','save','Save Book');

// Add a validation rule: title is required
$form->addRule('title','Please Enter a Book Title','required');

// Call the processing function if the submitted form
// data is valid; otherwise, display the form
if ($form->validate()) {
    $form->process('praise_book');
} else {
    $form->display();
}

// Define a function to process the form data
function praise_book($v) {
    global $subjects;
    // Entity-encode any special characters in $v['title']
    $v['title'] = htmlentities($v['title']);
    print "<i>$v[title]</i> is a great book about ";
    print $subjects[$v['subject']] . '.';
}
```

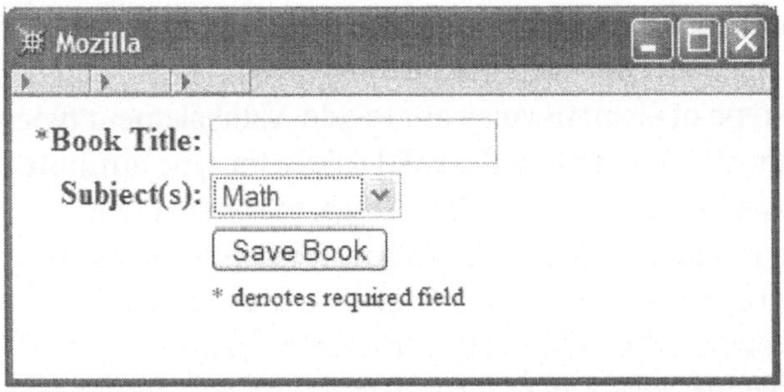

Figure 3-1. HTML_QuickForm produces a form for the browser to display.

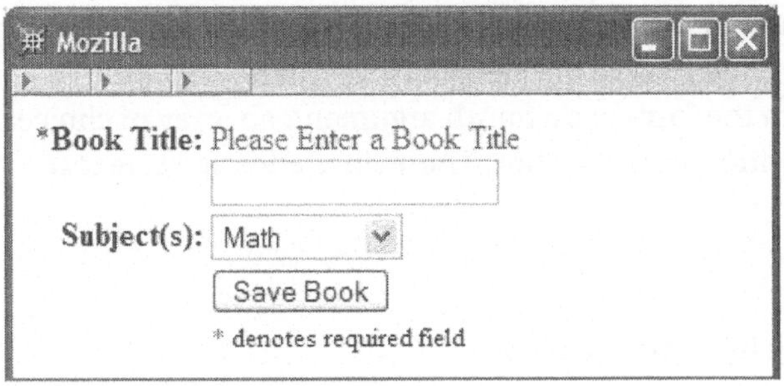

Figure 3-2. If you don't enter a title, an error is printed.

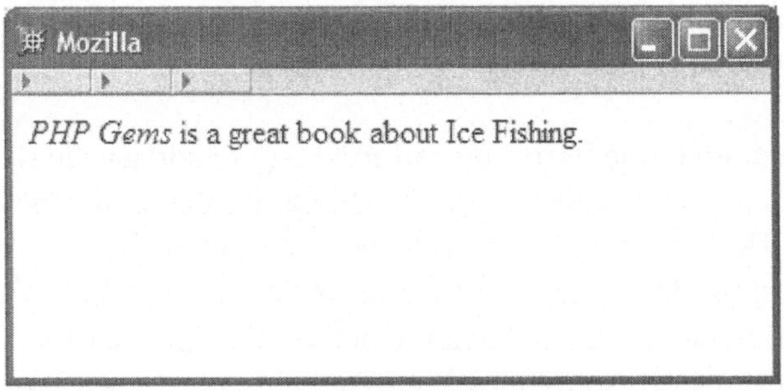

Figure 3-3. The `praise_book()` *function prints a message when a title is submitted.*

The first step when using HTML_QuickForm is to load the code that defines the module with `require` or `include`. HTML_QuickForm is installed under your PEAR base directory at `HTML/QuickForm.php`.

Next, you create a new `HTML_QuickForm` object. The `HTML_Quickform()` constructor takes one argument: the name of the form. This string is used as the value for the `name` and `id` attributes of the `<form>` tag in the page.

The addElement() method adds a new element to the form. The order in which you add elements is the order in which they are displayed. The first argument to addElement() is the type of element you want to add. Valid element types for HTML_QuickForm are mostly the same as the valid values for type attribute of an HTML <input> tag: hidden, reset, checkbox, file, image, password, radio, button, submit, and text. Also valid are select and textarea, which correspond to the HTML <select> and <textarea> tags. HTML_QuickForm also has a few special element types of its own: hiddenselect, link, advcheckbox, date, static, header, and html. The next section covers all of these element types. This example form just uses three: text, select, and submit.

The second argument to each addElement() call is the name of the form element. This string is used as the value for the name attribute of the HTML tag for the element. The third argument to addElement() is a label for the form element. Each element's label is displayed next to the element. The call to addElement() that adds a select element to the form has a fourth argument: an array of choices to display as <option> tags within the select box. These lines add the title text box to the form:

```
// Add a text box
$form->addElement('text','title','Book Title:');
```

These lines add the subject <select> menu, with three choices, to the form:

```
// Add a select box
$subjects = array('Math','Ice Fishing','Anatomy');
$form->addElement('select','subject','Subject(s): ',$subjects);
```

After the elements are added to the form, you call addRule() to add a validation rule. HTML_QuickForm includes many common validation rules, and you can write your own as well. The first argument to addRule() is the element to which the rule applies. The second argument is the error text to display when the rule is broken, and the third argument is the name of the rule. The required rule used in this example ensures that something is entered in the title text box.

Once all of the elements and rules are defined, you can display or process the form as necessary. This example first calls the form's validate() method. This returns true if form data has been submitted, and it passes all the rules defined by addRule(). It returns false if the submitted data fail one or more of the rules or if no data was submitted. If validate() succeeds, the process() method runs the specified form-processing callback function. If validate() fails, the display() method displays the form. The first time the page is loaded, the form is displayed because validate() fails when no form data is submitted. On subsequent submissions of the form, it is only redisplayed if the submitted data fails at least one rule. The process() method calls the praise_book() function and passes it one argument: an array of the submitted form data. The keys in this array correspond to the names of the form elements. The `praise_book()` function uses this array to display a message about the submitted book.

The `display()` method lays out the form elements and their labels in a table. The HTML source code of the example form looks like this:

```
<table border="0">
  <form action="qf-intro-example.php" method="post" name="book" id="book">
  <tr>
  <td align="right" valign="top"><font color="red">*</font><b>Book
Title:</b></td>
  <td valign="top" align="left"><input name="title" type="text" /></td>
  </tr>
  <tr>
  <td align="right" valign="top"><b>Subject(s): </b></td>
  <td valign="top" align="left"><select name="subject">
    <option value="0">Math</option>
    <option value="1">Ice Fishing</option>
    <option value="2">Anatomy</option>
  </select></td>
  </tr>
  <tr>
  <td align="right" valign="top"><b></b></td>
  <td valign="top" align="left">
    <input name="save" value="Save Book" type="submit" />
  </td>
  </tr>
  <tr>
  <td></td>
  <td align="left" valign="top"><font size="1" color="#FF0000">*</font>
    <font size="1"> denotes required field</font>
  </td>
  </tr>
  </form>
</table>
```

By default, HTML_QuickForm uses the POST method and sets the action of the form to the value of `$_SERVER['PHP_SELF']`. You can override these settings by passing arguments to the `HTML_QuickForm` constructor. Remember that the first argument to the constructor is the form name. The second argument is the method to use. To create a form that uses the GET method, pass GET:

```
$form = new HTML_QuickForm('myform','GET');
```

The third argument to the constructor is an alternate URL to use as the form action:

```
$form = new HTML_QuickForm('myform','POST','/store/purchase.php');
```

To give the form a target attribute, which submits the form to a named frame or window, pass the frame or window name as a fourth argument to the constructor:

```
$form = new HTML_QuickForm('myform','POST','/store/purchase.php','shopframe');
```

If you want default values for the method and action URL, you can pass empty strings for those arguments:

```
// use the default method (POST), but change the action URL
$form = new HTML_QuickForm('myform','','/store/purchase.php');
// submit the form to a new blank window, but use the default method and URL
$form = new HTML_QuickForm('myform','','','_blank');
```

To include arbitrary attribute/value pairs in the `<form>` tag, pass those as a fifth argument to the constructor. You can specify the attributes and values as a string:

```
$form = new HTML_QuickForm('myform','','','','class="big" style="bold"');
```

Or, you can specify the attributes as an array:

```
$form = new HTML_QuickForm('myform','','','',
                           array('class' => 'big', 'style' => 'bold'));
```

Individual Elements

There are two ways to add elements to a form. The first is to use the `addElement()` method of the form object. This is how you built the form in the previous section. Because you can pass `addElement()` arguments that control various aspects and attributes of the form element, it's a flexible one-step way to populate your form. The other way to add elements to a form is to create elements as separate objects with the `createElement()` static method. This method takes the same arguments as `addElement()` but returns an object. You can then add the element to the form by passing the object to `addElement()`. In this example, two text elements are added to the form: the first using just `addElement()` and the second using `createElement()` with `addElement()`.

```
// $form is an HTML_QuickForm object
// add the text field in one step with addElement()
```

```
$form->addElement('text','first_name','First Name:');
// create the element with createElement() and then pass it to addElement()
$element =& HTML_QuickForm::createElement('text','last_name','Last Name:');
$form->addElement($element);
```

To avoid making copies of the object as it is created, it is necessary to retrieve the result of `createElement()` by reference with the `&` operator. This is not necessary in PHP 5. Using `createElement()` adds an extra step, but it also gives you access to the element object. You can call methods on the element object to alter its behavior. For example, the text element has methods called `setSize()` and `setMaxlength()`, which set the size and `maxlength` attributes of the element, respectively:

```
$element =& HTML_QuickForm::createElement('text','last_name','Last Name:');
$element->setSize(10); // Render the element as ten characters wide
$element->setMaxlength(30); // Allow no more than 30 characters of input
$form->addElement($element);
```

If you add elements to the form without using `createElement()`, you can retrieve element objects later with `getElement()`. Pass it the name of an element, and it returns the corresponding element object. You must retrieve the object by reference so that any changes you make to it are accurately reflected in the form:

```
$form->addElement('text','first_name','First Name:');
$element=& $form->getElement('first_name');
$element->setSize(40);
```

Some element methods retrieve information about the element instead of modifying it. For example, `getName()` returns an element's name:

```
$form->addElement('text','first_name','First Name:');
$element=& $form->getElement('first_name');
// this sets $name to "first_name"
$name = $element->getName();
```

All elements have the methods `setName()`, `getName()`, `setValue()`, `getValue()`, `setLabel()`, and `getLabel()`.

text

The `text` element produces the single-line text-entry box displayed by the HTML tag `<input type="text">`.

These are the valid arguments when creating a `text` element:

- `$elementName`: The `name` attribute of the element's `<input>` tag
- `$elementLabel`: The label of the element in the form
- `$attributes`: Arbitrary element attributes, as a string or an associative array

These are its methods:

- `setSize()`: The `size` attribute controls the width of the displayed text box.
- `setMaxlength()`: The `maxlength` attribute tells the browser how many characters can be typed into the text box.

The following is a sample usage:

```
$form->addElement('text','first_name','First Name:','class="big"');
```

This is the sample HTML:

```
<tr>
  <td align="right" valign="top"><b>First Name:</b></td>
  <td valign="top" align="left"><input class="big" name="first_name" type="text"
   /></td>
</tr>
```

password

The `password` element behaves just like the `text` element, but it is displayed with the `<input type="password">` tag instead of `<input type="text">`. This means that text entered into a password box isn't displayed as it's entered. Instead, an asterisk or other symbol is shown in place of each character.

textarea

The `textarea` element produces the multiple-line text-entry area displayed by the HTML tags `<textarea></textarea>`.

These are the valid arguments when creating a `textarea` element:

- `$elementName`: The `name` attribute of the element's `<input>` tag
- `$elementLabel`: The label of the element in the form
- `$attributes`: Arbitrary element attributes, as a string or an associative array

The following are its methods:

- `setWrap()`: The `wrap` attribute controls how lines are wrapped inside the textarea. `soft` means that the browser displays wrapped text but doesn't send the line breaks with submitted data, `hard` means that wrapped text is displayed and sent to the server, and `off` means the browser does no wrapping on its own.

- `setRows()`: The `rows` attribute controls how many lines of text are visible in the textarea at one time.

- `setCols()`: The `cols` attribute controls the width of the textarea.

The following is a sample usage:

```
$form->addElement('textarea','profile','Describe yourself:','wrap="soft"');
```

The following is the sample HTML:

```
<tr>
  <td align="right" valign="top"><b>Describe yourself:</b></td>
  <td valign="top" align="left"><textarea wrap="soft" name="profile">
   </textarea></td>
</tr>
```

hidden

The `hidden` element produces an HTML `<input type="hidden">` tag. The browser doesn't display any input widget when it sees this tag. Hidden elements are useful for passing values from page to page in a form. Remember, though, that a user can see the value of a `hidden` element by viewing the source code to a Web page. They are displayed without a label or other formatting.

These are the valid arguments when creating a `hidden` element:

- `$elementName`: The `name` attribute of the element's `<input>` tag.

- `$elementValue`: The default value to use for the element. This is overridden by a submitted form value.

- `$attributes`: Arbitrary element attributes, as a string or an associative array.

The following is a sample usage:

```
$form->addElement('hidden','code',120374);
```

This is the sample HTML:

```
<input name="code" type="hidden" value="120374" />
```

select

The select element produces the drop-down box displayed by the HTML <select> tag.

These are the valid arguments when creating a select element:

- $elementName: The name attribute of the element's <input> tag
- $elementLabel: The label of the element in the form
- $options: An array holding choices to display in the menu
- $attributes: Arbitrary element attributes, as a string or an associative array

The following are its methods:

setMultiple(): This sets the multiple attribute, which controls whether the user can select more than one element from the menu.

getMultiple(): This gets the value of the multiple attribute.

setSelected(): This sets an array containing the selected value or values from the menu.

getSelected(): This gets the array of selected values from the menu.

setSize(): This sets the size attribute, which controls how many options to display at once if multiple is set.

getSize(): This gets the value of the size attribute.

getPrivateName(): This returns the element name as displayed in the form. When multiple is set, this is the result of getName() with [] appended to it.

addOption($text, $value, $attributes): This adds an option to the end of the element's menu. The $attributes argument is optional.

`loadArray($arr, $values)`: This adds the options in the associative array `$arr` to the end of the element's menu. The values of the new options are taken from the keys of `$arr`. The text of the new options is taken from the values of `$arr`. The optional `$values` argument holds an array or comma-separated string of values to set as selected in the menu. For example:

```
$s =& $form->createElement('select','animal','Animal: ');
$opts = array('dog' => 'woof', 'cat' => 'meow', 'cow' => 'moo');
$s->loadArray($opts,'cat');
$form->addElement($s);
```

The menu is displayed with the following HTML:

```
<tr>
  <td align="right" valign="top"><b>Animal: </b></td>
  <td valign="top" align="left"><select name="animal">
    <option value="dog">woof</option>
    <option value="cat" selected="selected">meow</option>
    <option value="cow">moo</option>
</select></td>
</tr>
```

`loadDbResult($result, $textCol, $valueCol, $values)`: This adds options from the PEAR DB `DB_Result` object to the end of the element's menu. The `$textCol` argument holds the name of the column in the `DB_Result` object to use as the text of each option, and the `$valueCol` argument holds the name of the column to use as the value of each option. Both `$textCol` and `$valueCol` are optional. If they are omitted (or NULL), then the text of each option is the first column in the `DB_Result` object, and the value of each option is the second column. As in `loadArray()`, the optional `$values` argument holds an array or comma-separated string of values to set as selected in the menu.

`loadQuery($conn, $sql, $textCol, $valueCol, $values)`: This runs a database query and adds options from the query results to the end of the element's menu. The `$conn` argument is either a valid PEAR DB database connection handle or a string containing a PEAR DB Data Source Name (DSN). If `$conn` is a connection handle, then the SQL query in `$sql` is sent to the database using that connection handle. If `$conn` is a DSN, then a connection is established using the DSN, and the query in `$sql` is sent to the database using that new connection handle. The optional `$textCol`, `$valueCol`, and `$values` arguments behave as they do in the `loadDbResult()` method. Because `loadQuery()` accepts its first argument by reference, you can't pass a DSN as a string literal but must instead pass a variable that holds the DSN. For example:

```
// The right way to do it
$dsn = 'mysql://user:password@host/db';
$s->loadQuery($dsn,'SELECT flavor,id FROM ice_cream');
// The wrong way to do it:
$s->loadQuery('mysql://user:password@host/db','SELECT flavor,id FROM➥
ice_cream');
```

If you pass `$options` as indexed array, the values in the array appear as choices, and the `value` attribute of each `<option>` tag is set to the numeric key of each array element. For example:

```
$subjects = array('Math','Ice Fishing','Anatomy');
$form->addElement('select','subject','Subject(s): ',$subjects);
```

When this form is displayed, the select element is expressed with the following HTML:

```
<select name="subject">
    <option value="0">Math</option>
    <option value="1">Ice Fishing</option>
    <option value="2">Anatomy</option>
</select>
```

The first element of the `$subjects` array has the key 0 and the value `Math`. So the first `<option>` tag displayed has its `value` attribute set to `0`, and the text between the `<option>` and `</option>` tags is `Math`. If you select `Math` from the list of choices and submit the form, the value of the submitted form variable `subject` is 0. If you select `Anatomy` from the list of choices and submit the form, the value of `subject` is 1.

To specify `<option>` values explicitly, define both keys and values in the `$options` array:

```
$elevator = array(22 => 'Rooftop Dining Room',
                   4 => 'Library',
                   1 => 'Lobby');
$form->addElement('select','which_floor','Your Floor: ',$elevator);
```

This produces the following HTML:

```
<select name="which_floor">
    <option value="22">Rooftop Dining Room</option>
    <option value="4">Library</option>
    <option value="1">Lobby</option>
</select>
```

Note that the order in which the choices appear in the drop-down box is the same as the order in which they are defined in the array. To have string `<option>` values, use string keys in the array:

```
$elevator = array('Rooftop Dining Room' => '22nd Floor',
                  'Library' => '4th Floor',
                  'Lobby' => '1st Floor');
$form->addElement('select','which_floor','Your Floor: ',$elevator);
```

Just as before, the `<option>` value attributes are set to the keys of the `$elevator` array. Because those keys are strings in this example, the `value` attributes are strings as well:

```
<select name="which_floor">
    <option value="Rooftop Dining Room">22nd Floor</option>
    <option value="Library">4th Floor</option>
    <option value="Lobby">1st Floor</option>
</select>
```

checkbox

The `checkbox` element produces an HTML `<input type="checkbox">` tag. The `value` attribute of this input tag is always set to `1`.

These are the valid arguments when creating a `checkbox` element:

- `$elementName`: The `name` attribute of the element's `<input>` tag
- `$elementLabel`: The label of the element in the form
- `$text`: The display text
- `$attributes`: Arbitrary element attributes, as a string or an associative array

It takes the following methods:

- `setChecked()`: Sets the `checked` attribute, which causes a check to be displayed inside the checkbox
- `getChecked()`: Gets the value of the `checked` attribute
- `setText()`: Sets the display text printed to the right of the checkbox
- `getText()`: Gets the display text printed to the right of the checkbox

The following is the sample usage:

```
$form->addElement('checkbox','redeye','Red Eye OK?',
                  '(Check if a late night flight is acceptable.)');
```

This is the sample HTML:

```
<input name="redeye" type="checkbox" value="1" id="qf_ca4d9a" />
<label for="qf_ca4d9a">(Check if a late night flight is acceptable.)
</label>
```

The `for` attribute of the `<label>` tag corresponds to the `id` attribute of the `<input>` tag. This ID value is generated internally by HTML_QuickForm.

If a checkbox is left unchecked in a submitted form, then an element with the name of the checkbox isn't defined at all in the array of submitted form variables. If the checkbox is checked, then the element with the same name as the checkbox has a value of `1` in the array of submitted form variables.

radio

The `radio` element produces an HTML `<input type="radio">` tag. Radio buttons are like checkboxes, but if you put multiple radio buttons with the same name in one form, the browser only lets one radio button be selected at a time.

These are the valid arguments when creating a `radio` element:

- `$elementName`: The `name` attribute of the element's `<input>` tag
- `$elementLabel`: The label of the element in the form
- `$text`: The display text
- `$value`: The `value` attribute of the element's `<input>` tag
- `$attributes`: Arbitrary element attributes, as a string or an associative array

The following is the sample usage:

```
$form->addElement('radio','when','Departure:','Depart in the morning','morning');
$form->addElement('radio','when',null,'Depart in the afternoon','afternoon');
$form->addElement('radio','when',null,'Depart in the evening','evening');
```

The following is the sample HTML:

```
<tr>
  <td align="right" valign="top"><b>Departure:</b></td>
  <td valign="top" align="left"><input name="when" value="morning"
type="radio" id="qf_27dde5" /><label for="qf_27dde5">Depart in the
morning</label></td>
</tr>
<tr>
  <td align="right" valign="top"><b></b></td>
  <td valign="top" align="left"><input name="when" value="afternoon"
type="radio" id="qf_2316ca" /><label for="qf_2316ca">Depart in the
afternoon</label></td>
</tr>
<tr>
  <td align="right" valign="top"><b></b></td>
  <td valign="top" align="left"><input name="when" value="evening"
type="radio" id="qf_f7bf3f" /><label for="qf_f7bf3f">Depart in the
evening</label></td>
</tr>
```

Each radio button `<input>` element has the same name but a different value. If the user chooses the `Depart in the morning` radio button, then the value of the `when` element of the submitted form variable array is `"morning"`. If the user chooses the `Depart in the afternoon` or `Depart in the evening` radio buttons, the value of the submitted form variable is `afternoon` or `evening`, respectively.

submit

The `submit` element produces an HTML `<input type="submit">` tag. This is typically displayed by the browser as a button that, when clicked, submits the form to the server.

These are the valid arguments when creating a `submit` element:

- `$elementName`: This is the `name` attribute of the element's `<input>` tag.
- `$value`: The `value` attribute of the element's `<input>` tag. This is displayed on the button.
- `$attributes`: Arbitrary element attributes, as a string or an associative array

The following is a sample usage:

```
$form->addElement('submit','save','Save Data');
```

The following is the sample HTML:

```
<tr>
  <td align="right" valign="top"><b></b></td>
  <td valign="top" align="left"><input name="save" value="Save Data"
   type="submit" /></td>
</tr>
```

reset

The `reset` element produces an HTML `<input type="reset">` tag. This element is identical to the `submit` element except that the reset button resets all elements in the form to their default values instead of submitting the form.

button

The `button` element produces an HTML `<input type="button">` tag. This element is identical to the `submit` element except that the button has no default action associated with it. Typically, an action is linked to a `button` element by setting its `onClick` attribute to JavaScript that runs when the button is clicked.

The following is the sample usage:

```
$form->addElement('button','check','Check the Page','onClick="checkPage();"');
```

The following is the sample HTML:

```
<tr>
  <td align="right" valign="top"><b></b></td>
  <td valign="top" align="left"><input onclick="checkPage();" name="check"
value="Check the Page" type="button" /></td>
</tr>
```

image

The image element produces an HTML <input type="image"> tag. This displays an image in the form. A user can click the image to submit the form. The x and y coordinates of the pixel the user clicked in the image are submitted with the form as well.

These are the valid arguments when creating an image element:

- $elementName: The name attribute of the element's <input> tag.
- $src: The src attribute is a relative or absolute URL of the image to display.
- $attributes: Arbitrary element attributes, as a string or an associative array

The following is the sample usage:

```
$form->addElement('image','state_map','/usa-states.png');
```

The following is the sample HTML:

```
<tr>
  <td align="right" valign="top"><b></b></td>
  <td valign="top" align="left"><input name="state_map" type="image"
   src="/usa-states.png" /></td>
</tr>
```

If a user submits the form by clicking in the upper-leftmost corner of the image, the submitted form variables state_map_x and state_map_y are both set to 0. A click ten pixels to the right and eight pixels down sets state_map_x to 10 and state_map_y to 8. Because the name attribute of the <input type="image"> tag is state_map, the submitted form variable state_map_x is set to the horizontal position in the image of the user's click. Similarly, the submitted form variable state_map_y is set to the vertical position in the image of the user's click.

The same rules apply for URLs in the src attribute of <input type="image"> tags as they do in the src attribute of an <img> tag. If you specify a full URL, beginning with http://, the browser fetches the image from that location. If you just specify a pathname, the browser looks for the image relative to the URL of the page in which the form appears.

file

The file element produces an HTML <input type="file"> tag. This displays a text box and a button that, when clicked, brings up a file selection dialog box. The file element lets users upload a file to your server.

These are the valid arguments when creating a file element:

- $elementName: The name attribute of the element's <input> tag
- $elementLabel: The label of the element in the form
- $attributes: Arbitrary element attributes, as a string or an associative array

It takes the following methods:

- setSize(): Sets the size attribute, which controls how wide the input field is in the browser
- getSize(): Gets the value of the size attribute

The following is the sample usage:

```
$form->addElement('file','data','Your File:');
```

The following is the sample HTML:

```
<tr>
  <td align="right" valign="top"><b>Your File:</b></td>
  <td valign="top" align="left"><input name="data" type="file" /></td>
</tr>
```

When your form contains a file element, HTML_QuickForm adds an enctype attribute with the value multipart/form-data to the <form> tag. This instructs the browser to properly package the submitted form data, including the contents of the uploaded file, so that the server can parse it. Additionally, HTML_QuickForm adds a hidden element called MAX_FILE_SIZE to the form. This defaults to 1MB (1,048,576 bytes). You can change this by calling the setMaxFileSize() method on the form object with a new value. The MAX_FILE_SIZE variable is used by well-behaved browsers to prevent uploads of too-large files. A malicious user could circumvent the MAX_FILE_SIZE limitation. The maximum uploaded file size that PHP accepts is controlled by PHP's upload_max_filesize configuration directive.

advcheckbox

The advcheckbox element generates a checkbox with a value that you can specify. This differs from the checkbox element, whose value attribute is always set to 1. The advcheckbox element creates a regular checkbox element in the form but also a hidden element. When the checkbox is checked, the value of the hidden element is updated, using JavaScript, to the specified value.

These are the valid arguments when creating an `advcheckbox` element:

- `$elementName`: The name for HTML_QuickForm's internal element array
- `$elementLabel`: The label of the text in the form
- `$text`: The text to display in the form
- `$attributes`: Arbitrary element attributes, as a string or an associative array
- `$values`: The specified value to submit when the checkbox is checked

It takes the following method:

- `setValues()`: This sets the values stored in the `hidden` element. You can pass a `false` value to `setValues()` to make the checkbox act like a regular checkbox. Otherwise, the number or string passed in is stored in the `hidden` element.

The following is the sample usage:

```
$form->addElement('advcheckbox','window_seat','Seat Location:',
                  'Check if you want a window seat',null,'yes');
```

The following is the sample HTML:

```
<tr>
  <td align="right" valign="top"><b>Seat Location:</b></td>
  <td valign="top" align="left"><input name="__window_seat"
  type="checkbox" value="1" onclick="if (this.checked) {
this.form['window_seat'].value='yes'; }else { this.form['window_seat'].value='';
}" />Check if you want a window seat<input type="hidden" name="window_seat"
value="" /></td>
</tr>
```

static

The `static` element generates plain text that is paired with a label in the form layout. This element isn't a form widget like a text box or select menu but is useful for displaying information about or a description of a neighboring element.

These are the valid arguments when creating a `static` element:

- `$elementName`: The name for HTML_QuickForm's internal element array
- `$elementLabel`: The label of the text in the form
- `$text`: The text to display in the form
- `$attributes`: Arbitrary element attributes, as a string or an associative array

The following is the sample usage:

```
$form->addElement('static','info','Information:',"Don't run with scissors");
```

This is the sample HTML:

```
<tr>
  <td align="right" valign="top"><b>Information:</b></td>
  <td valign="top" align="left">Don't run with scissors</td>
</tr>
```

header

The `header` element is similar to the `static` element but only its label is displayed, and it has different formatting. This makes it useful for a header that sets off a section of a form.

These are the valid arguments when creating a `header` element:

- `$elementName`: The name for HTML_QuickForm's internal element array
- `$text`: The text to display in the form

The following is the sample usage:

```
$form->addElement('header','episode_4','A New Hope');
```

The following is the sample HTML:

```
<tr>
  <td nowrap="nowrap" align="left" valign="top" colspan="2" bgcolor="#CCCCCC">
<b>A New Hope</b></td>
</tr>
```

link

The `link` element generates an HTML `<a>` tag that is paired with a label in the form layout.

These are the valid arguments when creating a `link` element:

- `$elementName`: The `name` attribute of the element's `<a>` tag
- `$elementLabel`: The label of the link in the form
- `$href`: The target of the link
- `$text`: The text to display in the form
- `$attributes`: Arbitrary element attributes, as a string or an associative array

The following is the sample usage:

```
$form->addElement('link','pp_link','Privacy Policy:',
                  'http://www.example.com/privacy.html', 'Click Here',
                  '_target="blank"');
```

The following is the sample HTML:

```
<tr>
  <td align="right" valign="top"><b>Privacy Policy:</b></td>
  <td valign="top" align="left"><a _target="blank" name="pp_link"
href="http://www.example.com/privacy.html">Click Here</a></td>
</tr>
```

html

The `html` element inserts unmodified HTML into the rendering of the form. Because HTML_QuickForm displays form elements in table rows, take care to format HTML inserted with this element properly so that it fits into the form's table.

This is the valid argument when creating an `html` element:

- `$text`: The HTML to display in the form

The following is the sample usage:

```
$form->addElement('html','<img src="spacer.png">');
```

The following is the sample HTML:

```
<img src="spacer.png">
```

Element Groups

You can present elements in groups with HTML_QuickForm. This changes their layout. Instead of each element having its own label and table row, all the elements in a group are displayed in the same table row. They share a label. To group elements, first create each of them using the createElement() method. Store the created elements in an array. Then, add the group of elements to the form by passing the array to the addGroup() method. For example, here's how to create a group of three text fields:

```
$name[] = &HTML_QuickForm::createElement('text','firstname');
$name[] = &HTML_QuickForm::createElement('text','middlename');
$name[] = &HTML_QuickForm::createElement('text','lastname');
$form->addGroup($name,'user_name','Your Name: ',' ');
```

This adds the following HTML to the form:

```
<tr>
  <td align="right" valign="top"><b>Your Name: </b></td>
  <td valign="top" align="left"><input name="user_name[firstname]" type="text"
/> <input name="user_name[middlename]" type="text" /> <input
name="user_name[lastname]" type="text" /></td>
</tr>
```

Each call to createElement() adds another element to the $name array. You can specify null for arguments such as label when you call createElement() because these elements take their label from the group.

The first argument to addGroup() is the array of elements that make up the group. The second argument is the name of the group, and the third argument is the single label used for the entire group. The individual element names in the HTML are constructed from the group name passed to addGroup() and the element name passed to createElement(). The group is treated as an array, and each text field is an element of that array. This results in individual element names of user_name[firstname], user_name[middlename], and user_name[lastname].

The <input type="text"> HTML tags for each element of the user_name group are separated by a space because the third argument to the addGroup() call is a space. Specify any string to separate the elements by passing it to addGroup(). For phone numbers, a hyphen is a good separator:

```
$phone[] = &HTML_QuickForm::createElement('text','areacode',null,'size="3"');
$phone[] = &HTML_QuickForm::createElement('text','exchange',null,'size="3"');
$phone[] = &HTML_QuickForm::createElement('text','last4',null,'size="4"');
$form->addGroup($phone,'phone_number','Phone: ','-');
```

This group displays the following HTML:

```
<tr>
  <td align="right" valign="top"><b>Phone: </b></td>
  <td valign="top" align="left"><input size="3" name="phone_number[areacode]"
type="text" />-<input size="3" name="phone_number[exchange]" type="text" />-
<input size="4" name="phone_number[last4]" type="text" /></td>
</tr>
```

In addition to using - as the element separator, this example passed attributes to `createElement()` as a fourth argument. These attributes adjust the size of each text field. The third argument, where a label would go, was left as the empty string. You can also use HTML as a group element separator. For example, make `<br />` the group element separator to display a line break between each element in the group.

Grouping Radio Buttons

Creating a group of radio buttons with the same name but different values requires a slightly different syntax. The radio buttons should be created with no name or label, just text and value. For example, the following are three radio buttons in a group, each corresponding to one meal:

```
$meals[] =& HTML_QuickForm::createElement('radio',null,null,'Breakfast','br');
$meals[] =& HTML_QuickForm::createElement('radio',null,null,'Lunch','lu');
$meals[] =& HTML_QuickForm::createElement('radio',null,null,'Dinner','di');
$form->addGroup($meals,'meal','Meal: ','<br>');
```

Because each of the radio buttons in the group have no name of their own, they each take their name from the group name: `meal`. They have identical names but different values. Only one of the values is submitted with the form. For example, if the Breakfast radio button is selected, then the submitted form variable `meal` has the value `br`. The following is what the HTML looks like for this group of radio buttons:

```
<tr>
  <td align="right" valign="top"><b>Meal: </b></td>
  <td valign="top" align="left"><input value="br" type="radio" id="qf_a8704d"
```

```
name="meal" /><label for="qf_a8704d">Breakfast</label><br>
<input value="lu" type="radio" id="qf_39a433" name="meal" /><label
 for="qf_39a433">Lunch</label><br>
<input value="di" type="radio" id="qf_c5fabd" name="meal" /><label
 for="qf_c5fabd">Dinner</label></td>
</tr>
```

Processing Submitted Data

Displaying a form is only half of the picture. When a user submits a form, you need to validate and process the data entered in all of the form elements. HTML_QuickForm gives you two ways to handle that data: with or without a callback function.

Using a Callback Function

The `process()` method accepts the name of a callback function that is passed an array of submitted form variables. Call `process()` when you want to do something with the form data. Like the example at the beginning of the chapter, code that uses HTML_QuickForm often has the following `if` statement that processes the form if data has been submitted and displays the form otherwise:

```
// Call the processing function if the submitted form data is valid
// Otherwise, display the form
if ($form->validate()) {
    $form->process('praise_book');
} else {
    $form->display();
}
```

When you call `$form->process('praise_book')`, it in turn calls a function named `praise_book()` and passes it an associative array of submitted form data. The following is an example where the processing callback sends an e-mail message to `webmaster@example.com` with the subject and body entered in the form:

```
$form = new HTML_QuickForm('send_email');
$form->addElement('text','subject','Subject: ','size="30" maxlength="128"');
$form->addElement('textarea','body','Message Body: ','rows="10" cols="30"');
$form->addElement('submit','send','Send Message');
if ($form->validate()) {
    $form->process('send_message');
```

```
} else {
    $form->display();
}
function send_message($data) {
    mail('webmaster@example.com',$data['subject'],$data['body']);
    print "Your message has been sent.";
}
```

The `$data` array in `send_message()` is populated with the submitted form data. The value of the array element with the key `subject` is the value of the submitted form element subject. The same is true for the other elements in the form: `body` and `send`.

By default `process()` includes information about uploaded files in the array it passes to the callback. To exclude uploaded file-related information, pass `process()` a second argument of `false`.

When a file is uploaded via a form, the server saves it in a temporary file. Before opening or processing the uploaded file, you should move it to a separate directory with the `moveUploadedFile()` method. Using this method protects you from accidentally moving a file that wasn't uploaded via an HTML form. The `moveUploadedFile()` method is a method of the file upload form element. To call `moveUploadedFile()`, first access the form element with `getElement()` and then pass `moveUploadedFile()` two arguments: the directory to move the file to and the new filename in the destination directory. This moves the file uploaded via the form element `myfile` to `/tmp/processed.txt`:

```
$file =& $form->getElement('myfile');
$file->moveUploadedFile('/tmp','processed.txt');
```

Take care to use `=&` with `getElement()` so that `$file` is a reference to the appropriate form element and not a copy.

In the array of submitted form data passed to `process()`, file elements have more information than other input elements. Instead of a scalar value, there's an array of data about the uploaded file. Table 3-1 lists the elements of this array.

Table 3-1. Uploaded File Information

Array Key	Description
name	Filename on the client
type	MIME type of file
tmp_name	Temporary filename on the server
size	File size
error	Error when uploading, if any

You should treat this information about the uploaded file with some skepticism. The values for name and type come from the browser. They are not calculated by the server. Although most browsers report this data correctly, nothing prevents a malicious user from constructing a file upload form submission that includes false values for this data. If you use the reported name to construct a filename on the server for the uploaded file, filter out strings such as .., /, and \. Table 3-2 lists the possible values for the error array element.

Table 3-2. Upload File Error Codes

Error Code	Description
0	No error; upload successful.
1	The file size is bigger than `upload_max_filesize` configuration directive.
2	The file size is bigger than `MAX_FILE_SIZE` form variable.
3	The file was partially uploaded.
4	No file was uploaded.

The following code shows a complete file upload example:

```
$form = new HTML_QuickForm('uploader');

// File upload needs an element of type "file"
$form->addElement('file','uploaded_file','Your File:');

// We want files of 128kbytes or less
$max_size = 131072;

// Make sure that a file is uploaded
$form->addRule('uploaded_file','Please upload a file','uploadedfile');

// Have HTML_QuickForm test, after the file is uploaded, that it is
// less than 128k
$form->addRule('uploaded_file','Your file is too big','maxfilesize',$max_size);
$form->addElement('submit','save','Send It');

// Tell well-behaved browsers not to allow upload of a file larger than
// 128k
$form->setMaxFileSize(131072);
```

```
// Display or process the form
if ($form->validate()) {
    $form->process('move_file');
} else {
    $form->display();
}

function move_file($data) {
    global $form;

    // Remove backslashes and forward slashes from new filename
    $new_name = strtr($data['uploaded_file']['name'],'/\\','');
    // Remove ".." from new filename
    $new_name = str_replace('..','',$new_name);

    $file =& $form->getElement('uploaded_file');
    if ($file->moveUploadedFile('/tmp',$new_name)) {
        print "The file has been uploaded to /tmp/$new_name.";
    } else {
        print "The file could not be uploaded to /tmp/$new_name.";
    }
}
```

This example puts acceptable uploaded files in the `/tmp` directory. There are two calls to `addRule()`, which implement built-in HTML_QuickForm form validation rules. These are explained in more detail in the "Setting Validation Rules" section. The two rules used here are `uploadedfile`, which ensures that the specified field contains an uploaded file and not other form data, and `maxfilesize`, which checks the size of an uploaded file against a limit. The call to `setMaxFileSize()` adjusts the `MAX_FILE_SIZE` hidden element in the form. As discussed previously, this field is used by well-behaved browsers to prevent an oversized file from being sent with the form submission.

Once a file is uploaded, the example calls the `move_file()` function to process it. This function massages the supplied filename for the uploaded file to remove special characters and then moves the file into the `/tmp` directory.

Without a Callback Function

If you don't want to use the `process()` method and a callback function, you can access submitted form data directly with the `getSubmitValues()` method. It returns an array of submitted form data. The keys in the array are the names of the form elements, and the values in the array are the corresponding values of each form element. Once you retrieve the array of submitted form data with `getSubmitValues()`, you can process the information from the form. The following is the simple e-mail message sending example using `getSubmitValues()` instead of `process()`:

```
$form = new HTML_QuickForm('send_email');
$form->addElement('text','subject','Subject: ','size="30" maxlength="128"');
$form->addElement('textarea','body','Message Body: ','rows="10" cols="30"');
$form->addElement('submit','send','Send Message');
$data = $form->getSubmitValues();
if ($data['send']) {
    mail('webmaster@example.com',$data['subject'],$data['body']);
    print "Your message has been sent.";
} else {
    $form->display();
}
```

After adding appropriate elements to the form, the program puts any submitted form data into `$data` by using `getSubmitValues()`. The submit button in the form is named `send`, so if that element of data has a value, the program assumes the form has been submitted. It uses the `mail()` function to send an e-mail message. If `$data['send']` is `false`, then the program displays the form instead.

The `getSubmitValues()` method of an `HTML_QuickForm` object only returns data submitted via the method (GET or POST) that the object uses. Variables in the query string aren't included in what `getSubmitValues()` returns for a POST form. Similarly, variables in POST data aren't included in what `getSubmitValues()` returns for a GET form. Also, the array `getSubmitValues()` returns doesn't include any information on uploaded files.

Setting Validation Rules

HTML_QuickForm provides a flexible structure to incorporate data validation rules into your form. A number of common rules are included, and you can write your own as well. The `addRule()` method tells HTML_QuickForm to check the value in an element against a rule. For example, the `required` rule makes sure that the form element has a value:

```
$form->addElement('text','subject','Subject: ','size="30" maxlength="128"');
$form->addRule('subject','Enter a subject','required');
```

The first argument to addRule() is the name of the element to which the rule should be applied. The second argument is the message displayed if the rule isn't satisfied, and the third argument is the rule to apply. You must add an element to a form with addElement() before adding a rule for that element with addRule(). When the required rule is applied to an element, a small red asterisk appears next to the element and a note explaining that the asterisk denotes a required field is displayed at the bottom of the form. Figure 3-4 shows what the browser displays when the form is submitted without a value in the subject field.

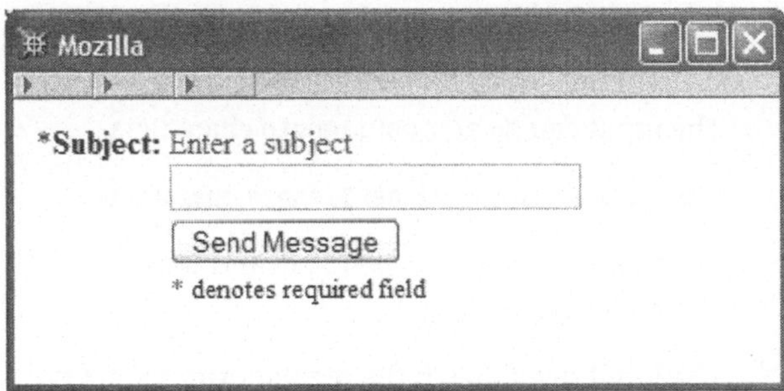

Figure 3-4. An error message is displayed when a validation rule is not satisfied.

HTML_QuickForm checks if submitted form data passes the rules when you call the validate() method. This method returns true if all the rules are satisfied or if no data was submitted. This makes it a useful condition in the if statement that decides whether to display or process the form. Instead of checking the value of a submitted element, you just call $form->validate():

```
if ($form->validate()) {
    mail('webmaster@example.com',$data['subject'],$data['body']);
    print "Your message has been sent.";
} else {
    $form->display();
}
```

If no data is submitted, then validate() returns false and the form is displayed. Similarly, if one or more of the validation rules isn't satisfied, validate() also returns false. This causes the form to be redisplayed, but this time it is displayed with error messages. If all of the validation rules are satisfied, then the form processing code that sends the e-mail message runs.

Built-in Validation Rules

The rules that HTML_QuickForm supports are `required`, `maxlength`, `minlength`, `rangelength`, `regex`, `email`, `emailorblank`, `lettersonly`, `alphanumeric`, `nopunctuation`, and `nonzero`. It also supports four rules for checking uploaded files: `uploadedfile`, `maxfilesize`, `mimetype`, and `filename`. Table 3-3 explains the built-in rules.

Table 3-3. Built-in Validation Rules

Rule Name	Argument	Rule Description
`required`		Some input is required in the field.
`maxlength`	`$length`	The input can be at most `$length` characters.
`minlength`	`$length`	The input must be at least `$length` characters.
`rangelength`	`$min,$max`	The input must be between `$min` and `$max` characters (inclusive).
`regex`	`$rx`	The input must match the regular expression `$rx`.
`email`		The input must be a likely syntactically valid e-mail address.*
`emailorblank`		The input must be blank or satisfy the `email` rule.
`lettersonly`		The input must contain only alphabetic characters.
`alphanumeric`		The input must contain only letters and numbers.
`numeric`		The input must contain a valid positive or negative integer or decimal number.
`nopunctuation`		The input must not contain any of these characters: `( ) . / * ^ ? # ! @ $ % + = , " ' > < ~ [ ] { }`.
`nonzero`		The input must not begin with zero.
`uploadedfile`		The element must contain a successfully uploaded file.
`maxfilesize`	`$size`	The uploaded file must be no more than `$size` bytes.

Table 3-3. Built-in Validation Rules (continued)

Rule Name	Argument	Rule Description
`mimetype`	`$mime`	The uploaded file must have a MIME type of `$mime`. If `$mime` is an array of MIME types, the uploaded file must have a MIME type equal to one of the elements in `$mime`.
`filename`	`$file_rx`	The uploaded file must have a filename that matches the regular expression `$file_rx`.

* The regular expression that the `email` and `emailorblank` rules use to determine a valid e-mail address is `/^[a-zA-Z0-9\._-]+\@(\[?)[a-zA-Z0-9\-\.]+\.([a-zA-Z]{2,4}|[0-9]{1,3})(\]?)$/'`.

To pass an argument to rules that use one, use the fourth argument of `addRule()`. The argument for `rangelength` should be a string containing the minimum and maximum lengths:

```
// subject must be at least 5 characters
$form->addRule('subject','Enter a valid subject','minlength',5);
// subject must be between 5 and 25 characters
$form->addRule('subject','Enter a valid subject','rangelength',"5,25");
```

Except for `required`, elements with no value submitted aren't tested against any validation rules assigned to them. This means that if you assign a `minlength` rule to an element and a user leaves the element blank when the form is submitted, HTML_QuickForm won't alert you that the rule isn't satisfied. To avoid this problem, assign both the `required` rule and the `minlength` rule to the element:

```
// subject must be at least 5 characters and must be filled in
$form->addRule('subject','Enter a subject of at least 5 characters',
               'minlength',5);
$form->addRule('subject','Enter a valid subject','required');
```

This way, a blank subject is caught by the validator because the `required` rule is broken. If subject has a value that is fewer than five characters, the validator catches the broken `minlength` rule.

Custom Validation Rules

You can add your own validation rules with registerRule(). These rules are one of two types: function or regex. Custom function rules have their logic in a specific user-defined function. To create a custom function rule, first define a function that performs the test for the rule. This function must return true if the rule is satisfied and false otherwise. Then, tell HTML_QuickForm about the function with registerRule(). Once it's registered, you can add the rule to an element with addRule() just like any other rule. This example checks to see whether the first and last letters of an input element are the same:

```
function compare_firstlast($element_name,$element_value) {
    $len = strlen($element_value);
    // If the string is empty, then return false
    if ($len == 0) { return false; }
    $first_letter = $element_value{0};
    $last_letter = $element_value{$len-1};
    if ($first_letter == $last_letter) {
        return true;
    } else {
        return false;
    }
}
$form->registerRule('same_firstandlast','function','compare_firstlast');
$form->addRule('user_name','The first and last letters must be the same',
               'same_firstandlast');
```

Custom regex rules check whether a form element matches a specific Perl-compatible regular expression. To create a custom regex rule, call registerRule() with a second argument of regex and pass the regular expression as the third argument to registerRule(). Once it's registered, add the custom regex rule to an element with addRule(). This custom regex rule checks for a valid U.S. ZIP or ZIP+4 code:

```
$form->registerRule('us_zip','regex','/^\d{5}(-\d{4})?$/');
$form->addRule('zip','Enter a valid US ZIP code','us_zip');
```

Custom rules can access the fourth argument to addRule() just like minlength or maxlength built-in rules. If it is specified when addRule() is called, this extra value is passed to a custom function rule as a second argument. For example, the custom function rule compare is used to make sure the values of the two password fields match:

```
$form->addElement('text','password','Password:');
$form->addElement('text','password2','Password (again):');
$form->registerRule('compare','function','compare_field');
$form->addRule('password','Passwords do not match','compare','password2');
function compare_field($element,$value,$arg) {
    global $form;
    if ($value == $form->getElementValue($arg)) {
        return true;
    } else {
        return false;
    }
}
```

The fourth argument to `addRule()`, `password2`, is passed to `compare_field()` as `$arg`. Because `password` and `password2` aren't hard-coded into the `compare_field()` function, you could use the same function and custom rule to compare other fields, such as e-mail address fields. The only difference would be in the second call to `addRule()`: You would add the rule to a different element and pass a different comparison element name.

A custom regex rule can use the extra value passed to `addRule()` by having the string `%data%` in its regular expression. The `%data%` is replaced by the extra value. In this example, the regular expression in the `emaildomain` rule as applied to the `name` element becomes `@(example.org)$/`:

```
$form->addElement('text','name','Name:');
$form->registerRule('emaildomain','regex','/@(%data%)$/');
$form->addRule('name','Enter an e-mail address from the example.org domain',
               'emaildomain','example.org');
```

Group Rules

To add a validation rule to a group, use the `addGroupRule()` method instead of the `addGroup()` function. If you want to apply the same validation rule individually to each member of the group, the syntax for calling `addGroupRule()` is the same as `addRule()`. This rule checks to see if each text field in the name group has input at least five characters long:

```
$group[] =& HTML_QuickForm::createElement('text','first');
$group[] =& HTML_QuickForm::createElement('text','middle');
$group[] =& HTML_QuickForm::createElement('text','last');
$form->addGroup($group,'name','Your Name:');
$form->addGroupRule('name','Enter a valid name','minlength',5);
```

If any one of the group members doesn't pass the validation check, then the `Enter a valid name` error message is displayed next to the group. To apply different rules to individual elements of a group, the syntax for `addGroupRule()` is more complicated:

```
$form->addGroupRule('name',
                    array(array(array('Invalid First Name', 'minlength',3)),
                          array(array('Invalid Middle Name','minlength',3)),
                          array(array('Last Name is required','required'),
                                array('Invalid Last Name','maxlength',20))));
```

The first argument to `addGroupRule()` is the same: the group to apply the rules against. The second argument to `addGroupRule()` is now an array. This array holds all of the rules that are applied against the individual elements. This array of rules has one value for each element in the group. That value is in turn an array of rules to apply to the element. Finally, each rule is expressed as a two- or three-element array, consisting of an error message, rule name, and optional argument to pass to the rule. The previous example adds the following rules to the group:

- The first name must be at least three characters (but is not required).
- The middle name must be at least three characters (but is not required).
- The last name is required.
- The last name can't be more than 20 characters.

Storing each of the subarrays in separate variables for clarity, you can also add these rules to the group like this:

```
// Define the rules for each element in the group
$first_name_rule = array('Invalid First Name','minlength',3);
$middle_name_rule = array('Invalid Middle Name','minlength',3);
$last_name_rule_1 = array('Last Name is required','required');
$last_name_rule_2 = array('Invalid Last Name','maxlength',20);

// Collect together the rules for each element
$first_rules = array($first_name_rule);
$middle_rules = array($middle_name_rule);
$last_rules = array($last_name_rule_1, $last_name_rule_2);

// Add the rules to the group
$form->addGroupRule('name',array($first_rules, $middle_rules, $last_rules));
```

Client-Side Validation

By default, the validation rules check submitted data once it has been sent to the server. You can also enable client-side validation for some rules. To have a rule checked by the browser, before the data is submitted, add `client` as a fifth argument to `addRule()`. For example, to make sure a value is entered in the subject field that is at least five characters long, you'd use this:

```
// subject is required and must be at least 5 characters
$form->addRule('subject','Enter a valid subject','required',null,'client');
$form->addRule('subject','Enter a valid subject','minlength',5,'client');
```

The client-side validation is accomplished by JavaScript functions added to the form by HTML_QuickForm. When a user clicks the form's submit button, the JavaScript functions run the client-side validation rules and pop up an alert box if any of the rules are not satisfied. Client-side validation is available for all of the built-in rules except for `uploadedfile`, `maxfilesize`, `mimetype`, and `filename`. It is also available for any custom regex rules. You can enable client-side validation on custom function rules if you also define a JavaScript function in the page with the same name as the custom function. That JavaScript function must duplicate the checks that the server-side PHP validation function does.

Filters

HTML_QuickForm provides a way to automatically modify submitted form data. This is useful to trim whitespace from user input or perform other prevalidation tasks. Use the `applyFilter()` method to run a function on an element or group of elements:

```
// Trim whitespace from the value of subject
$form->applyFilter('subject','trim');
// Trim whitespace from subject and body
$form->applyFilter(array('subject','body'),'trim');
//Trim whitespace from all elements
$form->applyFilter('__ALL__','trim');
```

The first argument to `applyFilter()` specifies the fields to filter. You can pass a string containing a field name, an array containing a list of field names, or the special string `__ALL__`. The string `__ALL__` tells `applyFilter()` to run the filter function on all submitted form elements. The second argument to `applyFilter()` is the filter function to run. This can be a built-in function, such as `trim()`, or a user-defined function. A user-defined filter function should take one argument—the submitted value—and return the modified value. For example, the following is a custom filter function that cleans up a message board post subject line by removing multiple instances of `Re:` from its beginning:

```
function clean_re($s) {
    return preg_replace('/^(re:\s*)+/i','Re: ',$s);
}
$form->applyFilter('subject','clean_re');
```

The `applyFilter()` function modifies the values in the internal array that HTML_QuickForm uses to keep track of submitted form data. This is the same array that is passed to a callback function invoked by `process()`. If you want the submitted data to be modified by the filter functions before it is validated, you must call `applyFilter()` before you call `validate()` because `validate()` uses that same internal array. Even after calling `applyFilter()`, you can access the prefilter value of an element with the `getElementValue()` function. Pass it the name of an element, and it returns the submitted value, unaffected by any filters.

Group Rules and Filters: An Example

The following code implements a form that contains an element group and applies a filter to a `<select>` menu to prevent out-of-range submissions:

```
$form = new HTML_QuickForm('info');

// Add a Header for formatting
$form->addElement('header','','Enter Your Information');

// Create an element group of three textboxes for phone number
$phone[] = &HTML_QuickForm::createElement('text','areacode',null,'size="3"');
$phone[] = &HTML_QuickForm::createElement('text','exchange',null,'size="3"');
$phone[] = &HTML_QuickForm::createElement('text','last4',null,'size="4"');

// Add the group with a separator of "-"
$form->addGroup($phone,'phone_number','Phone: ','-');

// Add rules for phone number parts: each is required and must be
// specific lengths
$form->addGroupRule('phone_number',
                    array(array(array('Area code is required', 'required'),
                                array('Area code must be 3 numbers',
                                      'rangelength',array(3,3))),
                          array(array('Exchange is required','required'),
                                array('Exchange must be 3 numbers',
                                      'rangelength',array(3,3))),
```

```
                            array(array('Phone number is required','required'),
                                  array('Phone number must be 7 digits',
                                        'rangelength',array(4,4)))));

// Add a select menu for choosing number type
// First, define the choices, with the zero'th choice being a prompt
$number_types = array('[ Select One ]','Home','Business','Mobile');

// Add the element to the form
$form->addElement('select','number_type','Number Type: ',$number_types);

// Prevent users from selecting the zero'th choice
$form->addRule('number_type','Please Select a Number Type','nonzero');

// Add a filter that prevents out of range submissions
$form->applyFilter('number_type','filter_number_type');

// Every good form needs a submit button
$form->addElement('submit','submit','Send Information');


// The main logic: display or process
if ($form->validate()) {
    $form->process('display_info');
} else {
    $form->display();
}

// The filter function that ensures a submitted number type is in the
// $number_types array
function filter_number_type($i) {
    return (array_key_exists($i,$GLOBALS['number_types']) ? $i : 0);
}

// Format the submitted data nicely for printing
function display_info($data) {
    $number_type_string = $GLOBALS['number_types'][$data['number_type']];
    printf("Your %s number is (%03d) %03d-%04d.",
           strtolower($number_type_string),
           $data['phone_number']['areacode'],
           $data['phone_number']['exchange'],
           $data['phone_number']['last4']);
}
```

The phone_number group contains three text elements: one for the area code, one for the exchange (the first three digits of the phone number), and one for the last four digits of the phone number. Each element of this group has two rules applied to it. First, they each get a required rule. Next, they each have a rangelength rule with the same number for the minimum and maximum length: three for the area code and exchange and four for the last four digits. This ensures that the area code and exchange are each exactly three characters long and the last four digits field is, as its name implies, exactly four digits long.

The number_type select element offers choices as to what kind of number has been entered: Home, Business, or Mobile. The nonzero rule applied to number_type makes the first choice in the $number_types array, [Select One], invalid. The filter function applied to number_type prevents an out-of-range submission. Even though the menu displayed in the form offers choices from zero to three, a malicious user could construct a request that submits a different value for number type. This filter rule, using the filter_number_type() function, maps any number type value to 0 that isn't 0, 1, 2, or 3.

When this form is submitted and validated, the code runs the display_info() function. This function uses printf() to format and display the submitted information. The submitted numeric value for number_type is turned back into a string by looking it up in the global $number_types array, and the components of the phone number are also printed.

CHAPTER 4

Templating with Smarty

IN MANY WAYS, PHP itself is a template engine. Text outside the `<?php` and `?>` tags is displayed unmodified, and commands inside those tags are parsed and executed. A PHP page that displays a static header, retrieves some rows from a database, formats them in an HTML table, and displays a static footer is plugging dynamic data into a static template.

A specialized template engine such as Smarty is valuable because it enforces the discipline of separating presentation logic from application logic. Although you can use PHP alone to build templated pages, it's difficult to prevent programmers and page designers from getting in each other's way when PHP is your template language. Smarty makes it easier to keep designers focused on implementing layout and presentation logic in templates and keep programmers focused on implementing application logic in separate PHP classes and functions.

This separation is valuable for reasons beyond improved workplace discipline. A template-based site is a flexible site: Only the templates have to change when you want to update your site's design. The core logic that displays articles, searches a database, or shows a product catalog can remain untouched; what the results look like can vary. Hence, templates also streamline the creation of multiple interfaces to the same content. Unique interfaces could be deployed for different browsers, different languages, or different cobranding partners. Each browser, language, or partner gets its own set of templates, but all interfaces share the same application logic.

Most of this chapter explains the details of building a template-based site with Smarty. This chapter also explores caching, an additional benefit of using Smarty. Caching improves your site performance by storing static copies of unchanged dynamic information. For example, if you display news headlines on your front page and your headline feed only changes every 15 minutes, there's no need to pull headlines from the feed every time you generate that front page. You can use Smarty's caching features to keep a copy of the headlines for 15 minutes and automatically rebuild the headline list when necessary.

Installing and Configuring Smarty

There are four steps to installing and configuring Smarty:

1. Download the Smarty distribution, and uncompress it.
2. Copy the library files from the distribution to a deployment directory.
3. Create directories for templates, compiled templates, and cached pages.
4. Determine the proper way to invoke Smarty from your PHP scripts.

To get Smarty, visit `http://smarty.php.net/download.php` and follow the link on the page to download the Smarty source code. This chapter describes Smarty version 2.6.0. Smarty is distributed as a gzipped tar file, so uncompress the archive and extract files from it with this:

```
% gunzip -c Smarty-2.6.0.tar.gz | tar xf -
```

If you're running Windows, you can use a utility such as WinZip to handle gzipped tar files.

The next step is to copy some files from the Smarty distribution into a deployment directory. This directory should not be underneath the document root of your Web site. If the deployment directory is not in your PHP include path, then you must set the `SMARTY_DIR` PHP constant to the name of the directory, including a trailing slash. This chapter uses `/usr/lib/php/smarty` as a deployment directory, but you can use any directory you want, as long as the user that the Web server runs as has read access to it. If the deployment directory doesn't exist yet, create it and then copy everything in the `libs` subdirectory of the Smarty distribution to this deployment directory:

```
# mkdir -p /usr/lib/php/smarty
# cp -pR Smarty-2.6.0/libs/* /usr/lib/php/smarty
```

After copying these files, you need to make some directories and ensure they have correct permissions. Directories must be created for templates, configuration files, compiled templates, and cached pages. The compiled templates and cached pages directories must be writable by the user that your Web server runs as. The templates and configuration files directories must be writable by any user that should be able to edit a template or configuration file—your Web site designers and editors.

The directory for templates is called templates:

```
# mkdir /usr/lib/php/smarty/templates
```

The directory for configuration files is called configs:

```
# mkdir /usr/lib/php/smarty/configs
```

The directory for compiled templates is called templates_c:

```
# mkdir /usr/lib/php/smarty/templates_c
```

The directory for cached pages is called cache:

```
# mkdir /usr/lib/php/smarty/cache
```

The easiest way to set proper permissions on the templates_c and cache directories is to, as superuser, change the owner of the directories to the user that your Web server runs as:

```
# chown nobody /usr/lib/php/smarty/templates_c
# chown nobody /usr/lib/php/smarty/cache
```

These directories need to be writable by the Web server user because Smarty puts files in them as it runs. Then, change the permissions of the templates and configs directories as appropriate. If all of the site designers are in the group siteedit, for example, execute the following commands:

```
# chgrp siteedit /usr/lib/php/smarty/configs
# chgrp siteedit /usr/lib/php/smarty/templates
# chmod g+w /usr/lib/php/smarty/configs
# chmod g+w /usr/lib/php/smarty/templates
```

This changes the group of the configs and templates directories to siteedit and allows all users that are members of the siteedit group to write to those directories.

If you've created the directories properly, listing your deployment directory should look like this (the modification times of the files have been omitted to shorten each line):

```
drwxr-xr-x    2 nobody   root        4096  cache
-rw-rw-r--    1 sklar    wheel       9946  Config_File.class.php
drwxrwxr-x    2 root     siteedit    4096  configs
```

```
drwxrwsr-x   2 sklar    wheel        4096  core
-rw-rw-r--   1 sklar    wheel        5017  debug.tpl
drwxrwsr-x   2 sklar    wheel        4096  plugins
-rw-rw-r--   1 sklar    wheel       65531  Smarty.class.php
-rw-rw-r--   1 sklar    wheel       76885  Smarty_Compiler.class.php
drwxrwxr-x   2 root     siteedit     4096  templates
drwxr-xr-x   2 nobody   root         4096  templates_c
```

The `cache` and `templates_c` directories are owned by `nobody` and are only writable by that user. The `configs` and `templates` directories are writable by everyone in the `siteedit` group. The rest of the files and directories are readable by all users.

The last step in setting up Smarty is determining the appropriate values for Smarty configuration settings. All interactions with Smarty in your PHP scripts are through an object, which is an instance of the `Smarty` class, which is defined in the `Smarty.class.php` file. Once the `Smarty` object is instantiated, some of its properties must be set to point to the directories you've created:

```
define('SMARTY_DIR','/usr/lib/php/smarty/');
require SMARTY_DIR.'Smarty.class.php';
$smarty = new Smarty;
$smarty->template_dir = SMARTY_DIR.'templates/';
$smarty->compile_dir = SMARTY_DIR.'templates_c/';
$smarty->config_dir = SMARTY_DIR.'configs/';
$smarty->cache_dir = SMARTY_DIR.'cache/';
```

After the Smarty object is instantiated and these properties are set, you can interact with `$smarty` to set variables and invoke templates, as described in the rest of the chapter. Although none of the examples in this chapter include these setup lines, each example assumes it is running in a script in which this setup has already occurred.

Understanding Basic Smarty Concepts

A Smarty template is like a life-size cutout of an astronaut or supermodel that you can have a picture taken of with your head sticking through a hole where the real astronaut or supermodel's head would be. In every photo, most of the image is the same. Only the face poking through the hole changes. A template contains presentation information that doesn't change, such as headers, menus, and footers. When building a page based on that template, Smarty adds some dynamic data to the template specific to that request—it pokes a particular face through the hole.

There are generally three steps to take in a PHP script that uses Smarty: instantiating the Smarty object (detailed in the previous section), assigning variables to the Smarty object, and displaying a template. The variables assigned to the Smarty object are interpolated into the template when the template is displayed.

Listing 4-1 is a template that displays information about a flavor of ice cream. It goes into the `templates` subdirectory of `SMARTY_DIR`. The formatting of the information is defined in the template, but the flavor-specific details are assigned to the Smarty object outside the template.

Listing 4-1. `icecream.tpl`

```
<html>
<head><title>Ice Cream: {$flavor}</title></head>
<body>
<h1>{$flavor}</h1>
<table border="1">
<tr><th colspan="2">About {$flavor}</th></tr>
<tr><td>Calories</td><td>{$calories}</td></tr>
<tr><td>Price</td><td>${$price}</td></tr>
</table>
</body>
</html>
```

In a template, curly braces indicate Smarty commands and functions. The most basic command is to insert the value of a variable. Putting a variable name in curly braces causes that variable's value to be interpolated in the template when it is displayed. To show some information about chocolate ice cream, you can invoke `icecream.tpl` with the PHP script in Listing 4-2. The script should be saved into the document root of the Web server.

Listing 4-2. `chocolate.php`

```
$smarty->assign('flavor','Chocolate');
$smarty->assign('calories',10);
$smarty->assign('price',4.55);
$smarty->display('icecream.tpl');
```

The three `$smarty->assign()` calls assign particular values in the `$smarty` object to the template variables named `flavor`, `calories`, and `price`. Calling `$smarty->display('icecream.tpl')` tells the `$smarty` object to load the template in the `icecream.tpl` file, execute any commands in it, and display the results. In this case, executing commands consists only of interpolating some variables' values. This results in the following HTML:

```
<html>
<head><title>Ice Cream: Chocolate</title></head>
```

```
<body>
<h1>Chocolate</h1>
<table border="1">
<tr><th colspan="2">About Chocolate</th></tr>
<tr><td>Calories</td><td>10</td></tr>
<tr><td>Price</td><td>$4.55</td></tr>
</table>
</body>
</html>
```

The usefulness and power of a templating engine asserts itself when it comes time to display a page about vanilla ice cream. Listing 4-3 creates such a page that has the same layout as the chocolate page.

Listing 4-3. vanilla.php

```
$smarty->assign('flavor','Vanilla');
$smarty->assign('calories',20);
$smarty->assign('price',4.25);
$smarty->display('icecream.tpl');
```

This displays an almost identical page—the only differences are the interpolated variable values. When it's time to change the layout of the ice cream information pages, only `icecream.tpl` needs to be updated. The PHP scripts that invoke the template benefit from the changed template without any modification.

Using Variables in a Template

The core of a templating system is variable interpolation. By combining different sets of variables with various templates, you can produce a variety of pages. Using the same variables with different templates is common when displaying output for different platforms or browsers. For example, imagine a news site that wants to tailor its content based on the browser and connection of a reader. This site has one template for Web browsers on high-bandwidth connections, one for Web browsers on low-bandwidth connections, and one for mobile devices such as phones and organizers. When an article is requested, the site gathers, from a database or file, the appropriate data for the article such as headline, byline, body, and image URLs. Then, depending on the browser that asked for the article, the site invokes a specific Smarty template. Each template formats the article data differently. For example, the high-bandwidth connection template includes all of the images, and the mobile device template excludes images and presents just stripped-down text.

This same news site uses different sets of variables with a single template when displaying different articles for the same kind of browser. When a high-bandwidth browser requests a specific article, that article's data is retrieved and plugged into the high-bandwidth article template. When another article is requested, different data is retrieved and plugged into the same template. Individual articles can be edited without affecting the template, and the template can be edited without touching a particular article's data. The template structure separates the content of the site (the articles) from the look and feel of the site.

As shown in the previous section, the `assign()` method assigns values to template variables, and the `display()` method displays a template. Instead of single name/value pairs, `assign()` also accepts an associative array as an argument. It uses the keys of the associative array elements as template variable names and the values of the elements as the template variable values. For example, you can create the vanilla page like this:

```
$smarty->assign(array('flavor' => 'Vanilla',
                      'calories' => 20,
                      'price' => 4.25));
$smarty->display('icecream.tpl');
```

Request Variables

Smarty makes request variables available through elements of the special `$smarty` variable. GET variables are in `$smarty.get`, POST variables are in `$smarty.post`, cookie variables are in `$smarty.cookies`, environment variables are in `$smarty.env`, server variables are in `$smarty.server`, and session variables are in `$smarty.session`. If the `request_use_auto_globals` Smarty configuration variable is `true`, then Smarty gets these request variables from superglobal arrays: `$_GET`, `$_POST`, `$_COOKIE`, `$_ENV`, `$_SERVER`, and `$_SESSION`, respectively. Otherwise, it uses the older global arrays: `$HTTP_GET_VARS`, `$HTTP_POST_VARS`, `$HTTP_COOKIE_VARS`, `$HTTP_ENV_VARS`, `$HTTP_SERVER_VARS`, and `$HTTP_SESSION_VARS`, respectively. Whether or not `request_use_auto_globals` is `true`, Smarty makes the elements in the superglobal array `$_REQUEST` available in `$smarty.request`.

Variable Modifiers

Frequently, variables need to be interpolated with slight modifications. That's where modifiers come in. Variable modifiers are tiny, limited-use functions that produce a new result based on a variable. They don't change the original variable but instead supply a new version of it—one that's all uppercase, contains the number of characters in the variable, or is otherwise formatted. To use a modifier, put a | and the modifier name after the variable.

Smarty doesn't do any entity encoding or other modification of request variables, so you still need to be cautious of cross-site scripting attacks or other vulnerabilities of unchecked user input. To safely display submitted data, use the escape variable modifier. For example, if $_REQUEST['link'] is <a href="/chocolate.php">Yum!</a>, then the following:

```
{$smarty.request.link|escape}
```

displays the value of $_REQUEST['link'] with HTML entities encoded:

```
&lt;a href=&quot;/chocolate.php&quot;&gt;Yum!&lt;/a&gt;
```

Some variable modifiers take arguments. These go in a colon-delimited list after the modifier name. For example, the cat modifier appends a string to a variable. The string to append is specified as an argument:

```
{$flavor|cat:" Fudge"}
```

If the template variable $flavor has been assigned Vanilla, then the template displays this:

```
Vanilla Fudge
```

Variable modifiers can also be chained together. To have the output of one modifier processed by another, put a | and the second modifier after the first modifier:

```
{$flavor|cat:" Fudge"|upper}
```

If the template variable $flavor has been assigned Vanilla, then the template displays this:

```
VANILLA FUDGE
```

Text Processing

The examples of text-processing modifiers are based on the following variable assignments:

```
$smarty->assign(array('flavor' => 'Chocolate Smoked Oyster',
                      'quote' => 'Everyone says, "I love Chocolate Smoked Oyster!"',
                      'quote2' => "It's my favorite flavor!",
```

```
                    'price' => 5,
                    'spaced_flavor' => "     Chocolate   Smoked\n\nOyster",
                    'link' => '<a href="oyster.php">Oyster</a>'),
                    'address' => 'oyster@example.com',
                    'description' =>
'Mixing the earthiness of smoked oyster and the intensity of chocolate,
Chocolate Smoked Oyster ice cream simultaneously conjures feelings of the
steamy jungle where cacao pods grow and the salty breeze of New England
oyster beds.'));
```

Some of the Smarty text-processing modifiers are similar to PHP built-in functions. Table 4-1 lists the relationship between these text-processing modifiers and PHP functions.

Table 4-1. Smarty Text-Processing Modifiers and Native PHP Equivalents

PHP Function or Operator	**Modifier**	**Description**
ucwords()	capitalize	Capitalizes the first letter of each word in a string
. (string concatenation operator)	cat	Combines two strings
htmlspecialchars()	escape	Entity-escapes quotes, angle brackets, and ampersand
htmlentities()	escape	Entity-escapes all HTML entities
urlencode()	escape	Hex-escapes nonalphanumeric characters (except _)
strtolower()	lower	Lowercases all characters in a string
nl2br()	nl2br	Turns newlines to tags
str_replace()	replace	Replaces a substring
preg_replace()	regex_replace	Replaces a substring that matches a regular expression
sprintf()	string_format	Prints a field-formatted string
strtoupper()	upper	Capitalizes all characters in a string
wordwrap()	wordwrap	Inserts newlines in a string to wrap it at a certain line length

capitalize

The `capitalize` modifier capitalizes the first letter of each word in a variable. For example:

```
{$quote|capitalize}
```

This is the example's output:

```
Everyone Says, "I Love Chocolate Smoked Oyster!"
```

cat

The `cat` modifier appends a string to a variable. For example:

```
{$flavor|cat:" Sauce"}
```

This is the example's output:

```
Chocolate Smoked Oyster Sauce
```

escape

The `escape` modifier escapes special characters in a variable. The parameter passed to `escape` controls what kind of escaping it does. By default, or with a parameter of `html`, it escapes the characters `<`, `>`, `&`, `"`, and `'`. With a parameter of `quotes`, single quotes are escaped. With a parameter of `htmlall`, all HTML entities are escaped. With a parameter of `url`, special characters are URL-encoded. With a parameter of `javascript`, quotes, backslashes, and newlines are escaped. With a parameter of `hex`, every character is turned into a URL-encoded hex escape. With a parameter of `hexentity`, every character is turned into an entity-encoded hex escape. This can provide limited masking of e-mail addresses from harvesting robots.

This is the example usage:

```
{* The first two are the same *}
{$link|escape}
{$link|escape:"html"}
{$quote2|escape:"quotes"}
{$link|escape:"htmlall"}
{$quote|escape:"url"}
{$quote2|escape:"javascript"}
{$flavor|escape:"hex"}
{$address|escape:"hexentity"}
```

This is the example output:

```
&lt;a href=&quot;oyster.php&quot;&gt;Oyster&lt;/a&gt;
&lt;a href=&quot;oyster.php&quot;&gt;Oyster&lt;/a&gt;
It\'s my favorite flavor!
&lt;a href=&quot;oyster.php&quot;&gt;Oyster&lt;/a&gt;
Everyone+says%2C+%22I+love+Chocolate+Smoked+Oyster%21%22
It\'s my favorite flavor!
%43%68%6f%63%6f%6c%61%74%65%20%53%6d%6f%6b%65%64%20%4f%79%73%74%65%72
&#x6f;&#x79;&#x73;&#x74;&#x65;&#x72;&#x40;&#x65;&#x78;&#x61;&#x6d;&#x70;&#x6c;
&#x65;&#x2e;&#x63;&#x6f;&#x6d;
```

indent

The `indent` modifier indents a string at each line break. (It doesn't insert line breaks into a string.) By default, `indent` inserts four spaces for an indentation. You can specify how many characters to indent as a first parameter and a character other than space to use as an indenting character as a second parameter.

This is the example usage:

```
{$description|indent}
{$description|indent:2}
{$description|indent:2:"-"}
```

This is the example output:

```
    Mixing the earthiness of smoked oyster and the intensity of chocolate,
    Chocolate Smoked Oyster ice cream simultaneously conjures feelings of the
    steamy jungle where cacao pods grow and the salty breeze of New England
    oyster beds.
  Mixing the earthiness of smoked oyster and the intensity of chocolate,
  Chocolate Smoked Oyster ice cream simultaneously conjures feelings of the
  steamy jungle where cacao pods grow and the salty breeze of New England
  oyster beds.
--Mixing the earthiness of smoked oyster and the intensity of chocolate,
--Chocolate Smoked Oyster ice cream simultaneously conjures feelings of the
--steamy jungle where cacao pods grow and the salty breeze of New England
--oyster beds.
```

lower

The `lower` modifier lowercases a variable. For example:

```
{$flavor|lower}
```

This is the example's output:

```
chocolate smoked oyster
```

nl2br

The nl2br modifier adds a <br /> tag before each newline in a string. This is useful for preserving hard line breaks in a text file when it is displayed as HTML.

This is the example usage:

```
{$description|nl2br}
```

This is the example output:

```
Mixing the earthiness of smoked oyster and the intensity of chocolate,<br />
Chocolate Smoked Oyster ice cream simultaneously conjures feelings of the<br />
steamy jungle where cacao pods grow and the salty breeze of New England<br />
oyster beds.
```

regex_replace

The regex_replace modifier replaces text in a variable that matches a regular expression. It uses PHP's preg_replace() function, so it should be supplied with a Perl-compatible regular expression. The first parameter to regex_replace is a regular expression, including delimiters, for which to search. The second parameter is the string that replaces text that matches the regular expression.

This is the example usage:

```
{$flavor|regex_replace:"/[aeiou]/":"*"}
```

This is the example output:

```
Ch*c*l*t* Sm*k*d Oyst*r
```

replace

The replace modifier uses PHP's str_replace() function to replace one string with another in a variable. The first parameter to replace is the string for which to search. The second parameter is the string that replaces the text that matches the first parameter.

This is the example usage:

```
{$flavor|replace:"e":"3"}
```

This is the example output:

```
Chocolat3 Smok3d Oyst3r
```

spacify

The `spacify` modifier separates each character of a variable with a space. You can pass an alternate separator character as a parameter.

This is the example usage:

```
{$flavor|spacify}
{$flavor|spacify:"-"}
```

This is the example output:

```
C h o c o l a t e   S m o k e d   O y s t e r
C-h-o-c-o-l-a-t-e- -S-m-o-k-e-d- -O-y-s-t-e-r
```

string_format

The `string_format` modifier uses PHP's `sprintf()` function to provide string formatting. Pass the format you want to use as a parameter.

This is the example usage:

```
{$price:"%.2f"}
```

This is the example output:

```
5.00
```

strip

The `strip` modifier turns all whitespace sequences in a string into a single space. Each group of multiple tabs, newlines, or spaces is turned into a single space. If you pass a string as a parameter, that string is used to replace whitespace.

This is the example usage:

```
{$spaced_flavor|strip}
{$spaced_flavor|strip:" "}
```

This is the example output:

```
Chocolate Smoked Oyster
 Chocolate Smoked Oyster
```

strip_tags

The `strip_tags` modifier removes HTML markup from a string.

This is the example usage:

```
{$link|strip_tags}
```

This is the example output:

```
Oyster
```

truncate

The `truncate` modifier cuts off a string at 80 characters. If it removed characters from the string, it adds three periods to the end of the string to indicate the truncation. You can pass a different cutoff length as a first parameter and an alternate truncation indicator as a second parameter. By default, `truncate` doesn't break words when it truncates a string. If you want it to break words, pass `true` as a third parameter.

This is the example usage:

```
{$description|truncate}
{$description|truncate:40}
{$description|truncate:40:" ! "}
{$description|truncate:40:" ! ":true}
```

This is the example output:

```
Mixing the earthiness of smoked oyster and the intensity of chocolate,...
Mixing the earthiness of smoked...
Mixing the earthiness of smoked !
Mixing the earthiness of smoked oyste !
```

upper

The `upper` modifier uppercases a variable.

This is the example usage:

```
{$flavor|upper}
```

This is the example output:

```
CHOCOLATE SMOKED OYSTER
```

wordwrap

The `wordwrap` modifier inserts line breaks into a string so that each line isn't too long. By default, it wraps a string at 80 characters, uses `\n` as a linebreak character, and doesn't end lines in the middle of a word. It accepts an alternate line length as a first parameter and alternate line break string as a second parameter.

This is the example usage:

```
{$description|wordwrap}
{$quote|wordwrap:20}
{$quote|wordwrap:20:"\n\n"}
```

This is the example output:

```
Mixing the earthiness of smoked oyster and the intensity of chocolate,
Chocolate Smoked Oyster ice cream simultaneously conjures feelings of the
steamy jungle where cacao pods grow and the salty breeze of New England
oyster beds.
Everyone says, "I
love Chocolate
Smoked Oyster!"
Everyone says, "I

love Chocolate

Smoked Oyster!"
```

Text Counting

These modifiers provide statistics about the length of a variable that are useful in calculating appropriate display parameters. The examples use the following variable assignment:

```
$smarty->assign('testimonial',"This is the best ice cream ever. I've never had
anything that tastes as smoky, as chocolatey, or as oystery.
You better believe that I'll happily eat two scoops of this every day!");
```

count_characters

The count_characters modifier reports the number of characters in a variable, excluding whitespace. To include whitespace, pass true as a parameter.

This is the example usage:

```
{$testimonial|count_characters}
{$testimonial|count_characters:true}
```

This is the example output:

```
147
179
```

count_words

The count_words modifier reports the number of words in a variable by counting the number of substrings, separated by whitespace, that contain alphanumeric characters. The string 2 plus 2 has three words; the string 2 + 2 has two words.

This is the example usage:

```
{$testimonial|count_words}
```

This is the example output:

```
33
```

count_sentences

The count_sentences modifier calculates the number of sentences in a variable by finding the number of periods in the variable that have a word character before them but not after them. According to the count_sentences modifier, example.com is great! example.net is alright. contains one sentence. The periods in the host names are ignored because they have word characters immediately after them, and the exclamation is ignored because it doesn't end with a period.

This is the example usage:

```
{$testimonial|count_sentences}
```

This is the example output:

```
2
```

count_paragraphs

The `count_paragraphs` modifier computes the number of paragraphs in a variable by counting the number of newline and line break characters in the variable.

This is the example usage:

```
{$testimonial|count_paragraphs}
```

This is the example output:

```
2
```

Other Modifiers

Two other modifiers also provide useful features: `default` and `date_format`.

default

The `default` modifier supplies a value when an interpolated variable hasn't been defined.

This is the example usage:

```
{* Nothing has been assigned to $exotic_flavor *}
{* "Chocolate" has been assigned to $flavor *}
{$exotic_flavor|default:"Vanilla"}
{$flavor|default:"Green Tea"}
```

This is the example output:

```
Vanilla
Chocolate
```

date_format

The `date_format` modifier uses PHP's `strftime()` function to provide formatted date and time strings. You can use `date_format` with the special `$smarty.now` variable, which holds the current time as an epoch time stamp. The default format string for `date_format` is `%b %e, %Y`. Specify a different format string as the first parameter to `date_format`. Additionally, you can specify a default time as a second parameter to `date_format`. This is used if the variable that `date_format` is modifying is empty. The second parameter is parsed internally by `strtotime()`, so you can specify relative times such as `yesterday` or `last Thursday`.

This is the example usage:

```
{$smarty.now|date_format}
{$smarty.now|date_format:"%c"}
{$missing_date|date_format:"%c":"next Tuesday"}
```

This is the example output:

```
Sep 12, 2003
Fri Sep 12 15:37:17 2003
Tue Sep 23 00:00:00 2003
```

Comments

Smarty templates can include comments. These comments aren't visible in generated pages. To put a comment in a template, surround the comment text with {* and *}:

```
{* Here's the name in uppercase *}
{$name|upper}
```

Comments can span multiple lines:

```
{* Mandatory information about a user:
    - name
    - rank
    - serial number *}
<ul>
<li>Name: {$name|upper}</li>
<li>Rank: {$rank}</li>
<li>Serial Number: {$serial_number}</li>
</ul>
```

Implementing Conditional Logic

Logic is essential in a template for making decisions about what to display. For example, you may want to display a personalized page header if a user is logged in and otherwise show a generic header. If a database result set contains more than ten rows, you can display the entire thing. If the result set is larger, you can display the first ten rows with a link to a page that contains a full listing.

Although necessary, conditional logic in templates is potentially dangerous. Only logic that determines what to display should go into the template. Any code that makes decisions about program flow should be in PHP and should happen before you call display() to render the template. For example, although the template may do different things depending on the size of a database result set, all of the code and logic that executes the database query and retrieves the results should be in PHP, outside the template. The template language is a way for interface designers to implement their ideas without having to rely on site programmers. It requires careful coordination and ongoing vigilance to make sure that the in-template logic doesn't grow beyond its presentation-related boundaries.

Use the {if} function to put a conditional statement in a template. The qualifier in the test expression must be surrounded with spaces so Smarty can parse it properly. Also, the end of the conditional statement must be denoted with {/if}. Otherwise, test expressions look like their counterparts in PHP if() statements:

```
{* Test the value of $_REQUEST['choice'] *}
{if $smarty.request.choice > 5}
You've submitted a choice more than 5.
{/if}

{* is today a monday? *}
{if $smarty.now|date_format:"%u" == 1}
It's Monday: don't forget to take out the trash!
{else}
It's not Monday: don't bother taking out the trash.
{/if}

{* how many elements are there in the $flavor array? *}
{assign var="flavor_count" value=$flavor|@count}
{if $flavor_count == 0}
There are no flavors.
{elseif $flavor_count == 1}
There is only one flavor: {$flavor[0]}.
{else}
There are multiple flavors.
{/if}
```

Smarty understands {elseif} and {else}, which act just like elseif() and else in PHP. Smarty also supports some test expressions that PHP doesn't, such as is even, is odd, and is div by. These test a number's divisibility:

```
{* "is even" tests for an even number *}
{if $smarty.request.choice is even}
You've submitted a number divisible by two.
{/if}
```

```
{* is odd" tests for an odd number *}
{if $smarty.request.choice is odd}
You've submitted a number that's not divisible by two.
{/if}

{* is div by tests for divisibility *}
{$smarty.request.numerator} divided by {$smarty.request.denominator}
{if $smarty.request.numerator is div by $smarty.request.denominator}
is
{else}
is not
{/if}
an integer.
```

Smarty also understands alphabetic synonyms for many operators (see Table 4-2).

Table 4-2. Operator Equivalencies

Operator	Meaning	Synonyms
=	Equal to	eq
!=	Not equal to	ne, neq
!	Not	not
<	Less than	lt
<=	Less than or equal to	le, lte
>	Greater than	gt
>=	Greater than or equal to	ge, gte
&&	Logical and	and
||	Logical or	or
%	Modulus division	mod

You can use the alphabetic operators just like their punctuated versions:

```
{* Test the value of $_REQUEST['choice'] *}
{if $smarty.request.choice gt 5}
You've submitted a choice more than 5.
{/if}
```

```
{* is today a monday? *}
{if $smarty.now|date_format:"%u" eq 1}
It's Monday: don't forget to take out the trash!
{else}
It's not Monday: don't bother taking out the trash.
{/if}
```

Looping and Cycling Through Data

Displaying sets and tables of data is a popular task for a template. Smarty provides a few constructs to help. The `{foreach}` and `{section}` functions are ways to process each element in an array. The `{foreach}` function is simpler, but the `{section}` function is more powerful. The `{cycle}` function rotates through an array, displaying a new element of the array each time it is invoked.

Iterating Through an Array with {foreach}

The `{foreach}` function is the simplest way to iterate through an array in Smarty. With `{foreach}`, you can display a block of text once for each element in an array, usually incorporating the value of that array element in the block of text. The two mandatory arguments to `{foreach}` are `from`, which is the array variable you want to iterate through, and `item`, which is the name that each element of the array is assigned to as Smarty iterates. For example, this template prints each element of the array assigned to the template variable `$loop`:

```
{foreach from=$loop item=flavor}{$flavor}{/foreach}
```

If this template is invoked from a PHP script like this:

```
$smarty->assign('loop',array('Vanilla','Chocolate','Strawberry'));
$smarty->display('foreach.tpl');
```

then the template prints this:

```
VanillaChocolateStrawberry
```

For each element in the array, the template displays whatever is between the `{foreach}` and `{/foreach}` tags. In this simple template, the only thing to display is a variable interpolation command. Because the item argument of `{foreach}` is set to `flavor`, `$flavor` contains each array element's value and `{$flavor}` interpolates that value into the output.

{foreach} loops also have properties that indicate the iteration number of the loop and whether the current iteration is the first or last one. To access these properties, give the loop a name in the {foreach} declaration and then use the special $smarty.foreach variable. This template prints the elements of an array as a list. It uses the first and last properties to determine when to display the <ul> and </ul> tags and uses the iteration property to display flavor numbers:

```
{foreach from=$loop item=flavor name=flavorloop}
{if $smarty.foreach.flavorloop.first} <ul> {/if}
<li> Flavor number {$smarty.foreach.flavorloop.iteration} is {$flavor}
{if $smarty.foreach.flavorloop.last} </ul> {/if}
{/foreach}
```

Invoking this template with the same array assigned to $loop previously produces the following output:

```
<ul> <li> Flavor number 1 is Vanilla
<li> Flavor number 2 is Chocolate
<li> Flavor number 3 is Strawberry
 </ul>
```

You can combine a {foreach} block with {foreachelse}, which indicates text to display if there are no elements in the block's array. For example:

```
{foreach from=$other_loop item=flavor name=flavorloop}
{if $smarty.foreach.flavorloop.first} <ul> {/if}
<li> Flavor number {$smarty.foreach.flavorloop.iteration} is {$flavor}
{if $smarty.foreach.flavorloop.last} </ul> {/if}
{foreachelse}
There are no flavors.
{/foreach}
```

Because there is nothing assigned to the template variable $other_loop, this template prints There are no flavors.

{foreach} loops also have a total property, which contains the number of iterations that the loop goes through. This template uses the total property to indicate before the list the number of flavors listed:

```
{foreach from=$loop item=flavor key=flavor_key name=flavorloop}
{if $smarty.foreach.flavorloop.first}
There are {$smarty.foreach.flavorloop.total} flavors:
<ul> {/if}
<li> Flavor number {$smarty.foreach.flavorloop.iteration} is {$flavor}
{if $smarty.foreach.flavorloop.last} </ul> {/if}
{/foreach}
```

The template displays the following:

```
There are 3 flavors:
<ul> <li> Flavor number 1 is Vanilla
<li> Flavor number 2 is Chocolate
<li> Flavor number 3 is Strawberry
 </ul>
```

When iterating through an associative array, you can access the array keys with the key argument to the {foreach} function. Each time through the loop, the array element key is copied to the variable specified by the key argument. For example, this template prints elements of the associative array assigned to the template variable $colors, storing each element key in the $flavor variable and each element value in the $color variable:

```
{foreach from=$colors key=flavor item=color}
The color of {$flavor} ice cream is {$color}.
{/foreach}
```

If this template is invoked from a PHP script like this:

```
$smarty->assign('colors',
                array('vanilla' => 'white',
                      'chocolate' => 'brown',
                      'strawberry' => 'pink'));
$smarty->display('foreach.tpl');
```

then it prints this:

```
The color of vanilla ice cream is white.
The color of chocolate ice cream is brown.
The color of strawberry ice cream is pink.
```

Iterating with {section}

The {section} function provides a more flexible iteration method than {foreach}. It supports the same name, item, and from arguments and has first, last, iteration, and total properties. However, with {section}, you don't have to start iterating at the first array element, and each iteration can jump to another array element by steps larger than one. Although the loop variable in a {foreach} block holds an array element value, the loop variable in a {section} block holds an array index. This template uses a {section} block to display the contents of an associative array in an HTML table:

```
<table>
{section name=icecream loop=$flavors}
<tr>
 <td>{$flavors[icecream].name}</td>
 <td>{$flavors[icecream].calories}</td>
 <td>${$flavors[icecream].price|string_format:"%.02f"}</td>
</tr>
{/section}
</table>
```

The template can be invoked from a PHP script like this:

```
$flavors = array(array('name' => 'Vanilla',
                       'calories' => 20,
                       'price' => 4.25),
                 array('name' => 'Chocolate',
                       'calories' => 30,
                       'price' => 4.50),
                 array('name' => 'Strawberry',
                       'calories' => 30,
                       'price' => 3.50),
                 array('name' => 'Salmon Butter',
                       'calories' => 200,
                       'price' => 9.44),
                 array('name' => 'Guava Mint Bouillon',
                       'calories' => 50,
                       'price' => 3.75));
$smarty->assign('flavors',$flavors);
$smarty->display('section.tpl');
```

which results in the following output:

```
<table>
<tr>
 <td>Vanilla</td>
 <td>20</td>
 <td>$4.25</td>
</tr>
<tr>
 <td>Chocolate</td>
<td>30</td>
 <td>$4.50</td>
</tr>
```

```
<tr>
 <td>Strawberry</td>
 <td>30</td>
 <td>$3.50</td>
</tr>
<tr>
 <td>Salmon Butter</td>
 <td>200</td>
 <td>$9.44</td>
</tr>
<tr>
 <td>Guava Mint Bouillon</td>
 <td>50</td>
<td>$3.75</td>
</tr>
</table>
```

The name of the section is `icecream`, and the `loop` variable is `$flavors`. This means that for each element in the template variable `$flavors`, `icecream` is assigned an index, starting at zero. Elements of `$flavors` are accessed with the `$flavors[icecream]` syntax, which refers to the current element of the array. Because each element of `$flavors` is an associative array, you use an expression such as `$flavors[icecream].name` to retrieve a particular subarray element value. `{section}` blocks also support accessing the current array element through the `index` property, the previous element through the `index_prev` property, and the next element through the `index_next` property.

`{section}` blocks share the `first`, `last`, `iteration`, and `total` properties of `{foreach}` blocks. You can use these properties in a template to display a header row and move the `<table></table>` tags inside the `{section}` block:

```
{section name=icecream loop=$flavors}
{if $smarty.section.icecream.first}<table>
<tr><th colspan="4" align="center">
Displaying {$smarty.section.icecream.total} flavors</th></tr>
{/if}
<tr>
 <td>Flavor {$smarty.section.icecream.iteration}</td>
 <td>{$flavors[icecream].name}</td>
 <td>{$flavors[icecream].calories}</td>
 <td>${$flavors[icecream].price|string_format:"%.02f"}</td>
</tr>
{if $smarty.section.icecream.last}</table>{/if}
{/section}
```

The variable $smarty.section.icecream.first is true only the first time through the {section} block, so the <table> tag and header row are printed immediately before the first data row. Each row uses the iteration property to print a flavor number. The $smarty.section.icecream.last property is true only the last time through the {section} block, so the </table> tag is printed immediately after the last data row. Conditionally displaying the <table> and </table> tags makes it easy to use a {sectionelse} block to display alternate text when there is no data in the loop array:

```
{section name=icecream loop=$flavors}
{if $smarty.section.icecream.first}<table>
<tr><th colspan="4" align="center">
Displaying {$smarty.section.icecream.total} flavors</th></tr>
{/if}
<tr>
 <td>Flavor {$smarty.section.icecream.iteration}</td>
 <td>{$flavors[icecream].name}</td>
 <td>{$flavors[icecream].calories}</td>
 <td>${$flavors[icecream].price|string_format:"%.02f"}</td>
</tr>
{if $smarty.section.icecream.last}</table>{/if}
{sectionelse}
There are no flavors to display.
{/section}
```

If $flavors has no elements, only the template between {sectionelse} and {/section} is displayed. Because the <table> and </table> tags are inside the {section} block, they are not displayed when the {sectionelse} template part is.

The max property of a {section} block limits the number of iterations. This template only displays (at most) three flavors because the value of max is 3:

```
{section name=icecream loop=$flavors max=3}
{if $smarty.section.icecream.first}<table>{/if}
<tr>
 <td>{$flavors[icecream].name}</td>
 <td>{$flavors[icecream].calories}</td>
 <td>${$flavors[icecream].price|string_format:"%.02f"}</td>
</tr>
{if $smarty.section.icecream.last}</table>{/if}
{/section}
```

The step property of a {section} block changes how the array index is incremented each time through the block. By default, the array index is incremented by one. With step, you can set that to another value. This template uses a step of 2 to display two flavors per table row:

```
{section name=icecream loop=$flavors step=2}
{if $smarty.section.icecream.first}<table>{/if}
<tr>
 <td>{$flavors[icecream].name}</td>
 <td>{$flavors[icecream].calories}</td>
 <td>${$flavors[icecream].price|string_format:"%.02f"}</td>
{assign var="next_flavor" value=`$smarty.section.icecream.index+1`}
{if $flavors[$next_flavor]}
 <td>{$flavors[$next_flavor].name}</td>
 <td>{$flavors[$next_flavor].calories}</td>
 <td>${$flavors[$next_flavor].price|string_format:"%.02f"}</td>
{else}
 <td> </td><td> </td><td> </td>
{/if}
</tr>
{if $smarty.section.icecream.last}</table>{/if}
{/section}
```

In this template, the `icecream` index takes on the values `0`, `2`, and `4` instead of `0`, `1`, `2`, `3`, and `4`. The first part of the table row display is unchanged: It displays table cells with the name, calories, and price of the current flavor. Then, you use `assign` to calculate the index of the next flavor: one more than the current index. If an element with the `$next_flavor` index exists in the array, you display table cells with information about that flavor. If not (which means that `icecream` currently points to the last element in the array), then you display three empty table cells instead.

A `{section}` block also has a `start` property, which controls at which array element the index starts. By default, `start` is `0`, which starts the `{section}` block at the first element in the array. To start on the third element, set `start` to `2`:

```
{section name=icecream loop=$flavors start=2}
{if $smarty.section.icecream.first}<table>{/if}
<tr>
 <td>{$flavors[icecream].name}</td>
 <td>{$flavors[icecream].calories}</td>
 <td>${$flavors[icecream].price|string_format:"%.02f"}</td>
</tr>
{if $smarty.section.icecream.last}</table>{/if}
{/section}
```

Iterating with {cycle}

The `{cycle}` function is intended for use inside another looping construct when you want to repeatedly display a set of values. Perhaps the most common use of {cycle} is to display alternating table row background colors. The most straightforward way to do this is to specify the colors to {cycle} as a comma-separated string:

```
<table>
{section name=icecream loop=$flavors}
<tr bgcolor="{cycle values="#cccc33,#eeee33"}">
 <td>{$flavors[icecream].name}</td>
 <td>{$flavors[icecream].calories}</td>
 <td>${$flavors[icecream].price|string_format:"%.02f"}</td>
</tr>
{/section}
</table>
```

Using the $flavors array from previous sections, the template produces the following output:

```
<table>
<tr bgcolor="#cccc33">
 <td>Vanilla</td>
 <td>20</td>
 <td>$4.25</td>
</tr>
<tr bgcolor="#eeee33">
 <td>Chocolate</td>
 <td>30</td>
 <td>$4.50</td>
</tr>
<tr bgcolor="#cccc33">
 <td>Strawberry</td>
 <td>30</td>
 <td>$3.50</td>
</tr>
<tr bgcolor="#eeee33">
 <td>Salmon Butter</td>
 <td>200</td>
 <td>$9.44</td>
</tr>
<tr bgcolor="#cccc33">
 <td>Guava Mint Bouillon</td>
 <td>50</td>
 <td>$3.75</td>
</tr>
</table>
```

Each time through the {section} block, the {cycle} tag prints the next value from its values list. When the end of the list is reached, {cycle} starts at the beginning again. The set of values to cycle through can be specified as a template variable as well. This template variable can be an array or a comma-separated list:

```
// You can assign a cycle list as an array
 $smarty->assign('row_colors',array('#eeee33','#cccc33'));
// Or as a comma-separated list in a string
$smarty->assign('row_colors',"#eeee33,#cccc33");
```

To use a template variable as the cycle list, specify it with the values parameter to {cycle}:

```
<tr bgcolor="{cycle values=$row_colors}">
```

The advance parameter controls when {cycle} advances to the next element in its list. If advance is false, then {cycle} prints the same value the next time it is called. If advance is true, which is the default, then a new value is printed the next time {cycle} is called. One use of advance is to switch to a new value only when a piece of information that's being displayed changes. For example, this code uses the same row color for all consecutive elements with the same calories value:

```
<table>
{section name=icecream loop=$flavors}
{* Check if the calories value for the next element is the same as
   the calories value for the current element *}
{if $flavors[icecream.index_next].calories eq $flavors[icecream].calories}
{assign var="do_advance" value=false}
{else}
{assign var="do_advance" value=true}
{/if}
<tr bgcolor="{cycle name=rowcycle values=$row_colors advance=$do_advance}">
 <td>{$flavors[icecream].name}</td>
 <td>{$flavors[icecream].calories}</td>
 <td>${$flavors[icecream].price|string_format:"%.02f"}</td>
</tr>
{/section}
</table>
```

The do_advance variable is set to false when the calories value in the current element of the $flavors array is the same as the calories value for the next element.

This ensures that the same {cycle} value is printed when that next element is displayed. Because Chocolate and Strawberry are adjacent in $flavors and they each have 30 calories, they are displayed with the same background color:

```
<table>
<tr bgcolor="#00ff00">
 <td>Vanilla</td>
 <td>20</td>
 <td>$4.25</td>
</tr>
<tr bgcolor="#99ff99">
 <td>Chocolate</td>
 <td>30</td>
 <td>$4.50</td>
</tr>
<tr bgcolor="#99ff99">
 <td>Strawberry</td>
 <td>30</td>
 <td>$3.50</td>
</tr>
<tr bgcolor="#00ff00">
 <td>Salmon Butter</td>
 <td>200</td>
 <td>$9.44</td>
</tr>
<tr bgcolor="#99ff99">
 <td>Guava Mint Bouillon</td>
 <td>50</td>
 <td>$3.75</td>
</tr>
</table>
```

The print parameter controls whether {cycle} displays anything at all. The default, true, means that {cycle} prints a value. If print is set to false, {cycle} doesn't print a value, but it still advances to the next value in its list. This example uses the print parameter to merely highlight with a background color those rows with prices cheaper than $4:

```
<table>
{section name=icecream loop=$flavors}
{if $flavors[icecream].price < 4}
{assign var="do_print" value=true}
{else}
{assign var="do_print" value=false}
{/if}
```

```
<tr bgcolor="{cycle name=rowcycle values=$row_colors
             advance=$do_print print=$do_print}">
 <td>{$flavors[icecream].name}</td>
 <td>{$flavors[icecream].calories}</td>
 <td>${$flavors[icecream].price|string_format:"%.02f"}</td>
</tr>
{/section}
</table>
```

When the `price` value in the current element of the `$flavors` array is less than four, `advance` and `print` parameters are both set to `true`. Otherwise, they are set to `false`. Setting `advance` as well as `print` to `false` ensures that the background color alternates among only rows that have a color, not all rows. The HTML that this code prints is as follows:

```
<table>
<tr bgcolor="">
 <td>Vanilla</td>
 <td>20</td>
 <td>$4.25</td>
</tr>
<tr bgcolor="">
 <td>Chocolate</td>
 <td>30</td>
 <td>$4.50</td>
</tr>
<tr bgcolor="#00ff00">
 <td>Strawberry</td>
 <td>30</td>
 <td>$3.50</td>
</tr>
<tr bgcolor="">
 <td>Salmon Butter</td>
 <td>200</td>
 <td>$9.44</td>
</tr>
<tr bgcolor="#99ff99">
 <td>Guava Mint Bouillon</td>
 <td>50</td>
 <td>$3.75</td>
</tr>
</table>
```

Although {cycle} uses a comma as its default delimiter for values specified in a string, you can change that with the delimiter parameter. This example uses the vertical bar as a delimiter character:

```
<tr bgcolor="{cycle values=$colorlist delimiter="|"}">
```

This corresponds to the values being assigned to a template variable like this:

```
$smarty->assign('colorlist', '#00ff00|#eeee33');
```

Including Other Files and Templates

Smarty provides a number of ways to incorporate information from other files into your template output. These functions help you make your template organization modular and reusable. You can put common functions or display patterns into small templates and then combine those functions and templates into larger templates for output.

Configuration Files

Configuration files define variables. Load a config file to set the variables defined in the file. You can also just load a section of a file to set the variables defined in that section. Configuration files are useful for defining bits of text or HTML attributes, especially if you want to select among different sets of definitions. For example, you can create two configuration files that define elements of a page header, as shown in Listing 4-4 and Listing 4-5.

Listing 4-4. plumbers.conf

```
who=Plumber
tool=wrench
```

Listing 4-5. carpenters.conf

```
who=Carpenter
tool=hammer
```

Load the values from a configuration file into a template with the {config_load} function. Then, access values defined in the loaded configuration file by surrounding the setting name you want with hash marks:

```
{config_load file="plumbers.conf"}
Welcome, {#who#}. Here are instructions on how to tune up your {#tool#}.
```

With the `plumbers.conf` configuration file loaded, this prints the following:

```
Welcome, Plumber. Here are instructors on how to tune up your wrench.
```

Smarty looks for configuration files in the directory defined by the `config_dir` configuration setting. If `config_dir` is set to `/usr/local/www/smarty/configs`, then `{config_load file="plumbers.conf"}` attempts to open `/usr/local/www/smarty/configs/plumbers.conf`.

Configuration files can be divided into sections. To indicate a section in a configuration file, put the section name in brackets at the beginning of a line. The section then contains variable definitions after the section name until the end of the file or the beginning of another section. Listing 4-6 shows a configuration file with a global portion and three sections.

Listing 4-6. `jobs.conf`

```
greeting=Welcome
[wood]
who=Carpenter
tool=hammer
[water]
who=Plumber
tool=wrench
[metal]
who=Welder
tool=torch
```

To load variables from a particular section, use the `section` parameter to `{config_load}`. This template loads the global variables (those outside of a section) and the variables in the `water` section:

```
{config_load file="jobs.conf" section="water"}
{#greeting#}, {#who#}. Here are instructions on how to tune up your {#tool#}.
```

The template outputs the following:

```
Welcome, Plumber. Here are instructions on how to tune up your wrench.
```

{include}

The `{include}` tag loads another template and displays its output. Any variables defined when the `{include}` tag is used are available to the included template. The `{include}` tag is useful for breaking common page elements such as headers, footers, and menus into subtemplates. This example selects what menu subtemplate to include based on the value of the $section variable:

```
{if $section == dessert}
{include file="dessert-menu.tpl"}
{else}
{include file="general-menu.tpl"}
{/if}
```

To assign the output of a subtemplate to a variable instead of displaying it, pass {include} the assign attribute with the name of the variable to be assigned to:

```
{include file="dessert-menu.tpl" assign="menucontents"}
{* display the menu as all uppercase *}
{$menucontents|upper}
```

You can also pass variable values to the subtemplate by specifying them inside the {include} tag:

```
{include file="dessert-menu.tpl" flavor="Chocolate" category="expensive"}
```

To the dessert-menu.tpl template, the variable $flavor is now set to Chocolate and the variable $category to expensive.

{capture}

The {capture} tag prevents template output from being displayed. Instead, anything that would be output between the {capture} and {/capture} tags is slurped up into a variable. The captured content is accessible via the special $smarty.capture variable. This is useful for displaying the same content more than once on a page:

```
{* capture the navigation bar, composed of two subtemplates *}
{capture name="navigation"}
{include file="general-navbar.tpl"}
{include file="specific-navbar.tpl"}
{/capture}

{* display navigation *}
{$smarty.capture.navigation}
{* page body goes here *}
{* display navigation again *}
{$smarty.capture.navigation}
```

Because the name parameter to the {capture} function is navigation, the output of the two include files is assigned to the $smarty.capture.navigation variable. Subsequently, that variable can be used again in the page.

{insert}

The {insert} tag runs a PHP function and displays the return value of the function in the template. The output of an {insert} tag is not cached. The name parameter to {insert} controls what PHP function is executed. For example, if name is set to functionname, then the PHP function insert_functionname() is run. This {insert} tag runs the PHP function insert_current_temp():

```
{insert name="current_temp" zip="60651"}
```

The PHP function is passed two arguments. The first argument is an associative array of the parameters inside the {insert} tag. The second argument is a reference to the currently active $smarty object. An insert function uses the parameters array to control its behavior and the $smarty object reference if it needs access to configuration settings. This insert_current_temp() function retrieves the current temperature for the provided ZIP code via a SOAP call:

```
function insert_current_temp($params, &$smarty) {
    require_once 'SOAP/Client.php';
    if (! $params['zip']) {
        return "No temperature available.";
    } else {
        $wsdl_url = 'http://www.xmethods.net/sd/2001/TemperatureService.wsdl';
        $wsdl = new SOAP_WSDL($wsdl_url);
        $client = $wsdl->getProxy();
        $temp = $client->getTemp($params['zip']);
        // This temperature server returns -999 if there was an error
        if ($temp == -999) {
            return "No temperature available.";
        } else {
            return "In ZIP Code $params[zip], it is $temp degrees Fahrenheit.";
        }
    }
}
```

The lone argument, zip, is accessible as $params['zip'] inside the function. The return value of the function is displayed in the template. You can have the returned value assigned to a variable instead of displayed by including the assign parameter in the {insert} tag:

```
{insert name="current_temp" zip="60651" assign="chicagotemp"}
```

You have a few choices for defining the PHP functions that are called by {insert} tags. The first is to define the function in your PHP script before the template is invoked with display(). This can be in the same file that calls display() or in another included file. The second method is to provide the {insert} tag with the name of a PHP file that defines the function by including a script parameter. With this method, Smarty looks for a function called smarty_insert_current_temp(), not insert_current_temp(). This {insert} usage declares that smarty_insert_current_temp() is defined in /usr/local/lib/php/temps.php:

```
{insert name="current_temp" zip="60651" script="/usr/local/lib/php/temps.php"}
```

The last way to define an {insert} tag's PHP function is to put the function in its own file in the plugins directory. If no script parameter is provided to the {insert} tag and insert_current_temp() isn't defined, then Smarty looks for a file called insert.current_temp.php in the plugins directory that defines the function smarty_insert_current_temp().

Whichever method you use to define PHP functions for {insert} tags, the function bodies are identical. The function names should start with insert_ if they are defined in PHP scripts before the template is invoked. If the functions are defined in a file loaded by the script parameter or in an autoloaded file in the plugins directory, then their names must start with smarty_insert_.

{fetch}

The {fetch} tag displays the contents of a file or URL. This is useful if you have content stored in a plain-text file that you want to display inside a template that contains layout and navigation. To display a file, specify the full path of a filename or a relative path from the location of the script invoking the template. Listing 4-7 shows a PHP script that invokes the template in Listing 4-8 to display a plain-text file.

Listing 4-7. fetch.php

```
$basedir = '/usr/local/share/textfiles';
// canonicalize pathname
$file = realpath($basedir.$_SERVER['PATH_INFO']);
// make sure $file is readable, is actually a file (not a directory)
// and is under $basedir (no ../.. stuff in PATH_INFO)
if (is_readable($file) && is_file($file) && preg_match("@^$basedir/@",$file)) {
    $smarty->assign('file',$file);
}
$smarty->display('fetch.tpl');
```

Listing 4-8. fetch.tpl

```
{if $file}
<pre>{fetch file="$file"}</pre>
{else}
<h1>Error</h2>
<i>{$smarty.server.PATH_INFO}</i> could not be found or is not readable.
{/if}
```

If fetch.php is accessed as http://www.example.com/fetch.php/story.txt, $_SERVER['PATH_INFO] is set to /story.txt, so $file is set to /usr/local/share/textfiles/story.txt. If that file exists and is readable, then the template variable file is set to /usr/local/share/textfiles/story.txt. The call to realpath() unravels any symbolic links or parent directory accessing within the path information. For example, if the supplied path information was /../../../../etc/passwd, realpath() translates /usr/local/share/textfiles/story.txt/../../../../etc/passwd into /etc/passwd. Because the filename /etc/passwd doesn't begin with /usr/local/share/textfiles, the preg_match("@^$basedir/@",$file) call fails and the template variable is not assigned. Then, fetch.php invokes the fetch.tpl template. In the template, if $file is set, the {fetch} function displays its contents. If it is not set, the template displays an error message.

Processing Text

This section describes Smarty's built-in text-processing functions that make some common tasks easier, such as trimming whitespace and populating form elements with data from template variables.

Removing Whitespace

The {strip} function removes extraneous whitespace from a block of text. This is especially useful if you add whitespace to a template to make it more readable. For example, consider this {section} block:

```
<table>
{section name=icecream loop=$flavors}
<tr>
 <td>{$flavors[icecream].name}</td>
 <td>
 {if $flavors[icecream].calories < 10}
  Not much
 {else}
```

```
  {$flavors[icecream].calories}
 {/if}
 </td>
 <td>${$flavors[icecream].price|string_format:"%.02f"}</td>
</tr>
{/section}
</table>
```

When this template runs, each <td> is on its own line in the output. Plus, the line breaks before the {if}, {else}, and {/if} tags add even more whitespace to the output. Surrounding the {section} block with {strip} removes the whitespace at the beginning and end of each line:

```
{strip}
<table>
{section name=icecream loop=$flavors}
<tr>
 <td>{$flavors[icecream].name}</td>
 <td>
 {if $flavors[icecream].calories < 10}
  Not much
 {else}
  {$flavors[icecream].calories}
 {/if}
 </td>
 <td>${$flavors[icecream].price|string_format:"%.02f"}</td>
</tr>
{/section}
</table>
{/strip}
```

Removing whitespace with {strip} also trims the size of your pages, saving you bandwidth and speeding up downloads for your users.

Generating HTML

Smarty provides functions that ease the creation of HTML tables, image tags, and some form elements: checkboxes, radio buttons, and select menus. You can, obviously, code HTML directly in your templates, but these functions help when you need to produce HTML based on template variables.

Tables

The {html_table} tag produces an HTML table containing values from an array. The following examples use these variable assignments:

```
$smarty->assign('bgcolors', array('bgcolor="#cccccc"',
                                   'bgcolor="#eeeeee"'));
$smarty->assign('flavornames',
                array('Vanilla','Chocolate','Strawberry',
                      'Salmon Butter','Guava Mint Bouillon'));
```

To generate a table, provide an array name to {html_table} in the loop parameter:

```
{html_table loop=$flavornames}
```

This produces a three-column table with a border. If the number of elements in the array is not a multiple of three, then extra table cells are filled with . The table looks like this:

```
<table border="1">
<tr>
<td>Vanilla</td>
<td>Chocolate</td>
<td>Strawberry</td>
</tr>
<tr>
<td>Salmon Butter</td>
<td>Guava Mint Bouillon</td>
<td> </td>
</tr>
</table>
```

To change the number of columns, use the cols parameter:

```
{html_table loop=$flavornames cols=2}
```

Setting cols to 2 produces a two-column table:

```
<table border="1">
<tr>
<td>Vanilla</td>
<td>Chocolate</td>
</tr>
```

```
<tr>
<td>Strawberry</td>
<td>Salmon Butter</td>
</tr>
<tr>
<td>Guava Mint Bouillon</td>
<td> </td>
</tr>
</table>
```

To set attributes of the `<table>` tag, use the `table_attr` parameter. What you provide in `table_attr` overrides the default `border="1"` attribute. Use single quotes to enclose an attribute string that itself contains double quotes. For example, this `{html_table}` tag:

```
{html_table loop=$flavornames table_attr='border="3" style="yummy"'}
```

produces a table with this opening tag:

```
<table border="3" style="yummy">
```

If you don't want any attributes in the opening table tag, including `border="1"`, set `table_attr` to the empty string:

```
{html_table loop=$flavornames table_attr=""}
```

Similar to `table_attr` is `tr_attr`, which controls attributes of each `<tr>` tag. This `{html_table}` tag:

```
{html_table loop=$flavornames tr_attr='bgcolor="#cccccc"'}
```

produces this table:

```
<table border="1">
<tr bgcolor="#cccccc">
<td>Vanilla</td>
<td>Chocolate</td>
<td>Strawberry</td>
</tr>
<tr bgcolor="#cccccc">
<td>Salmon Butter</td>
<td>Guava Mint Bouillon</td>
<td> </td>
</tr>
</table>
```

If you set `tr_attr` to an array, the array values are cycled through the `<tr>` tags. This tag:

```
{html_table loop=$flavornames cols=2 tr_attr=$bgcolors}
```

produces this table, in which the `<tr>` attributes alternate between the elements of `$bgcolors`:

```
<table border="1">
<tr bgcolor="#cccccc">
<td>Vanilla</td>
<td>Chocolate</td>
</tr>
<tr bgcolor="#eeeeee">
<td>Strawberry</td>
<td>Salmon Butter</td>
</tr>
<tr bgcolor="#cccccc">
<td>Guava Mint Bouillon</td>
<td> </td>
</tr>
</table>
```

In the same vein as `table_attr` and `tr_attr`, `td_attr` controls attributes for each `<td>` tag. You can specify a string to be used for all table cells. This tag:

```
{html_table loop=$flavornames td_attr='bgcolor="#cccccc"'}
```

produces this table:

```
<table border="1">
<tr>
<td bgcolor="#cccccc">Vanilla</td>
<td bgcolor="#cccccc">Chocolate</td>
<td bgcolor="#cccccc">Strawberry</td>
</tr>
<tr>
<td bgcolor="#cccccc">Salmon Butter</td>
<td bgcolor="#cccccc">Guava Mint Bouillon</td>
<td bgcolor="#cccccc"> </td>
</tr>
</table>
```

Like tr_attr, td_attr accepts an array of values to cycle through. This tag:

```
{html_table loop=$flavornames td_attr=$bgcolors}
```

produces a table of cells whose colors alternate:

```
<table border="1">
<tr>
<td bgcolor="#cccccc">Vanilla</td>
<td bgcolor="#eeeeee">Chocolate</td>
<td bgcolor="#cccccc">Strawberry</td>
</tr>
<tr>
<td bgcolor="#cccccc">Salmon Butter</td>
<td bgcolor="#eeeeee">Guava Mint Bouillon</td>
<td bgcolor="#cccccc"> </td>
</tr>
</table>
```

Note that at the beginning of each table row, the <td> attributes start over at the beginning of $bgcolors. Even though the last <td> in the first row has the attribute bgcolor="#cccccc", so does the first <td> in the second row.

The last parameter of {html_table} is trailpad, which controls what appears in padding cells added to the end of the table. By default, this is . To override this, specify a different value for trailpad. This {html_table} tag:

```
{html_table loop=$flavornames trailpad="[ None ]"}
```

produces a table whose last cell contains [None]:

```
<table border="1">
<tr>
<td>Vanilla</td>
<td>Chocolate</td>
<td>Strawberry</td>
</tr>
<tr>
<td>Salmon Butter</td>
<td>Guava Mint Bouillon</td>
<td>[ None ]</td>
</tr>
</table>
```

Images

The chief convenience of the {html_image} tag is that it automatically calculates image height and width values for you. This convenience is computationally expensive, though. If you're also using caching, then you pay the size calculation performance penalty only once, when the template output is put into the cache. If you are not using template caching, try to avoid {html_image}. Instead, write explicit <img> tags.

At a minimum, you need to specify an image filename to {html_image}:

```
{html_image file="email-address.png"}
```

All image filenames are relative to the Web server's document root directory. If invoked from a page in the document root directory (not a subdirectory of the document root), these two {html_image} usages are equivalent:

```
{* relative to the "current directory", which is document root *}
{html_image file="email-address.png"}
{* the "absolute path" beginning with a slash starts at the document root *}
{html_image file="/email-address.png"}
```

The {html_image} tag outputs an HTML <img> tag with src, alt, height, width, and border attributes:

```
<img src="email-address.png" alt="" border="0" width="107" height="13" />
```

If Smarty can't find the image file specified in an {html_image} tag, it reports an error. You can specify a different value for border, alt, height, and width with appropriately named parameters to {html_image}:

```
{html_image file="email-address.png" alt="me" border="9" width=36 height=402}
```

This outputs the following:

```
<img src="email-address.png" alt="me" border="9" width="36" height="402" />
```

To wrap the image in a hyperlink, specify the target URL with the link parameter to {html_image}:

```
{html_image file="email-address.png" link="http://www.example.com"}
```

This outputs the following:

```
<a href="http://www.example.com"><img src="email-address.png" alt="" border="0"
width="107" height="13" /></a>
```

Checkboxes and Radio Buttons

The {html_checkboxes} and {html_radios} functions create HTML checkbox and radio elements, <input type="checkbox"> and <input type="radio">. These two Smarty functions behave similarly. Aside from the type attribute of the <input> tags they output, their only difference is that {html_checkboxes} accepts an array to specify more than one checked item, but {html_radios} accepts only a string to specify a single checked item.

The example checkboxes and radio buttons in this section use these variable assignments:

```
$smarty->assign('flavornames',array('Vanilla','Chocolate','Strawberry'));
$smarty->assign('flavorcolors',array('white','brown','pink'));
$smarty->assign('flavorinfo',array('white' => 'Vanilla', 'brown' => 'Chocolate',
                                   'pink' => 'Strawberry'));
$smarty->assign('favorites', array('white','brown'));
```

The shortest way to generate radio buttons or checkboxes is to provide an associative array such as $flavorinfo, whose keys are used as form element values and whose values are used as form element labels:

```
{html_radios name="flavor1" options=$flavorinfo}
{html_checkboxes name="flavor2" options=$flavorinfo}
```

This template generates the following HTML:

```
<label><input type="radio" name="flavor1" value="white" />Vanilla</label>
<label><input type="radio" name="flavor1" value="brown" />Chocolate</label>
<label><input type="radio" name="flavor1" value="pink" />Strawberry</label>

<label><input type="checkbox" name="flavor2[]" value="white" />Vanilla</label>
<label><input type="checkbox" name="flavor2[]" value="brown" />Chocolate</label>
<label><input type="checkbox" name="flavor2[]" value="pink" />Strawberry</label>
```

Because the form element name of each checkbox is flavor2[] instead of just flavor2, submitting the form with multiple elements checked makes $_REQUEST['flavor2'] an array containing the values of all the checked checkboxes. A radio button group can have only one element selected on submission, so the radio button element names are unmodified.

If you don't have all of the value and label information in a single associative array, you can pass separate arrays for values and labels with the values and output parameters. This template generates identical output to the previous HTML:

```
{html_radios name="icecream" values=$flavorcolors output=$flavornames}
{html_checkboxes name="icecream" values=$flavorcolors output=$flavornames}
```

To separate each radio button or checkbox with a string, specify that string with the separator parameter. This template arranges the radio buttons in one table row and the checkboxes in another table row:

```
<table><tr><td>
{html_radios name="flavor1" options=$flavorinfo separator="</td><td>"}
</td></tr>
<tr><td>
{html_checkboxes name="flavor1" options=$flavorinfo separator="</td><td>"}
</td></tr></table>
```

The template outputs HTML with each form element in its own table cell:

```
<table><tr><td>
<label><input type="radio" name="flavor1" value="white" />Vanilla</label>
</td><td>
<label><input type="radio" name="flavor1" value="brown" />Chocolate</label>
</td><td>
<label><input type="radio" name="flavor1" value="pink" />Strawberry</label>
</td><td>
</td></tr>
<tr><td>
<label><input type="checkbox" name="flavor1[]" value="white" />Vanilla</label>
</td><td>
<label><input type="checkbox" name="flavor1[]" value="brown" />Chocolate</label>
</td><td>
<label><input type="checkbox" name="flavor1[]" value="pink" />Strawberry</label>
</td><td>
</td></tr></table>
```

Both {html_radios} and {html_checkboxes} accept a string in the checked parameter to indicate a single element that should be checked by default. This template:

```
{html_radios name="flavor1" options=$flavorinfo checked="pink"}
{html_checkboxes name="flavor2" options=$flavorinfo checked="pink"}
```

generates this output:

```
<label><input type="radio" name="flavor1" value="white" />Vanilla</label>
<label><input type="radio" name="flavor1" value="brown" />Chocolate</label>
<label><input type="radio" name="flavor1" value="pink" checked="checked" />➥
Strawberry
</label>

<label><input type="checkbox" name="flavor2[]" value="white" />Vanilla</label>
<label><input type="checkbox" name="flavor2[]" value="brown" />Chocolate</label>
<label><input type="checkbox" name="flavor2[]" value="pink" checked="checked" />➥
Strawberry
</label>
```

The {html_checkboxes} function also accepts an array in the checked parameter to indicate that multiple elements should be checked by default. This template:

```
{html_checkboxes name="flavor2" options=$flavorinfo checked=$favorites}
```

generates this output:

```
<label><input type="checkbox" name="flavor2[]" value="white" checked="checked"
/>Vanilla</label>
<label><input type="checkbox" name="flavor2[]" value="brown" checked="checked"
/>Chocolate</label>
<label><input type="checkbox" name="flavor2[]" value="pink" />Strawberry</label>
```

Select Menus

The {html_options} function makes it easy to display a full-fledged select menu containing labels and values from an array. To generate a menu with {html_options}, supply an associative array name in the options parameter and a name for the menu in the name parameter:

```
{html_options options=$flavorinfo name="flavor"}
```

This template generates the following:

```
<select name="flavor">
<option label="Vanilla" value="white">Vanilla</option>
<option label="Chocolate" value="brown">Chocolate</option>
<option label="Strawberry" value="pink">Strawberry</option>
</select>
```

Just like {html_radios} and {html_checkboxes}, you can supply the values and labels in separate arrays with the values and output parameters. This template generates an identical menu to the previous HTML:

```
{html_options values=$flavorcolors output=$flavornames name="flavor"}
```

If you don't supply a name parameter, then {html_options} just displays the <option></option> list without surrounding <select></select> tags. When you do include name, however, you can specify arbitrary attributes to appear inside the opening <select> tag by including them as parameters to {html_options}. For example, to apply a style and allow users to choose multiple options from the menu, use this:

```
{html_options options=$flavorinfo name="flavor" multiple="multiple" class="big"}
```

This template produces a <select> menu with this opening tag:

```
<select name="flavor" multiple="multiple" class="big">
```

The {html_options} function accepts default values to mark as selected in the selected parameter. You can supply a string to select one default or an array to select multiple defaults:

```
{html_options options=$flavorinfo name="flavor" selected="brown"}
{html_options options=$flavorinfo multiple=multiple name=flavor
selected=$favorites}
```

This template outputs the following:

```
<select name="flavor">
<option label="Vanilla" value="white">Vanilla</option>
<option label="Chocolate" value="brown" selected="selected">Chocolate</option>
<option label="Strawberry" value="pink">Strawberry</option>
</select>
<select name="flavor" multiple="multiple">
<option label="Vanilla" value="white" selected="selected">Vanilla</option>
<option label="Chocolate" value="brown" selected="selected">Chocolate</option>
<option label="Strawberry" value="pink">Strawberry</option>
</select>
```

If you pass an array in the selected parameter without specifying multiple to indicate that the <select> menu can accommodate multiple choices, {html_options} doesn't report an error, but a browser renders only one of the "selected" elements as selected.

Dates and Times

In addition to what is discussed in this section, there are two functions, {html_select_time} and {html_select_date}, that generate select menus for choosing a time and date. These functions are documented in the Smarty online manual at http://smarty.php.net/manual/en/language.function.html.select.time.php and http://smarty.php.net/manual/en/language.function.html.select.date.php.

Displaying Delimiter Characters

By default, Smarty tags are delimited with { and }. So what do you do when you want a literal curly brace character in your template? Use the {ldelim} or {rdelim} tag. The {ldelim} tag displays the left/opening delimiter, and the {rdelim} tag displays the right/closing delimiter. For example, consider this template:

```
Smarty uses {ldelim} and {rdelim} as delimiter characters.
```

which outputs the following:

```
Smarty uses { and } as delimiter characters.
```

You can also put text inside a {literal} block to prevent Smarty from parsing it. Everything between {literal} and {/literal} is printed as is. For example:

```
{literal}
Smarty uses {ldelim} and {rdelim} as delimiter characters.
{/literal}
```

This template prints the following:

```
Smarty uses {ldelim} and {rdelim} as delimiter characters.
```

The only thing you can't put inside a {literal} block is a {/literal} tag because that signals the end of the {/literal} block to Smarty. If you put {ldelim}/literal} inside a {literal} block, it comes out unmodified, as {ldelim}/literal}, because inside the {literal} block the {ldelim} tag isn't parsed. If you want to include the string {/literal} in page output, you need to do it with {ldelim} or {rdelim} outside of a {literal} block.

Caching Template Output

Smarty's template compiling mechanism provides one level of efficiency. The first time a template is invoked, Smarty turns the template into a PHP file and then executes the PHP file. As long as the template doesn't change, subsequent invocations of the same template use the already-generated PHP file instead of parsing the template again. This produces pages faster because template parsing involves lots of regular expressions and string handling, which can be slow on large, complicated templates.

Although template compilation saves expensive template parsing steps, the PHP file that the template is turned into still has to be executed on each request. Sometimes that's necessary: The PHP file produces different output on every request, so it always needs to run on demand. When the output of the PHP file won't change from request to request, however, Smarty's caching features increase your site's efficiency even more.

Smarty's caching saves the output from executing that PHP file. The next time a request comes in for a page that uses the same template, Smarty retrieves the cached results and displays them instead of re-executing the PHP file. Figure 4-1 illustrates the relationship between template compilation and template output caching. By default, the output of a template is cached for an hour, but you can adjust that on a global or per-template basis. You can also flush individual templates from the cache or flush the entire cache on demand. This is useful if you change a number of templates at once and want to repopulate the cache with updated information.

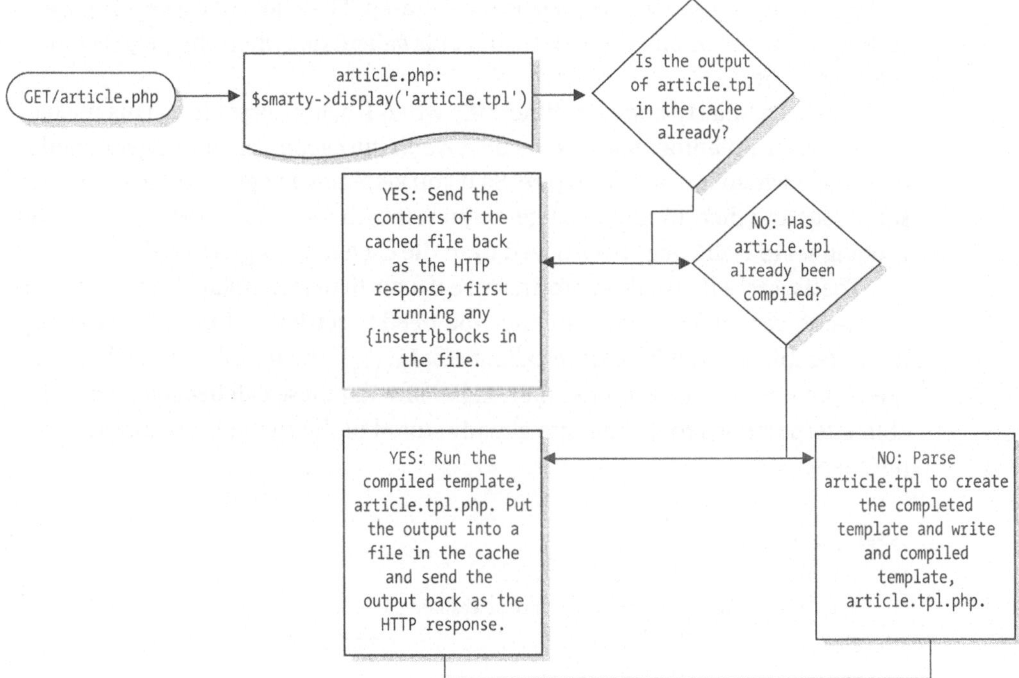

Figure 4-1. Template compilation and template output caching

To turn on caching, set the caching configuration setting to 1. Once $smarty->caching is set, calls to display() automatically use a cached copy of a template if available:

```
$smarty->caching = 1;
$smarty->display('article.tpl');
```

The output of {insert} tags is not cached. When a cached copy of a page that contains an {insert} tag is redisplayed, the {insert} tag is re-executed. If you have a page that is largely static but contains a few always-changing items such as ad banners or updated statistics, turn caching on but generate those changing items with {insert} tags. The bulk of the page is still pulled from the cache, making page generation faster.

To change the expiration time from one hour (3,600 seconds), set cache_lifetime before you call display():

```
$smarty->caching = 1;
$smarty->cache_lifetime = 600; // ten minutes
$smarty->display('article.tpl');
```

If a page doesn't exist in the cache when display() is called with cache_lifetime set to 3600 and, then 15 minutes later, the same page is requested with cache_lifetime set to 600, the page is regenerated. The relevant cache_lifetime setting is the one in place when display() is called, not when the page is put into the cache.

However, Smarty behaves differently when $caching is set to 2. This makes Smarty use the lifetime that was in effect when the cached page was generated to determine whether it should expire. So if you generate a page with cache_lifetime set to 3600 and then 15 minutes later request it with cache_lifetime set to 600 and caching set to 2, the page is retrieved from the cache, not regenerated.

The is_cached() method returns true if a particular template is cached. You can use is_cached() to check whether you need to retrieve information that populates template variables before calling display(). If the template is cached, then there's no need to make a potentially expensive database call because the variable interpolations that result are already stored in the cached copy of the template:

```
$smarty->caching = 1;
if (! $smarty->is_cached('article.tpl')) {
    $article_info = get_article_from_database($_REQUEST['article_name']);
    $smarty->assign('headline', $article_info->headline);
    $smarty->assign('byline',$article_info->byline);
    $smarty->assign('body',$article_info->body);
}
$smarty->display('article.tpl');
```

By default, caching is done on a per-template basis, independent of any variables that have been assigned. In the previous code, the first time this page is invoked with `$_REQUEST['article_name']` set to `constructionupdate`, data relevant to that article is pulled from the database, assigned to template variables, and included in the displayed (and cached) page. The next time the page is invoked, no matter what the value of `$_REQUEST['article_name']`, the cached copy of the template that has the `constructionupdate` article in it is displayed. To prevent this, pass a cache ID to `is_cached()` and `display()`. A cache ID is an integer or string that identifies the combination of things that are unique about a page to be cached. When you supply a cache ID, new cached template outputs are stored for each unique combination of template name and cache ID. With a cache ID, you can cache each article separately:

```
$smarty->caching = 1;
$cache_id = md5($_REQUEST['article_name']);
if (! $smarty->is_cached('article.tpl',$cache_id)) {
    $article_info = get_article_from_database($_REQUEST['article_name']);
    $smarty->assign('headline', $article_info->headline);
    $smarty->assign('byline',$article_info->byline);
    $smarty->assign('body',$article_info->body);
}
$smarty->display('article.tpl',$cache_id);
```

With `cache_id` supplied, requests with different values for `$_REQUEST ['article_name']` are cached separately. Because the cache ID is used in creating cache directory and filenames, you should restrict possible cache ID values and sanitize any input before passing a cache ID to `display()`. For example, in production, you should modify the previous example code to make sure `$_REQUEST['article_name']` corresponds to an existing database record before passing `$cache_id` to `display()`.

To clear Smarty's cache, use the `clear_all_cache()` method or the `clear_cache()` method. The `clear_all_cache()` method removes everything from Smarty's page cache. The `clear_cache()` method removes a specific template from the page cache. The following are some examples of how to use these methods:

```
// Clear everything from the cache
$smarty->clear_all_cache();
// Clear article.tpl from the cache
$smarty->clear_cache('article.tpl');
// Clear article.tpl with cache ID constructionupdate from the cache
// This leaves copies of article.tpl with other cache IDs in the cache
$smarty->clear_cache('article.tpl','constructionupdate');
// Clear copies of any template with cache ID constructionupdate from the cache
$smarty->clear_cache(null,'constructionupdate');
```

Two additional configuration settings affect how cached files are handled: compile_check and force_compile. The compile_check setting controls when Smarty recompiles templates into PHP pages. When compile_check is true, Smarty checks to see if a template file has changed when that template file is invoked with display(). If the file has changed since it was last compiled, then it is compiled again. It also clears the template from the cache. If compile_check is false, then the recompilation check doesn't happen and the cache is unaffected. The force_compile setting goes one step further. If force_compile is true, Smarty doesn't bother to check if a template has changed. Every time display() invokes a template, the template is recompiled and cleared from the cache. This process is resource intensive, so force_compile should only be used for development, never on a production site.

Putting It All Together

This section contains a small but complete example using Smarty. Listing 4-9 is a template that displays a table of ice cream information, and Listing 4-10 is the PHP script that connects to the database, retrieves information, and invokes the template. The template should be saved in the templates directory and the PHP script under the Web server's document root.

Listing 4-9. show-icecream.tpl*: Ice Cream Display Template*

```
{section name=icecream loop=$flavors}
{if $smarty.section.icecream.first}
<table>
{* Display a header row with the search term if there is one *}
<tr><th colspan="3">{if $search_term}Flavors Matching "{$search_term}</i>"
{else}All Flavors{/if}</th></tr>
<tr><td>Flavor</td><td>Calories</td><td>Price</td></tr>
{/if}
{* display each flavor, escaping entities in the flavor name *}
<tr>
 <td>{$flavors[icecream].flavor|escape}</td>
 <td>{$flavors[icecream].calories}</td>
 <td>${$flavors[icecream].price|string_format:"%.02f"}</td>
</tr>
{if $smarty.section.icecream.last}</table>{/if}
{sectionelse}
{* If there was no flavor data, say so *}
There are no flavors
{if $search_term}whose name contains "{$search_term}"{/if}.
{/section}
```

Listing 4-10. show-icecream.php: *Ice Cream Display PHP Script*

```
require 'DB.php';
// connect to the database
$dbh = DB::connect('mysql://phpgems:phpgems1@localhost/phpgems');
// we want our results back as associative arrays
$dbh->setFetchMode(DB_FETCHMODE_ASSOC);
// was a search term specified?
if ($_REQUEST['search_term']) {
    // make the search term accessible from the template -- we escape it
    // to avoid any XSS attacks
    $smarty->assign('search_term', htmlentities($_REQUEST['search_term']));
    // retrieve all rows from the ice_cream table where flavor contains
    // the search term
    $ice_cream = $dbh->getAll('SELECT * FROM ice_cream WHERE flavor LIKE ?',
                              array('%'.$_REQUEST['search_term'].'%'));
} else {
    // no search term, so retrieve all rows
    $ice_cream = $dbh->getAll('SELECT * FROM ice_cream');
}
// make the ice cream data accessible from the template
$smarty->assign('flavors',$ice_cream);
// display the template
$smarty->display('show-icecream.tpl');
```

Without a search term, show-icecream.php and show-icecream.tpl display all of the flavors in the table, as shown in Figure 4-2. Figure 4-3 shows the output when the search term V is supplied: just flavors that have the letter *V* or *v* in their name.

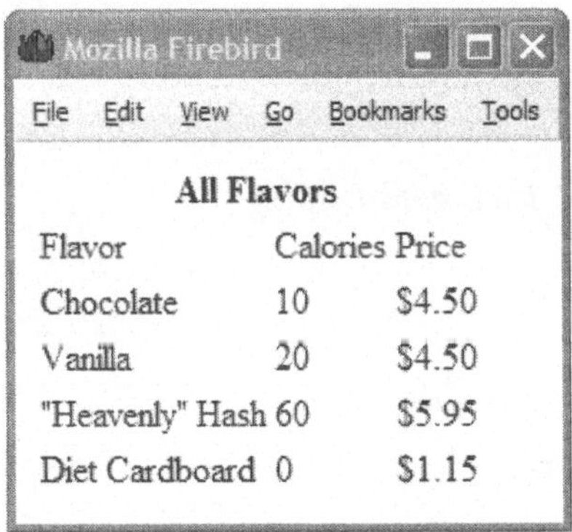

Figure 4-2. Displaying all flavors

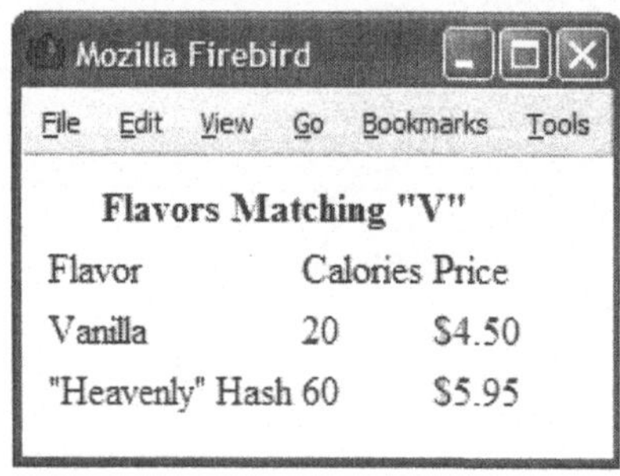

Figure 4-3. Displaying flavors with V *or* v *in their names*

The template and code in Listings 4-9 and 4-10 separate the data access and searching logic from the display and formatting of the data. I will extend this example with another template that displays the data in a different way. You can add a template that produces an XML rendering of the ice cream data with minimal modification of the PHP script. Listing 4-11 shows the template that outputs XML.

Listing 4-11. `show-icecream-xml.tpl`*: XML Ice Cream Display Template*

```
<flavors{if $search_term} search_term="{$search_term}"{/if}>
{section name=icecream loop=$flavors}
<flavor name="{$flavors[icecream].flavor|escape:htmlall}">
   <calories>{$flavors[icecream].calories}</calories>
   <price>${$flavors[icecream].price|string_format:"%.02f"}</price>
</flavor>
{/section}
</flavors>
```

Listing 4-12 is a modified `show-icecream.php` script that invokes the XML template instead of the standard one when the request variable `format` is set to `xml`.

Listing 4-12. `show-icecream.php`*: XML and HTML Ice Cream Display*

```
require 'DB.php';
// connect to the database
$dbh = DB::connect('mysql://phpgems:phpgems1@localhost/phpgems');
// we want our results back as associative arrays
$dbh->setFetchMode(DB_FETCHMODE_ASSOC);
// was a search term specified?
if ($_REQUEST['search_term']) {
    // make the search term accessible from the template -- we escape it
    // to avoid any XSS attacks
```

```
    $smarty->assign('search_term', htmlentities($_REQUEST['search_term']));
    // retrieve all rows from the ice_cream table where flavor contains
    // the search term
    $ice_cream = $dbh->getAll('SELECT * FROM ice_cream WHERE flavor LIKE ?',
                              array('%'.$_REQUEST['search_term'].'%'));
} else {
    // no search term, so retrieve all rows
    $ice_cream = $dbh->getAll('SELECT * FROM ice_cream');
}
// make the ice cream data accessible from the template
$smarty->assign('flavors',$ice_cream);
// display the template: XML or HTML
if ($_REQUEST['format'] == 'xml') {
    header('Content-Type: text/xml');
    $smarty->display('show-icecream-xml.tpl');
} else {
    $smarty->display('show-icecream.tpl');
}
```

The only changes required to `show-icecream.php` to accommodate the new template are at the very end. If `$_REQUEST['format']` is set to `xml`, then the program emits an XML-specific `Content-type` header and invokes the XML template. Otherwise, it invokes the HTML template. Adding a new template that displays the data differently doesn't require any modification to the logic that retrieves the data from the database. The data retrieval logic and each kind of display logic are completely independent: A programmer can alter the call to `DB::connect()` in `show-icecream.php` to point to a new database server without affecting the templates. A designer can spiff up the HTML table in `show-icecream.tpl` without disturbing any of the logic in `show-icecream.php`. An XML architect can change the schema in `show-icecream-xml.tpl` without affecting the HTML in `show-icecream.tpl` or the data access logic in `show-icecream.php`. Smarty makes it easy to keep the people responsible for these different tasks from stepping on each other's toes.

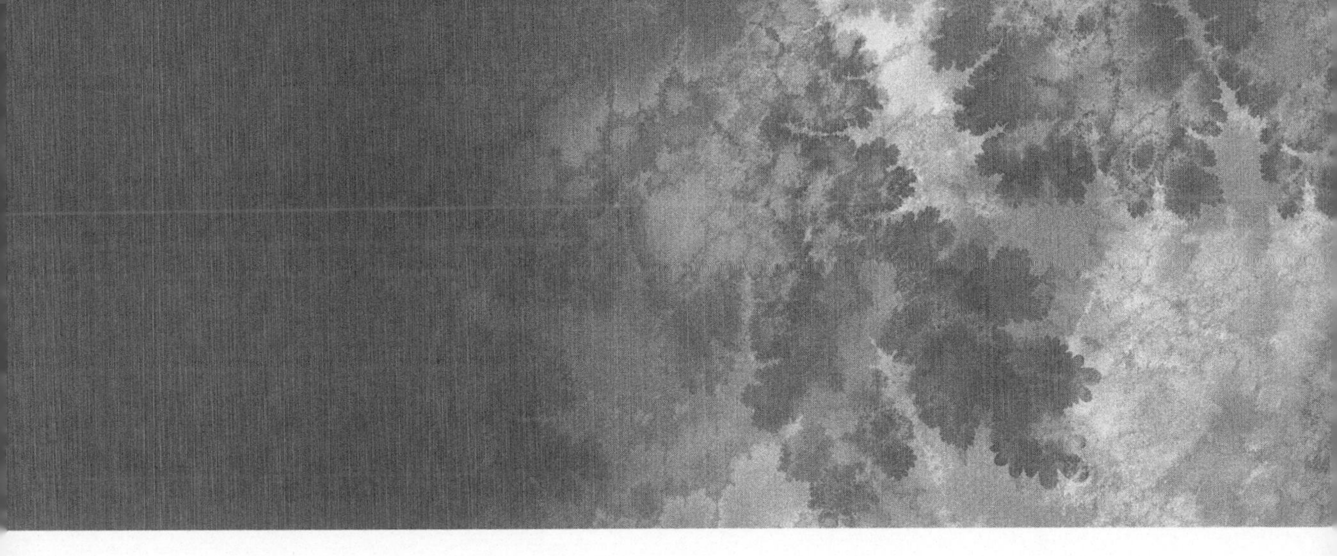

Part Three

XML

CHAPTER 5

Performing Event-Based XML Parsing with XML_Parser

XML_Parser is a module that simplifies parsing XML documents. It relies on PHP's xml extension and provides an object-oriented interface that makes it easier to work with the data in an XML document. In PHP 4, the xml extension uses the external expat library. In PHP 5, the XML extension uses the external libxml2 library.

There are two types of XML parsers. The xml extension and XML_Parser are SAX-style parsers.[1] PHP's domxml and simplexml extensions are DOM-style parsers.[2] SAX-style parsers, also called *event-based parsers*, scan an XML document and take action when they see certain events in the document such as opening tags, closing tags, or character data. DOM-style parsers build a tree representation of the document with parent and child elements and then let you examine or manipulate the tree to process the XML.

Because an event-based XML parser invokes callback functions to take the appropriate actions as it scans a document, it doesn't have to read in an entire XML file before it can get to work. As soon as the parser sees an item it understands, it invokes a function to handle the item. This saves time and memory, especially when parsing a large XML document. Event-based parsing with XML_Parser is best for XML manipulations where you can act discretely on relatively small chunks of data.

To use XML_Parser, you extend it and create callback methods in your subclass. You can create eight callback methods (see Table 5-1).

1. SAX stands for Simple API for XML, not to be confused with PHP5's SimpleXML extension.
2. DOM stands for Document Object Model.

Table 5-1. XML_Parser Callback Methods

Method Name	PHP Version	When Invoked	Example
startHandler	4 and 5	Start tag	`<flavor>`
endHandler	4 and 5	End tag	`</flavor>`
cdataHandler	4 and 5	Character data	Vanilla
piHandler	4 and 5	Processing instructions	`<?printer dpi:600 ?>`
entityrefHandler	5 only	External entity references	`<!ENTITY choco SYSTEM "http://www.example.com/chocolate.xml">`
unparsedHandler	4 and 5	Notations	`<!ENTITY doggie-picture SYSTEM "/images/violet-and-fig.gif" NDATA gif">`
notationHandler	4 and 5	Never	
defaultHandler	5 only	Entities	&
	4 only	Document prolog/preamble	`<?xml version="1.0" ?>`, `<!DOCTYPE dessert []>`
	4 only	External entity references	`<!ENTITY choco SYSTEM "http://www.example.com/chocolate.xml">`

This chapter shows you how to handle start and end tags, character data, and processing instructions. The other handlers are for rarely used elements of XML documents. Additionally, as you can see from Table 5-1, in different versions of PHP, the other element handlers work in different ways and not always correctly. For example, notations, which should cause the `notationHandler` to be invoked, are handled by `unparsedHandler`.

Handling Tags and Character Data

To handle tags, you need to define two methods: one that's called when the parser sees an opening tag such as `<flavor>` and one that's called when the parser sees a closing tag such as `</flavor>`. To handle character data, you define one method. It's called for each bit of uninterrupted text inside a tag.

For example, when parsing this XML:

```
<flavor>
Chocolate
</flavor>
```

the opening tag method is called for `<flavor>`, the character data method is called for `Chocolate`, and the closing tag method is called for `</flavor>`.

The callback function for an opening tag should be named `startHandler()`, the callback for the closing tag should be named `endHandler()`, and the character data callback should be called `cdataHandler()`.

The `startHandler()` method is passed three arguments. The first argument is a resource that points to the XML parser that invoked the callback. (This is the parser created by the underlying PHP function `xml_parser_create()`, not by the `XML_Parser` subclass.) The second argument passed to `startHandler()` is a string holding the name of the element whose start tag has been encountered, and the third argument is an associative array of attributes found in the start tag. The `endHandler()` method takes two arguments: the parser resource and a string holding the name of the element whose end tag has been encountered. The `cdataHandler()` also takes two arguments: the parser resource and a string holding the character data encountered.

The following is an `XML_Parser` subclass whose handlers let you know each time they are called:

```
require 'XML/Parser.php';
class demo_parser extends XML_Parser {
    function startHandler($xp, $element, $attribs) {
        print "START [$element]\n";
        var_dump($attribs);
    }
    function endHandler($xp, $element) {
        print "END [$element]\n";
    }
    function cdataHandler($xp, $data) {
        print "CDATA [$data]\n";
    }
}
```

To use this parser, instantiate it, call `setInputFile()` with a filename, and call the `parse()` method:

```
$parser =& new demo_parser;
$parser->setInputFile($argv[1]);
$parser->parse();
```

Before you instantiate a class that extends `XML_Parser`, you must `include` or `require` the `XML/Parser.php` file that defines the `XML_Parser` base class. The previous code that defines `demo_parser` has the necessary `require` statement. Subsequent examples in this chapter omit the line that loads `XML/Parser.php` for brevity, but you must always `require XML/Parser.php` in your code when you create a subclass of `XML_Parser`.

When using the `XML_Parser` class with PHP 4, you must instantiate a parser with `$parser =& new parser_class` and not `$parser = new parser_class`. Without the ampersand, PHP 4 assigns a copy of the newly created object to `$parser`. This causes problems when the parser invokes callback functions. In PHP 5, you don't need the ampersand because the object is not copied when it is created.

The `setInputFile()` method tells the parser to parse the XML in a given file. In the previous example, you pass `$argv[1]` to `setInputFile()` so the XML filename can be specified on the command line. There are two other ways to specify input XML to a parser. The `setInput()` method accepts a file handle returned from `fopen()` and causes the XML parser to read XML from that file handle until End of File (EOF). Both `setInput()` and `setInputFile()` don't actually read anything from the files until the `parse()` method is called. You can also parse XML in a string by passing the string to `parseString()`. The string is parsed when `parseString()` is called, so you don't need to subsequently call `parse()`.

The following three examples all parse the XML in a file called `flavors.xml`:

```
$parser =& new demo_parser;
$parser->parseString(file_get_contents('flavors.xml'));

$parser =& new demo_parser;
$parser->setInputFile('flavors.xml');
$parser->parse();

$parser =& new demo_parser;
$fh = fopen('flavors.xml') or die("Can't open flavors.xml");
$parser->setInput($fh);
$parser->parse();
```

The `parse()` method closes the open file handle of the file being parsed, whether it was specified with `setInputFile()` or `setInput()`.

By default, XML_Parser turns all element and attribute names to uppercase. Character data inside elements and attribute values are left unchanged. This process is called *case folding*. If your input XML may have element and attribute names with mixed, inconsistent capitalization styles, then case folding is helpful because it standardizes these strings so you can compare an `<icecream>` tag with an `<IceCream>` tag. However, if you don't want your input XML modified, turn case folding off by declaring a `$folding` property in your subclass and initializing it to `false`. The following is a version of the `demo_parser` class without case folding:

```
class demo_parser_no_case_folding extends XML_Parser {
    var $folding = false; // Turn off case folding
    function startHandler($xp, $element, &$attribs) {
        print "START [$element]\n";
        var_dump($attribs);
    }
    function endHandler($xp, $element) {
        print "END [$element]\n";
    }
    function cdataHandler($xp, $data) {
        print "CDATA [$data]\n";
    }
}
```

The character data handler may be invoked more than once to capture all of the character data between tags. To properly capture character data, use the character data handler to concatenate each piece of text together and then do something with the accumulated text in the end handler.

This `XML_Parser` subclass prints information about ice cream:

```
class ice_cream_parser_immediate extends XML_Parser {
    var $cdata;
    function startHandler($xp, $element, &$attribs) {
        switch ($element) {
        case 'FLAVOR':
            print "Flavor ID: $attribs[ID]\n";
            break;
        case 'NAME':
        case 'CALORIES':
        case 'PRICE':
            print '  '.ucfirst(strtolower($element)).': ';
            break;
        }
        $this->cdata = '';
    }

    function cdataHandler($xp, $data) {
        $this->cdata .= $data;
    }

    function endHandler($xp, $element) {
        switch ($element) {
        case 'NAME':
```

```
            case 'CALORIES':
                print "$this->cdata\n";
                break;
            case 'PRICE':
                printf("\$%.02f\n",$this->cdata);
                break;
            }
        }
    }
```

When it reaches a start tag, ice_cream_parser_immediate prints an appropriate string for the tag. For a <flavor> tag, it prints the tag's ID attribute. For other tags, it formats and prints the tag's name. The cdataHandler accumulates text in $this->cdata, and the endHandler prints the values of the name, calories, and price tags. Each value is printed on its own line. If given this data:

```
<icecream>
<flavor id="6">
 <name>Chocolate</name>
 <calories>10</calories>
 <price>4.50</price>
</flavor>
<flavor id="5">
 <name>Vanilla</name>
 <calories>20</calories>
 <price>4.50</price>
</flavor>
<flavor id="19">
 <name>Heavenly Hash</name>
 <calories>60</calories>
 <price>5.95</price>
</flavor>
<flavor id="12">
 <name>Diet Cardboard</name>
 <calories>0</calories>
 <price>1.15</price>
</flavor>
</icecream>
```

then ice_cream_parser_immediate prints the following:

```
Flavor ID: 6
  Name: Chocolate
  Calories: 10
  Price: $4.50
```

```
Flavor ID: 5
  Name: Vanilla
  Calories: 20
  Price: $4.50
Flavor ID: 19
  Name: Heavenly Hash
  Calories: 60
  Price: $5.95
Flavor ID: 12
  Name: Diet Cardboard
  Calories: 0
  Price: $1.15
```

This kind of parsing is the simplest you can do with XML_Parser. The only thing the class keeps track of between callback invocations is the accumulated character data for the current tag. This method is fast and simple, but you can't sort or format the data in relation to each other. The information inside each tag is displayed immediately when the closing tag appears. The name, calories, and price information for a given flavor are printed in the order that the tags appear in the file.

However, you can modify the handlers to accumulate more than just character data. The `ice_cream_parser_table` parser stores the information about each flavor in an array and then prints one line about the flavor when it sees a closing `</flavor>` tag:

```
class ice_cream_parser_table extends XML_Parser {
    var $cdata;
    var $flavor;
    function startHandler($xp, $element, &$attribs) {
        switch ($element) {
        case 'FLAVOR':
            $this->flavor = array ('ID' => $attribs['ID']);
             break;
        case 'NAME':
        case 'CALORIES':
        case 'PRICE':
            $this->cdata = '';
            break;
        }
    }

    function cdataHandler($xp, $data) {
        $this->cdata .= $data;
    }
```

```
    function endHandler($xp, $element) {
        switch ($element) {
        case 'NAME':
        case 'CALORIES':
        case 'PRICE':
            $this->flavor[$element] = $this->cdata;
            break;
        case 'FLAVOR':
            printf("%2d %-15s %3d \$%.02f\n",
                   $this->flavor['ID'], $this->flavor['NAME'],
                   $this->flavor['CALORIES'], $this->flavor['PRICE']);
            break;
        }
    }
}
```

This class has an additional variable, `$flavor`, in which the flavor information is stored. In the `startHandler`, the `$flavor` array is initialized with the flavor's `ID` attribute when the parser encounters a `<flavor>` tag. The `endHandler` adds elements to `$flavor` when encountering closing `</name>`, `</calories>`, and `</price>` tags. When the parser sees a closing `</flavor>` tag, the `endHandler` prints a formatted line of information about the flavor.

This parser collects all the information about a given flavor before printing anything. The printed information for one flavor is always in the same order: ID, name, calories, price, even if a `<calories>` tag pair follows a `<price>` tag pair for a flavor in the XML file. This is how `ice_cream_parser_table` displays the same information about flavors:

```
 6 Chocolate        10 $4.50
 5 Vanilla          20 $4.50
19 Heavenly Hash    60 $5.95
12 Diet Cardboard    0 $1.15
```

The `ice_cream_parser_table` parser can't do comparisons between different flavors. Each time it sees a `<flavor>` tag, the internal `$flavor` array is reset. It only knows about one flavor at a time.

The `ice_cream_parser_array` parser, however, accumulates data about all of the flavors and doesn't print anything. This makes the flavor data available for manipulation such as sorting that involves multiple flavors. The `ice_cream_parser_array` parser prints the flavors in the same format as `ice_cream_parser_table` but sorted by calorie count:

```
class ice_cream_parser_array extends XML_Parser {
    var $cdata;
    var $id;
```

```
    var $flavor;
    var $ice_cream;
    function startHandler($xp, $element, &$attribs) {
        switch ($element) {
        case 'FLAVOR':
            $this->id = $attribs['ID'];
            $this->flavor = array();
            break;
        case 'NAME':
        case 'CALORIES':
        case 'PRICE':
            $this->cdata = '';
            break;
        }
    }

    function cdataHandler($xp, $data) {
        $this->cdata .= $data;
    }

    function endHandler($xp, $element) {
        switch ($element) {
        case 'NAME':
        case 'CALORIES':
        case 'PRICE':
            $this->flavor[$element] = $this->cdata;
            break;
        case 'FLAVOR':
            $this->ice_cream[$this->id] = $this->flavor;
          break;
        }
    }
}
```

The ice_cream_parser_array parser uses two additional variables to accumulate data: $id and $ice_cream. The $id variable holds the ID attribute of the current flavor being parsed. The $ice_cream variable is an array of flavor information. On each starting <flavor> tag, the $id variable is reset to the new ID attribute and the $flavor array is cleared. On each closing </name>, </calories>, or </price> tag, the tag-specific information is put into an element of $flavor. On a closing </flavor> tag, the $flavor array is put into the $ice_cream array. After all <flavor></flavor> tag pairs have been processed, $ice_cream is an array whose keys are flavor IDs and whose values are arrays of flavor information.

Once the parsing is done, the $ice_cream array is treated just like any other PHP array. You sort it with uasort() and then iterate through it with foreach for printing:

```
function calorie_sort($a, $b) {
    return $a['CALORIES'] > $b['CALORIES'];
}

uasort($parser->ice_cream, 'calorie_sort');

foreach ($parser->ice_cream as $id => $data) {
    printf("%2d %-15s %3d \$%.02f\n",
           $id, $data['NAME'], $data['CALORIES'], $data['PRICE']);
}
```

This is the output:

```
12 Diet Cardboard     0 $1.15
 6 Chocolate         10 $4.50
 5 Vanilla           20 $4.50
19 Heavenly Hash     60 $5.95
```

A parser such as ice_cream_parser_array produces a flexible data structure that you can use with other parts of your programs that don't have to be "XML-aware." The downside of such a parser is memory usage and perceived speed. If you are parsing a large XML document, then you create a large array. Also, because the parser doesn't take any action until it has parsed the entire document, it may appear slower. Parsing the entire document doesn't actually take any longer, but you (and your users) won't see results as immediately as with a simpler parser.

Handling Processing Instructions

Processing instructions (PIs) are parts of XML documents that pass information to the program processing the XML, potentially to pass to other applications. Processing instructions often contain information for page-layout programs. The <?xml version="1.0" ?> string you see at the top of many XML documents is an example of a processing instruction. It tells the XML processor what version of XML the document is. Processing instructions begin with <? and end with ?>. Immediately after the <? comes a string called the *target* and then whitespace. This identifies to whom the information in the processing instruction should be passed. Target strings follow the same rules as element names, but the target xml is reserved. Everything after the target and whitespace until the closing ?> is the processing instruction's content. This data is application specific and can be whatever is appropriate for the program identified by the target.

PHP tags of the form `<?php ?>` are interpreted by the XML parser as processing instructions with a target of `php`. By adding a processing instruction handler to an `XML_Parser` subclass, you can make a simple templating language that runs arbitrary PHP. The `template_parser` class implements a templating language that understands three tags: `<page>`, `<header>`, and `<footer>`. It also runs PHP commands embedded in a page:

```
class template_parser extends XML_Parser {
    var $cdata;
    var $attribs;
    function startHandler($xp, $element, $attribs) {
        $this->cdata = '';
        $this->attribs = $attribs;
    }

    function cdataHandler($xp, $data) {
        $this->cdata .= $data;
    }

    function endHandler($xp, $element) {
        switch ($element) {
        case 'PAGE':
            break;
        case 'HEADER':
            printf("<html><head><title>%s</title></head><body><h1>%s</h1>\n",
                   $this->attribs['TITLE'],
                   $this->cdata);
            break;
        case 'FOOTER':
            printf('</body></html>');
            break;
        default:
            print "<$element";
            foreach ($this->attribs as $k => $v) {
                print " $k=\"" . htmlentities($v) . '"';
            }
            print ">$this->cdata</$element>";
            break;
        }
    }
```

```
    function piHandler($xp, $target, $data) {
        if ('php' == $target) {
            eval($data);
        }
    }
}
```

The template_parser class understands input XML like this:

```
<page>
<header title="Flavor List">
Ice Cream Flavors
</header>
<?php
$flavors = array('Vanilla','Chocolate','Steamed Banana');
foreach ($flavors as $f) { print "$f<p>\n"; }
?>
  <footer/>
</page>
```

which generates the following output:

```
<html><head><title>Flavor List</title></head><body><h1>
Ice Cream Flavors
</h1>
Vanilla<p>
Chocolate<p>
Steamed Banana<p>
</body></html>
```

In the template_parser class, the endHandler() method does the tag-specific work. The startHandler() method clears the $cdata variable and saves the tag attributes in $attribs. The endHandler() method does all of the printing. If the tag being closed is <header> or <footer>, then the appropriate HTML is printed. If the tag being closed is <page>, then nothing happens. This makes <page> the tag that wraps around the entire content of the page. If another tag is being closed, endHandler() uses the $attribs and $cdata variables to print the tag, its attributes, and its content, without modification.

The processing instruction handler, in the method piHandler(), takes care of evaluating PHP. If the target of the PI is php, then the handler calls eval() with the content of the PI. When using eval() in a piHandler() such as this, you should watch out for two concerns: security and variable scope. The entire content of the PI is passed to eval() for execution without any checks on what that content does. The PHP code in the PI content could display sensitive information, modify a database in an unexpected way, or write to a file. The code executes with the same permissions and access as the PHP script that is parsing the XML file. This means that permission to edit the XML files is equivalent to permissions to edit PHP scripts. If you're using this technique in a Web environment, make sure you put the same checks on XML file editing as you would on script editing.

The second concern is the variable scope for the PHP executed from inside the `piHandler()`. Because `eval()` is called from inside the method, the only local variables available are any you define inside that method. The `$this` variable is accessible to use methods or properties of the current instance of the `template_parser` object. Otherwise, you need to access variables through superglobal arrays such as `$_REQUEST` or `$GLOBALS`.

Handling Nested Tags

The parsers you've seen so far in this chapter handle only one level of nested tags because they just keep track of character data in a single variable. To properly handle more levels of tags, that information needs to be stored in an array. The parser in the `nested_tags` class treats `$cdata` as an array and uses `$level` to store the current tag nesting level:

```
class nested_tags extends XML_Parser {
    var $cdata = array();
    var $level = 0;

    function startHandler($xp, $element, $attribs) {
        print "\n" . str_repeat(' ',$this->level);
        print "<$element";
        foreach ($attribs as $k => $v) {
            print " $k=\"". htmlentities($v) . '"';
        }
        print '>';
        array_push($this->cdata,'');
        $this->level++;
    }

    function cdataHandler($xp, $data) {
        $this->cdata[$this->level-1] .= $data;
    }

    function endHandler($xp, $element) {
        $data = array_pop($this->cdata);
        $this->level--;
        if (strlen(trim($data))) {
```

```
            print htmlentities(trim($data));
        } else {
            print "\n" . str_repeat(' ',$this->level);
        }
        print "</$element>";
    }
}
```

The nested_tags parser prints its input XML formatted so that child tags are evenly indented from parent tags. It turns this input:

```
<icecream>
     <flavor id="6">
          <name>Chocolate</name>
          <calories>10</calories>
          <price>4.50</price>
</flavor><flavor id="5"><name>Vanilla</name><calories>20</calories>
<price>4.50</price></flavor><flavor id="19">
<name>Heavenly Hash</name>
<calories>60</calories>
<price>5.95</price>
</flavor>
<flavor id="12">
<name>Diet Cardboard &amp; Stuff</name><calories>0</calories>
<price>1.15</price></flavor></icecream>
```

into this output:

```
<ICECREAM>
 <FLAVOR ID="6">
  <NAME>Chocolate</NAME>
  <CALORIES>10</CALORIES>
  <PRICE>4.50</PRICE>
 </FLAVOR>
 <FLAVOR ID="5">
  <NAME>Vanilla</NAME>
  <CALORIES>20</CALORIES>
  <PRICE>4.50</PRICE>
 </FLAVOR>
 <FLAVOR ID="19">
  <NAME>Heavenly Hash</NAME>
  <CALORIES>60</CALORIES>
  <PRICE>5.95</PRICE>
 </FLAVOR>
 <FLAVOR ID="12">
```

```
  <NAME>Diet Cardboard &amp; Stuff</NAME>
  <CALORIES>0</CALORIES>
  <PRICE>1.15</PRICE>
 </FLAVOR>
</ICECREAM>
```

The `nested_tags` parser collects all character data in the `cdataHandler()` but only prints an element's character data if it consists of something other than whitespace:

```
if (strlen(trim($data))) {
    print htmlentities(trim($data));
} else {
    print "\n" . str_repeat(' ',$this->level);
}
```

This preserves internal whitespace in the character data but removes leading and trailing whitespace. For example, if an XML document contained this:

```
<flavor>
Vanilla


Bean
</flavor>
```

then the `nested_tags` parser prints this:

```
<FLAVOR>Vanilla

Bean</FLAVOR>
```

The whitespace between `<flavor>` and `Vanilla` and between `Bean` and `</flavor>` is removed by `trim()` in the `endElement()` handler before printing.

Using Per-Element Methods

The XML_Parser module has another mode in which all tags aren't handed by generic `startHandler()` and `endHandler()` methods. In this mode (called the *func* mode), each tag has its own methods for handling opening and closing. This mode is most useful for situations where you want to take very different actions for different tags, so a `switch()` block would be clumsy. The `template_parser_func` parser uses the func mode to make a templating system like the `template_parser` class. The method `xmltag_tagname()` is called when the `<tagname>` start tag is encountered, and the method `xmltag_tagname_()` is called when the `</tagname>` end tag is encountered. There is no default function called when a tag is encountered that doesn't have corresponding functions defined, so I've added methods to handle a tag named <content> that prints the character data inside the <content></content> tags:

```
class template_parser_func extends XML_Parser {
    var $cdata;

    function xmltag_page($xp, $element, $attribs) {}
    function xmltag_page_($xp, $element) {}

    function xmltag_header($xp, $element, $attribs) {
        printf('<html><head><title>%s</title></head><body>',
               $attribs['TITLE']);
        $this->cdata = '';
    }
    function xmltag_header_($xp, $element) {
        print $this->cdata;
    }

    function xmltag_footer($xp, $element) {
        print '</body></html>';
    }

    function xmltag_content($xp, $element, $attribs) {
        $this->cdata = '';
    }
    function xmltag_content_($xp, $element) {
        print $this->cdata;
    }

    function cdataHandler($xp, $data) {
        $this->cdata .= $data;
    }

    function piHandler($xp, $target, $data) {
        if ('php' == $target) {
            eval($data);
        }
    }
}
```

Set a parser to func mode by passing `func` as the second argument to the parser's constructor:[3]

```
$parser =& new template_parser_func(null,'func');
$parser->setInputFile('page.xml');
$parser->parse();
```

You can also specify func mode by calling the parser's `setMode()` method with an argument of `func`:

```
$parser =& new template_parser_func;
$parser->setMode('func');
$parser->setInputFile('page.xml');
$parser->parse();
```

If `page.xml` contains this:

```
<page>
<header title="Ice Cream Order Page">
Ice Cream Flavors
</header>

<content><![CDATA[
<ul style="creamy">
]]></content>

<?php
$flavors = array('Vanilla','Chocolate','Steamed Banana');
foreach ($flavors as $f) { print "<li> $f </li>\n"; }
?>

<content><![CDATA[</ul>]]></content>

<footer/>
</page>
```

then `template_parser_func` produces the following:

```
<html><head><title>Ice Cream Order Page</title></head><body>
Ice Cream Flavors
```

3. The first argument specifies a source encoding, discussed in the next section. Leaving the argument as `null` uses the default source encoding.

```
<ul style="creamy">
<li> Vanilla </li>
<li> Chocolate </li>
<li> Steamed Banana </li>
</ul></body></html>
```

The `<![CDATA[]]>` markers inside the `<content>` tags let you avoid entity-encoding less-than and greater-than signs in character data. Without `<![CDATA[]]>`, the `<content>` tags would look like `<content></ul></content>` instead of `<content><![CDATA[</ul>]]></content>`.

Specifying Character Sets

PHP's xml extension internally represents parsed documents in the UTF-8 character set. The XML_Parser module lets you specify a source encoding and a target encoding. The source encoding is the character set of an XML document to be read. The target encoding is the character set in which data passed to callback handlers is encoded.

The supported character sets for source and target encodings are UTF-8, ISO-8859-1, and US-ASCII. If you don't specify a source encoding, the xml extension assumes that incoming documents are encoded in ISO-8859-1.

Pass a source encoding as the first argument to a parser's constructor. For example, to create a parser that expects incoming documents to be encoded in UTF-8, use this:

```
$parser = new international_parser('UTF-8');
```

To specify a target encoding, pass it as the third argument to the constructor. For example, to create a parser that converts documents from UTF-8 to ISO-8859-1, use this:

```
$parser = new international_parser('UTF-8','event','ISO-8859-1');
```

The following parser, which just prints its input, illustrates these conversions:

```
class international_parser extends XML_Parser {
    function startHandler($xp, $e, $attribs) {
        print "<$e>";
    }
    function cdataHandler($xp, $data) {
        print $data;
    }
```

```
    function endHandler($xp, $e) {
        print "</$e>";
    }
}
```

The following are two versions of a file to parse with international_parser. The book-utf8.xml file encodes the ö in Gödel in the UTF-8 character set. This encoding is two bytes: 195 and 182. The book-iso8859.xml file encodes the ö in Gödel in the ISO-8859-1 character set. This encoding is one byte: 246. Both files, when rendered correctly, look like this:

```
<book>
<title>Gödel, Escher, Bach</title>
<author>Douglas A. Hofstadter</author>
</book>
```

Using international_parser with a source encoding that matches the character set of the input file produces correct results with either target encoding:

```
// Read the UTF-8 file and display results encoded as UTF-8: the two-byte
// sequence 195, 182 in the input file remains the same in the output.
$parser =& new international_parser('UTF-8','event','UTF-8');
$parser->setInputFile('book-utf8.xml');
$parser->parse();

// Read the UTF-8 file and display results encoded as ISO-8859-1: the two-byte
// sequence 195, 182 is converted to the byte 246 in the output.
$parser =& new international_parser('UTF-8','event','ISO-8859-1');
$parser->setInputFile('book-utf8.xml');
$parser->parse();

// Read the ISO-8859-1 file and display results encoded as ISO-8859-1: the
// 246 byte in the input remains the same in the output
$parser =& new international_parser('ISO-8859-1','event','ISO-8859-1');
$parser->setInputFile('book-iso8859.xml');
$parser->parse();

// Read in the ISO-8859-1 file and display results encoded as UTF-8: the
// 246 byte in the input is converted to the two-byte sequence 195, 182
// in the output
$parser =& new international_parser('ISO-8859-1','event','UTF-8');
$parser->setInputFile('book-iso8859.xml');
$parser->parse();
```

If the target encoding can't represent a character in the source encoding, the character is converted to a question mark. The US-ASCII encoding doesn't have an ö character, so displaying either file as US-ASCII produces this effect. For example, the following:

```
$parser =& new international_parser('UTF-8','event','US-ASCII');
$parser->setInputFile('book-utf8.xml');
$parser->parse();
```

prints the following output:

```
<BOOK>
<TITLE>G?del, Escher, Bach</TITLE>
<AUTHOR>Douglas A. Hofstadter</AUTHOR>
</BOOK>
```

If you are using the output from an XML parser in a Web page, make sure the character set of the Web page matches the target encoding of the XML parser. Use the `header()` command to specify the character set. For example, to tell the browser that the content is encoded with UTF-8, use this:

```
header('Content-Type: text/xml; charset=utf-8');
$parser =& new international_parser('ISO-8859-1','event','UTF-8');
$parser->setInputFile('book-iso8859.xml');
$parser->parse();
```

CHAPTER 6

Developing Lightweight Web Services with XML_RPC

XML-RPC IS A WAY to call a procedure on a remote computer. (RPC stands for Remote Procedure Call.) In your PHP programs, you can be both an XML-RPC client (calling functions on other computers) and an XML-RPC server (running functions in response to remote requests). XML-RPC accomplishes these remote procedure calls by passing XML messages over HTTP connections. An XML-RPC client packages information about the procedure it wants to call and the arguments to the procedure in an XML document. Then, it passes that XML document to an XML-RPC server over a regular HTTP POST request. The XML-RPC server looks at the XML document, calls the appropriate local function, and returns the results as another XML document as the response to the HTTP request.

The XML_RPC PEAR module takes care of the XML document formatting and HTTP request making for you. It gives you methods to specify what remote function you want and to turn the response into native PHP data types. It also provides methods for receiving XML-RPC requests and mapping them to functions written in PHP.

This chapter describes PEAR XML_RPC 1.0.4.

Choosing XML-RPC

XML-RPC aims to be a simple message-passing format for running remote procedures. It doesn't have the intricacy and power of SOAP, which is a good thing for smaller applications. The XML-RPC specification, at `http://www.xmlrpc.com/spec/`, is not very long and is easily digestible. One important section of the specification defines the various XML-RPC data types. There are six scalar types and two complex types. The six scalar types are `int` (also known as `i4`), `boolean`, `string`, `double`, `dateTime.iso8601`, and `base64`. The complex types are `array` and `struct`. The `array` type is a numerically indexed array, and the `struct` type is a string-indexed array. The values of each `array` or `struct` element can be any valid XML-RPC type, including another `struct` or `array`.

Each of these types is represented in an XML-RPC message by enclosing a value with the appropriate XML tag. For example, an integer is represented as `<value><int>15</int></value>`, and a string is represented as `<value><string>gargle</string></value>`. The XML_RPC module encodes values inside `XML_RPC_Value` objects. These objects hold information about type and value. To deal with arguments or return values in XML-RPC functions, you must first encapsulate a regular PHP scalar or array into an `XML_RPC_Value` object to pass an argument to a function or extract the value from an `XML_RPC_Value` object to access the return value from a function.

The classes and functions to handle XML-RPC types are defined in the `XML/RPC.php` include file, so the first step of any XML-RPC client operation is to `include` or `require` that file:

```
require 'XML/RPC.php';
```

Encoding XML-RPC Values

To create an `XML_RPC_Value` object, pass the value and type to the object constructor:

```
$name = new XML_RPC_Value('David','string');
$is_human = new XML_RPC_Value(true,'boolean');
$mass = new XML_RPC_Value(60,'int');
$temperature = new XML_RPC_Value(98.6,'double');
$expiration = new XML_RPC_Value('20090619T15:22:19', 'dateTime.iso8601');
```

If you don't specify a type, the value is treated as a `string`. These two lines are equivalent:

```
$name = new XML_RPC_Value('David','string');
$name = new XML_RPC_Value('David');
```

Use the `base64` type for binary data. First encode the data with the `base64_encode()` PHP built-in function and then pass it to the `XML_RPC_Value` constructor:

```
$my_file = file_get_contents('/tmp/some-file.bin');
$binary_data = new XML_RPC_Value(base64_encode($my_file), 'base64');
```

To create an `XML_RPC_Value` object that holds an array, pass the constructor a PHP array of `XML_RPC_Value` objects. For example, to create an array of integers, use this:

```
$ar = array(new XML_RPC_Value(60,'int'), new XML_RPC_Value(70,'int'),
            new XML_RPC_Value(80,'int'));
$masses = new XML_RPC_Value($ar, 'array');
```

Creating an XML-RPC `struct` is similar. You still pass an array to the `XML_RPC_Value` constructor for the `struct`, but it should have string keys. For example, to create a `struct` holding a `string`, an `integer`, and a `double`, use this:

```
$ar = array ('name' => new XML_RPC_Value('David'),
             'mass' => new XML_RPC_Value(60,'int'),
             'temperature' => new XML_RPC_Value(98.6,'double'));
$person = new XML_RPC_Value($ar,'struct');
```

When creating an `array` or `struct`, you don't have to store the array in a separate variable before passing it to the `XML_RPC_Value` constructor. You can put it all together in one statement:

```
$masses =
   new XML_RPC_Value(array(new XML_RPC_Value(60,'int'),
                           new XML_RPC_Value(70,'int'),
                           new XML_RPC_Value(80,'int')), 'array');
$person = new XML_RPC_Value(array('name' => new XML_RPC_Value('David'),
                                  'mass' => new XML_RPC_Value(60,'int'),
                      'temperature' => new XML_RPC_Value(98.6,'double')),
                      'struct');
```

Especially for complex types such as `array` and `struct`, converting PHP types to XML-RPC types can be cumbersome. The XML_RPC module includes an `XML_RPC_encode()` function to simplify this process. Pass `XML_RPC_encode()` a value, and it returns an `XML_RPC_Value` object with the passed value inside it. PHP `integers`, `doubles`, `strings`, and `booleans` turn into `XML_RPC_Value` objects of the corresponding type:

```
$name = XML_RPC_encode('David');
$is_human = XML_RPC_encode(true);
$mass = XML_RPC_encode(60);
$temperature = XML_RPC_encode(98.6);
```

PHP arrays and objects are turned into `XML_RPC_Value` objects of type `struct`. `XML_RPC_encode()` works recursively, so if you pass it an array of arrays of strings, you get back an `XML_RPC_Value` object of type `array` that contains more `XML_RPC_Value` objects of type `array` that each contain `XML_RPC_Value` objects of type `string`:

```
$clothes = array( 'top' => array('blue shirt', 'red shirt', 'green cape'),
                  'bottom' => array('plaid pants', 'yellow shorts',
                                    'magenta skirt'));
$encoded_clothes = XML_RPC_encode($clothes);
```

When operating on an object, XML_RPC_encode() uses property names for struct element names and property values for struct element values. The following object and array are turned into identical XML_RPC_Value structs. For example, an instance of this person class becomes a struct with a name element and a mass element:

```
class person {
    var $name;
    var $mass;
}
$me = new Person;
$me->name = 'David';
$me->mass = 60;
$encoded_me = XML_RPC_encode($me);
// This array encodes to an identical XML_RPC_Value as $me
$ar = array('name' => 'David', 'mass' => 60);
```

Decoding XML-RPC Values

To work with values stored in XML_RPC_Value objects, you must first extract the values into regular PHP variables. The XML_RPC_decode() function puts XML-RPC structs and arrays into PHP arrays, recursing as necessary. For example, decoding the $encoded_clothes XML_RPC_Value object created previously produces the original array:

```
$decoded_clothes = XML_RPC_decode($encoded_clothes);
var_dump($decoded_clothes);

array(2) {
  ["top"]=>
  array(3) {
    [0]=>
    string(10) "blue shirt"
    [1]=>
    string(9) "red shirt"
    [2]=>
    string(10) "green cape"
  }
  ["bottom"]=>
  array(3) {
    [0]=>
    string(11) "plaid pants"
```

```
    [1]=>
    string(13) "yellow shorts"
    [2]=>
    string(13) "magenta skirt"
  }
}
```

The `XML_RPC_decode()` function returns a scalar value (`double`, `integer`, or `string`) when decoding any scalar `XML_RPC_Value` type. However, the PHP type of the value returned may not match the `XML_RPC_Value` type. For example, you can create an `XML_RPC_Value` integer with this:

```
$i = new XML_RPC_Value('2732','int');
```

Because you've explicitly specified type `int`, `$i` is treated as a valid `integer` with value `2732` when passed to an XML-RPC procedure. However, because you passed `'2732'` (a `string`) to the `XML_RPC_Value` constructor instead of `2732` (an `integer`), its PHP type inside the object is `string`. This means that `XML_RPC_decode($i)` returns a `string`, not an `integer`. This can happen, for example, if you create `XML_RPC_Value` objects with values from submitted form variables. These values are always `strings`, even if their contents are numeric.

To convert the return values from `XML_RPC_decode()` into their proper type, use the `scalartyp()` method of the `XML_RPC_Value` object. It returns a string that indicates what type of scalar is stored in the object: `int`, `boolean`, `double`, `string`, `dateTime.iso8601`, or `base64`. Use that information to handle the value appropriately:

```
$val = XML_RPC_decode($encoded);
switch ($encoded->scalartyp()) {
case 'boolean':
    $val = (bool) $val;
    break;
case 'int':
    $val = (int) $val;
    break;
case 'string':
    $val = (string) $val;
    break;
case 'double':
    $val = (double) $val;
    break;
case 'dateTime.iso8601':
    // Convert to an epoch time stamp
    $val = XML_RPC_iso8601_decode($val);
    break;
```

```
case 'base64':
    $val = base64_decode($val);
    break;
}
```

To get finer control over extracting values from XML_RPC_Value objects, the objects have a few methods you can use instead of the XML_RPC_decode() function. The kindOf() method tells you whether an XML_RPC_Value object holds a scalar, array, or struct. It returns a string describing the object's type: scalar if the object contains a scalar, array if the object contains an array, or struct if the object contains a struct.

The scalarval() method returns a scalar value:

```
$xi = new XML_RPC_Value(273,'int');
$i = $xi->scalarval(); // $i  is 273
```

To extract an array, use the arraysize() method to find the size of the array and the arraymem() method to access each element of the array. The arraymem() method returns another XML_RPC_Value object that holds the value for a specified array element:

```
// We can't use XML_RPC_encode() to construct the array because
// XML_RPC_encode() turns PHP arrays into XML-RPC structs
$xar = new XML_RPC_Value(array(new XML_RPC_Value('clover'),
                               new XML_RPC_Value('wildflower'),
                               new XML_RPC_Value('daisy')), 'array');

for($i = 0, $j = $xar->arraysize(); $i < $j; $i++) {
    $el = $xar->arraymem($i);
    $flower = XML_RPC_decode($el);
    print "Element $i is $flower.\n";
}
```

This enumerates each element in the array and prints the following:

```
Element 0 is clover.
Element 1 is wildflower.
Element 2 is daisy.
```

The structreset() method resets the internal iterator to the beginning of a struct, and the structeach() method returns the next key/value pair in a struct. Use structreset() and structeach() to iterate through a struct:

```
$xs = XML_RPC_encode(array('apple' => 'green',
                           'lemon' => 'yellow',
                           'tie' => 'paisley'));
```

```
$xs->structreset();
while(list($k,$v) = $xs->structeach()) {
    $color = XML_RPC_decode($v);
    print "The color of $k is $color.\n";
}
```

This prints the following:

```
The color of apple is green.
The color of lemon is yellow.
The color of tie is paisley.
```

The `structmem()` method returns a particular element in a `struct`:

```
// This sets $tie_color to "paisley"
$tie_color = XML_RPC_decode($xs->structmem('tie'));
```

Calling XML-RPC Procedures on Another Server

The server `time.xmlrpc.com` offers a procedure called `currentTime.getCurrentTime()` that returns the time as an ISO8601 time stamp. To call an XML-RPC procedure on a remote server, you need an `XML_RPC_Client` object and an `XML_RPC_Message` object.

The `XML_RPC_Client` object holds information about the server to contact. The `XML_RPC_Message` object holds information about the procedure to call and its arguments. The `XML_RPC_Client` constructor takes two arguments: a path and a server name:

```
$client = new XML_RPC_Client('/RPC2', 'time.xmlrpc.com');
```

This means that the XML-RPC requests are going to be POSTed to the URL `http://time.xmlrpc.com/RPC2`. If you want to use a port other than the default (80), pass that as a third argument to the constructor.

Now you need to create a message to send to the XML-RPC server. This message, when sent to an XML-RPC server, calls the `currentTime.getCurrentTime()` procedure:

```
$message = new XML_RPC_Message('currentTime.getCurrentTime');
```

To send the message to the server, pass the message object to the client's `send()` method:

```
$response = $client->send($message);
```

The response is an XML_RPC_Response object. If something went wrong in calling the procedure, then it holds error information. If the procedure ran successfully, then it holds the return values. I'll talk about error handling soon, but for now, assume the call succeeded. To get at the return value, call the value() method on the response:

```
$return_value = $response->value();
```

You're not out of the woods yet. The $return_value variable is an XML_RPC_Value object, not a string or an array. The easiest way to turn an XML_RPC_Value object into a native PHP data type is to use the XML_RPC_decode() function:

```
$decoded_value = XML_RPC_decode($return_value);
```

Now you can see what time it is:

```
print $decoded_value;
20030820T07:42:48
```

The XML_RPC_iso8601_decode() function converts ISO8601 time stamps into standard seconds-since-epoch time stamps:

```
$now = XML_RPC_iso8601_decode($decoded_value);
```

And then you use strftime() to print a formatted date/time string:

```
print strftime('%c', $now);
Wed Aug 20 07:50:28 2003
```

Listing 6-1 shows all the steps for finding out the time via XML-RPC.

Listing 6-1. A Complete XML-RPC Request

```
// Load the class and function definitions
require 'XML/RPC.php';

// Create a client object to talk to the XML-RPC server
$client = new XML_RPC_Client('/RPC2', 'time.xmlrpc.com');

// Define a message that calls the procedure we want
$message = new XML_RPC_Message('currentTime.getCurrentTime');

// Send the message over the network and receive the response
$response = $client->send($message);
```

```
// Extract the return value object from the response
$return_value = $response->value();

// Turn the return value object into a PHP data type
$decoded_value = XML_RPC_decode($return_value);

// Turn the ISO8601 time stamp into a seconds-since-epoch value
$now = XML_RPC_iso8601_decode($decoded_value);

// Print out a formatted date/time string
print strftime('%c',$now);
```

> **NOTE** *The time returned by this function is U.S. Pacific Time because that's the time zone that the* `time.xmlrpc.com` *server observes.*

Arguments to an XML-RPC procedure should be passed as an array of `XML_RPC_Value` objects. Make this array the second argument to the `XML_RPC_Message` constructor. For example, to pass two arguments, an `int` and a `string` to a `shopping.purchase()` procedure, create the `XML_RPC_Message` object like this:

```
$message = new XML_RPC_Message('shopping.purchase',
                               array(new XML_RPC_Value(5, 'int'),
                                     new XML_RPC_Value('PHP Gems', 'string')));
```

To handle XML-RPC responses properly, you should check that the request completed successfully before retrieving a value from the response object. Do this with the `faultCode()` method. This returns `0` if the response was successful or an integer error code otherwise. If there was an error, the `faultString()` method returns a description of the error. Listing 6-2 augments the code in Listing 6-1 with error checking.

Listing 6-2. A Complete XML-RPC Request with Error Checking

```
// Load the class and function definitions
require 'XML/RPC.php';

// Create a client object to talk to the XML-RPC server
$client = new XML_RPC_Client('/RPC2', 'time.xmlrpc.com');
```

```
// Define a message that calls the procedure we want
$message = new XML_RPC_Message('currentTime.getCurrentTime');

// Send the message over the network and receive the response
$response = $client->send($message);

// Check if the response failed
if ($fault = ($response->faultCode())) {
    // Display an error message
    print "Error $fault: " . $response->faultString();
} else {
    // Extract the return value object from the response
    $return_value = $response->value();

    // Turn the return value object into a PHP data type
    $decoded_value = XML_RPC_decode($return_value);

    // Turn the ISO8601 time stamp into a seconds-since-epoch value
    $now = XML_RPC_iso8601_decode($decoded_value);

    // Print out a formatted date/time string
    print strftime('%c',$now);
}
```

For example, if you change the `$message` object to call the method `currentTime.thisMethodDoesNotExist`, then instead of a formatted time string, the program prints the following:

```
Error 7: Can't evaluate the expression because the name
"thisMethodDoesNotExist" hasn't been defined.
```

It's up to an individual XML-RPC server to define what fault codes and fault strings it uses. For `time.xmlrpc.com`, code `7` and the `Can't evaluate the expression` string are how it reports an unknown method.

Serving XML-RPC Methods

Only a few steps are required to set up an XML-RPC server with the XML_RPC module. First, include the `XML/RPC/Server.php` file:

```
require 'XML/RPC/Server.php';
```

Second, create a dispatch map that links XML-RPC procedure names with individual PHP functions. The dispatch map is an array whose keys are XML-RPC procedure names. The values of the dispatch map are associative arrays. The required element in these associative arrays is one whose key is `function` and whose value is the PHP function name to which the XML-RPC procedure name maps. For example, a dispatch map that indicates that the XML-RPC procedure `stooges.pickOne` maps to the function `pick_a_stooge()` looks like this:

```
$dispatch_map = array('stooges.pickOne' =>
                      array('function' => 'pick_a_stooge'));
```

When the server receives an XML-RPC request to call the procedure `stooges.pickOne`, it runs the `pick_a_stooge()` function and returns the results of the function in the XML-RPC response. The return value of the `pick_a_stooge()` function, however, must be an `XML_RPC_Response` object.

After defining the dispatch map, instantiate a new `XML_RPC_Server` object and pass the dispatch map to the constructor:

```
$server = new XML_RPC_Server($dispatch_map);
```

That's it. Now you can make XML-RPC requests to the server, and they'll be handled by the functions defined in the dispatch map. Listing 6-3 is a complete example, including the `pick_a_stooge()` function.

Listing 6-3. Serving XML-RPC Requests

```
// Load the class and function definitions
require 'XML/RPC/Server.php';

// Define the underlying PHP functions that the XML-RPC procedures call
$stooges = array('Moe','Larry','Curly');
function pick_a_stooge() {
    global $stooges;
    $which_stooge = mt_rand(0,2);
    $retval = new XML_RPC_Value($stooges[$which_stooge],'string');
    return new XML_RPC_Response($retval);
}

// Set up the dispatch map
$dispatch_map = array('stooges.pickOne' =>
                      array('function' => 'pick_a_stooge'));

// Start the server
$server = new XML_RPC_Server($dispatch_map);
```

The return value of pick_a_stooge() is an XML_RPC_Response object. This object is created by passing one XML_RPC_Value object to the XML_RPC_Response constructor. The XML_RPC_Value object contains the value you want to return from the function. Only one XML_RPC_Value object can be passed to the XML_RPC_Response object constructor. If you want to return multiple values from an XML-RPC procedure, package them in an XML_RPC_Value object using the XML-RPC type array or struct. Because pick_a_stooge() returns only one stooge name, you pass an XML_RPC_Value of type string to the XML_RPC_Response object.

A stooges.listAll() method, which returns an array of all the stooges, looks like this:

```
function list_all_stooges() {
    global $stooges;
    return new XML_RPC_Response(XML_RPC_encode($stooges));
}
```

The XML_RPC_encode() function creates an XML_RPC_Value object of type array containing XML_RPC_Value objects representing each element in the $stooges array.

You also have to modify the dispatch map to account for this new function:

```
$dispatch_map = array('stooges.pickOne' =>
                      array('function' => 'pick_a_stooge'),
                      'stooges.listAll' =>
                      array('function' => 'list_all_stooges'));
```

Listing 6-4 contains code to access the XML-RPC server in Listing 6-3. It assumes the server is accessible at http://www.example.com/xmlrpc.php.

Listing 6-4. Accessing the XML-RPC Server

```
// Load the class and function definitions
require 'XML/RPC.php';

// Create a client object to talk to the XML-RPC server
$client = new XML_RPC_Client('/xmlrpc.php', 'www.example.com');

// Define a message that calls the procedure we want
$message = new XML_RPC_Message('stooges.listAll');

// Send the message over the network and receive the response
$response = $client->send($message);

// Extract the return value object from the response
$return_value = $response->value();
```

```
// Turn the return value object into a PHP data type
$decoded_value = XML_RPC_decode($return_value);

// Display the results
print_r($decoded_value);
```

The stooges.listAll() and stooges.pickOne() methods do not accept any parameters.

Each XML-RPC function invoked is passed one argument, an object, that holds information about how it was called. The methodname property of the object is set to the XML-RPC procedure that invoked the function (for example, stooges.listAll or stooges.pickOne), and the params property of the object is an array of XML_RPC_Value objects holding any parameters supplied by the XML-RPC client when the procedure was called.

Now add a new procedure to select a particular stooge. Its integer parameter determines which stooge it returns:

```
function pick_this_stooge($request_info) {
    global $stooges;
    $which_stooge = XML_RPC_decode($request_info->params[0]);
    $retval = new XML_RPC_Value($stooges[$which_stooge],'string');
    return new XML_RPC_Response($retval);
}
```

You must add the new procedure to the dispatch map:

```
$dispatch_map = array('stooges.pickOne' =>
                      array('function' => 'pick_a_stooge'),
                      'stooges.listAll' =>
                      array('function' => 'list_all_stooges'),
                      'stooges.pickThis' =>
                      array('function' => 'pick_this_stooge'));
```

To get Larry, the second element in the $stooges array, you call stooges.pickThis() with a parameter of 1:

```
$message = new XML_RPC_Message('stooges.pickThis',
                               array(new XML_RPC_Value(1,'int')));
```

You may have noticed that the pick_this_stooge() function doesn't do any type checking to ensure that its one parameter is actually an integer (or even that it was passed a parameter). You can make sure that the correct number and type of parameters have been supplied for an XML-RPC procedure by adding a signature to the dispatch map. The signature for a particular function lists its return type and the type of each parameter it expects. The `stooges.pickThis()` procedure returns a string and wants one integer parameter. The following is what the dispatch map looks like with the signature added:

```
$dispatch_map = array('stooges.pickOne' =>
                      array('function' => 'pick_a_stooge'),
                      'stooges.listAll' =>
                      array('function' => 'list_all_stooges'),
                      'stooges.pickThis' =>
                      array('function' => 'pick_this_stooge',
                            'signature' => array(array('string','int'))));
```

The signature goes in an array element, with the key `signature`, in the array for a specific function. The value of the `signature` element is an array of arrays. This structure allows one procedure to have multiple acceptable signatures. Each subarray holds a list of types. First comes the return type and then each parameter type. To allow the `stooges.pickThis()` function to accept an integer or string parameter, add another signature to the array:

```
$dispatch_map = array('stooges.pickOne' =>
                      array('function' => 'pick_a_stooge'),
                      'stooges.listAll' =>
                      array('function' => 'list_all_stooges'),
                      'stooges.pickThis' =>
                      array('function' => 'pick_this_stooge',
                            'signature' => array(array('string','int'),
                                                 array('string','string'))));
```

If a procedure is called with parameters that don't match a valid signature, then the XML-RPC server returns a fault. Procedures with no signature accept any combination of parameters.

Adding an appropriate signature to the dispatch map prevents `pick_this_stooge()` from not having an parameter, but what if the argument passed is invalid? For example, it doesn't make any sense to ask for stooge `7` because there are only three of them in the `$stooges` array. When something such as this happens, the function should return a fault. To return a fault, pass `0` instead of an `XML_RPC_Value` object to the `XML_RPC_Response` constructor and add the fault code and fault description as additional arguments. Your fault codes should be greater than the value of the global variable `$XML_RPC_erruser` to avoid conflict with any system fault codes.[1] The following is a version of `pick_this_stooge()` that returns a fault if the parameter is out of range:

---

1. The `$XML_RPC_erruser` variable is set to 800.

```
function pick_this_stooge($request_info) {
    global $stooges, $XML_RPC_erruser;
    $which_stooge = XML_RPC_decode($request_info->params[0]);
    if (($which_stooge < 0) || ($which_stooge >= count($stooges))) {
       // The fault code returned is based on $XML_RPC_erruser to
       // avoid conflict with any system fault codes.
       return new XML_RPC_Response(0,
                                   $XML_RPC_erruser + 1,
                                   "Invalid stooge");
    } else {
        $retval = new XML_RPC_Value($stooges[$which_stooge],'string');
        return new XML_RPC_Response($retval);
    }
}
```

When writing a large application, store your fault codes and fault strings in a global array and then reference them inside individual functions. This makes it easier to reuse fault codes in multiple functions and provide for fault strings in different languages.

In addition to function names and signatures, the dispatch map can also hold documentation for each function. This goes in the array for a function under the key `docstring`. For example, to add a short description of what the `stooges.pickThis()` function does, you can modify the dispatch map to look like this:

```
$dispatch_map = array('stooges.pickOne' =>
                      array('function' => 'pick_a_stooge'),
                      'stooges.listAll' =>
                      array('function' => 'list_all_stooges'),
                      'stooges.pickThis' =>
                      array('function' => 'pick_this_stooge',
                            'signature' => array(array('string','int')),
                            'docstring' => 'Select a particular stooge.'));
```

You can access the documentation string, which can contain HTML markup, with the built-in `system.methodHelp()` procedure. This procedure isn't part of the XML-RPC specification, but many XML-RPC servers, including the PEAR XML_RPC module, support it. To find documentation for a particular function, pass the function name as an argument when calling `system.methodHelp()`:

```
$message = new XML_RPC_Message('system.methodHelp',
                               array(new XML_RPC_Value('stooges.pickThis')));
```

Normally, the `XML_RPC_Server` object handles any incoming request as soon as it is instantiated. The constructor parses the XML in the request and looks in the dispatch map to find a procedure to call. If you want to create the server object and then do some other task before the request is serviced, pass `false` as a second argument to the `XML_RPC_Server` constructor. Then, call the `XML_RPC_Server` object's `service()` method to service the request. For example, you could call a function that determines if access is allowed to the XML-RPC server:

```
$server = new XML_RPC_Server($dispatch_map, false);
if (check_xmlrpc_permissions($_SERVER['REMOTE_ADDR'])) {
    $server->service();
} else {
    // this IP address isn't allowed to access XML-RPC requests
}
```

CHAPTER 7

Developing Heavyweight Web Services with SOAP

If XML-RPC is a tricycle, SOAP is a pickup truck. They both help you go from one place to another, but you can just hop on a tricycle and start moving. Before you can get anywhere with a pickup truck, you've got to learn how to drive, make sure the tank is full of gas, and be sure that the bulky truck will fit down any alleys or tight squeezes along your route.

Of course, once you've got the hang of the truck, you can do a lot that you can't do with a tricycle: You can go fast, haul cargo, and honk the horn.

So it is with SOAP: It has a steeper learning curve than XML-RPC, especially if you want to write a SOAP server, but once you've chugged up that curve, you can do a lot more with it. XML-RPC is specifically focused on remote procedure calls. SOAP can handle those, too, but it is also a generalized framework for exchanging any kind of structured information.

You can use XML-RPC only over HTTP. SOAP can run, theoretically, over any transport protocol: HTTP, SMTP, FTP, or others. I'll just talk about HTTP in this chapter, though, because that makes up the bulk of current SOAP usage.

This chapter discusses PEAR SOAP 0.8RC3.

Choosing SOAP

Often you'll use SOAP because you have to—there's a Web service you want to access, and SOAP is the protocol the Web service uses. If you want to write a server, SOAP can be a good choice, too. One of the big differences between SOAP and XML-RPC is that SOAP supports ways for a server to enumerate its SOAP methods and their arguments. A SOAP client can autodiscover what methods a SOAP server offers and use the argument type information to format requests correctly.

This autodiscovery is enabled by two standards: DISCO and Web Service Description Language (WSDL). DISCO is a format for the automatic discovery of Web services, and WSDL is an XML format for specifying information about a Web service: its name, where it's located, what kinds of arguments it takes, and what kind of information it returns. A WSDL document describing a Web service can be complicated to read or write. Fortunately, you almost never have to do this. PHP SOAP clients can read a WSDL document and use it to create a PHP object with methods that correspond to the Web services in the WSDL document. PHP SOAP servers automatically generate WSDL that describes the methods they serve. The SOAP specification is at `http://www.w3.org/TR/SOAP/`. As you might expect from SOAP's pickup truck nature, reading the specification is a long and involved activity. You can find a gentler introduction to SOAP at `http://www.w3.org/TR/soap12-part0/`, which can also be a little rough going at times but is much friendlier than the actual specification.

Installing SOAP

Install PEAR SOAP with the PEAR package manager. Because version 0.8RC3 of the PEAR SOAP package is tagged as `beta` and not `stable`, first tell the package manager that you want to download a `beta` package:

```
# pear config-set preferred_state beta
```

Then, install SOAP with the `install` command. The `-a` argument tells the package manager to download and install all of the SOAP package's dependencies:

```
# pear install -a SOAP
```

The packages that SOAP depends on are Mail_mime, HTTP_Request, Net_URL, and Net_DIME.

After installing SOAP, reset the package manager to download `stable` versions of packages by default:

```
# pear config-set preferred_state stable
```

Making SOAP Requests

The easiest way to call a SOAP method from PHP is by starting with the URL of a WSDL document. Feed this to a `SOAP_WSDL` object, and PHP does the dirty work of figuring out method names and how the SOAP requests must be formatted. If a SOAP service that you want to use doesn't have an associated WSDL document, you can still access it with a little more work.

If you want to make a SOAP request over SSL (in other words, to an `https://` URL), your PHP build must have the `openssl` extension. It is not enough to dynamically load the `openssl` extension with `dl()`—it must be compiled into the PHP binary or Web server module you are using.

Making Requests with WSDL

With WSDL, a SOAP request is a breeze. Listing 7-1 demonstrates how to make a SOAP request when the Web service you are using has a WSDL file available.

Listing 7-1. SOAP Requests with WSDL

```
require 'SOAP/Client.php';
$wsdl = new SOAP_WSDL('http://www.webservicex.net/isbn.asmx?wsdl');
$client = $wsdl->getProxy();
$ret = $client->GetISBNInformation('0684181320');
```

After including the `SOAP/Client.php` file, which defines the classes you need, create a new `SOAP_WSDL` object, passing it the URL of a WSDL file. Then, call `getProxy()` on the `SOAP_WSDL` object. This returns another object whose methods correspond to the methods described in the WSDL file. Calling a method on the proxy object triggers a SOAP request. In this case, you pass an ISBN to the `GetISBNInformation()` method to get some information about a book.

The GetISBNInformation service returns a string containing an XML fragment you need to parse:

```
<ISBNORG>
<RECORD>
<ISBN>0684181320</ISBN>
<AUTHOR>Harold McGee</AUTHOR>
<FULLTITLE>On food and cooking : the science and lore of the kitchen /➥
Harold McGee</FULLTITLE>
<SHORTTITLE>On food and cooking :</SHORTTITLE>
<EDITION></EDITION>
<PUBLISHER>C. Scribner&amp;apos;s Sons,</PUBLISHER>
<DATE>1984</DATE>
<SUBJECT>Cookery</SUBJECT>
</RECORD>
</ISBNORG>
```

SOAP services can also return data in a format that doesn't require further parsing. Listing 7-2 shows a request to another SOAP service.

Listing 7-2. Another SOAP Request with WSDL

```
require 'SOAP/Client.php';
$wsdl = new SOAP_WSDL('http://webservices.instantlogic.com/zipcodes.ils?wsdl');
$client = $wsdl->getProxy();
$ret = $client->ZipCodes('19096');
```

Instead of being a document that requires additional parsing, `$ret` is an array containing information about the ZIP code:

```
array(8) {
  ["CITY"]=>
  string(9) "WYNNEWOOD"
  ["COUNTY"]=>
  string(10) "MONTGOMERY"
  ["LATITUDE"]=>
  string(10) "+40.051411"
  ["LONGITUDE"]=>
  string(11) "-075.164822"
  ["STATE"]=>
  string(2) "PA"
  ["ZIP"]=>
  string(5) "19096"
  ["ZIP_CLASS"]=>
  string(8) "STANDARD"
  ["Error"]=>
  string(0) ""
}
```

Every time you call the same Web service via WSDL, your program retrieves the WSDL file, parses it, and generates an appropriate PHP class. To save time, you can retrieve the WSDL file once and then save the generated PHP class to a file. Then, when you want to make a SOAP request defined by that generated class, just instantiate the class and call the appropriate method. The `generateProxyCode()` method returns the PHP source code for the proxy object instead of an instantiated object. Listing 7-3 shows how to save that code to a file.

Listing 7-3. Saving Generated Proxy Classes to a File

```
require 'SOAP/Client.php';
$wsdl = new SOAP_WSDL('http://www.webservicex.net/isbn.asmx?wsdl');
$client_code = $wsdl->generateProxyCode();
// Parse class name from code
if (preg_match('/class (\w+) extends SOAP_Client/',$client_code,$matches)) {
    $class_name = $matches[1];
    print "Saving class $class_name to $class_name.php...";
    // Open
    $fh = fopen("$class_name.php",'w') or die("Can't open $class_name.php");
    // Write header and code (but to prevent a parse error, no closing PHP tag)
    if (-1 === fwrite($fh,"<?php \$client_code")) {
        die("Can't write to $class_name.php");
    }
```

```
    // Close
    fclose($fh) or die("Can't close $class_name.php");
    print "done.\n";
} else {
    die("Couldn't get class name.");
}
```

With the book lookup Web service you've been using, the file WebService_ISBN_ISBNSoap.php is generated. To use that class in making an actual SOAP request, include the file, instantiate the class, and then call a method on the class. Listing 7-4 uses the WebService_ISBN_ISBNSoap class. It assumes that the current directory, which is where WebService_ISBN_ISBNSoap.php is stored, is in the PHP include_path.

Listing 7-4. Using a Generated Proxy Class

```
require 'SOAP/Client.php';
require 'WebService_ISBN_ISBNSoap.php';
$client = new WebService_ISBN_ISBNSoap();
$ret = $client->GetISBNInformation('0684181320');
```

If you are using a WSDL-described Web service with any frequency, you should generate static proxy classes as shown in Listing 7-3 and then use those class files in your code. It makes your program much faster, saves bandwidth, and reduces load on the remote server. If the WSDL file changes, however, your local class file is not automatically updated. Periodically regenerate your local class file and check for changes.

Making Requests Without WSDL

Whenever you can, use WSDL. Properly formatting a SOAP request requires attention to lots of details about namespaces, argument types, SOAPAction headers, and other arcana. Attention to the mind-numbing specifics of correctly building a request according to a complicated specification is exactly why computers are handy. So if a WSDL document describing the Web service you want to use is available, use it.

Without WSDL, it's your responsibility to pay attention to namespaces, argument types, and associated particulars. These get fed into the SOAP request in one of two ways: as SOAP_Value objects that make up the arguments to the SOAP method you are calling or as additional options specified when you call the SOAP method.

Listing 7-5 contains WSDL-less code to call the book information service you used previously.

Listing 7-5. Calling a Document-Style Service Without WSDL

```
require 'SOAP/Client.php';
$client = new SOAP_Client('http://www.webservicex.net/isbn.asmx');
$params = array('Code' =>
                new SOAP_Value('{http://www.webserviceX.NET}Code',
                                'string',
                                '0684181320'));
$options = array('soapaction' => 'http://www.webserviceX.NET/GetISBNInformation',
                 'namespace' => 'http://www.webserviceX.NET');
$ret = $client->call('GetISBNInformation', $params, $options);
```

Instead of creating a `SOAP_WSDL` object, you create a `SOAP_Client` object and pass the endpoint of the SOAP method to the constructor. An endpoint uniquely identifies the service that handles the SOAP method. For SOAP over HTTP, the endpoint is the URL that will process the SOAP request.

To call a SOAP method, use the `call()` method of the `SOAP_Client` object. This method takes three arguments. The first is the name of the method you want to call. In this case, it's `GetISBNInformation`.

The second argument is an array of parameters that should be passed to the SOAP method. This is an associative array in which the keys are the parameter names and the values are the parameter values. This array can take one of two forms: simple or complex. The simple form is when the parameter values are native PHP types. I'll tackle that in a few paragraphs. The complex form, used in Listing 7-5, is when the parameter values are `SOAP_Value` objects.

A `SOAP_Value` object is necessary when you need to instruct the SOAP client to encode the value as a particular type or you need to include a namespace in the name of the value. In this case, you need to include a namespace.

The three arguments to the `SOAP_Value` constructor are the name, the type, and the value. The `Code` argument to the `GetISBNInformation` method must be in the `http://www.webserviceX.NET` namespace. Including the namespace in curly braces at the beginning of the name tells the `SOAP_Value` object to put the value in that namespace.[1] The second and third arguments indicate that the `SOAP_Value` object holds a string and its value is `0684181320`.

The particular type required for any given argument is entirely application dependent. Like the namespace, argument types are handled automatically when WSDL is involved. Refer to documentation on the particular WSDL-less Web service you want to access to figure out what types are necessary for your arguments.

The reason why the `Code` argument to the `GetISBNInformation` method must be in the `http://www.webserviceX.NET` namespace is because the author of that

---

1. Even though namespaces look like URLs, they are case sensitive even in the hostname portion, unlike URLs.

SOAP service decided it should be so. Details such as the appropriate namespaces of arguments are documented in a WSDL file and handled transparently by the `SOAP_WSDL` object. Without WSDL, you need to get specific information about the service so you can construct arguments properly.

The third argument to `call()` is an associative array of options that modify the behavior of the `SOAP_Client` object. Table 7-1 lists the allowable options in this array.[2]

Table 7-1. `SOAP_Client::call()` *Options*

Name	**Default**	**Description**
`attachments`	`Dime`	How to encode attachments. Set to `Mime` for MIME encoding.
`namespace`	`--`	What to use as the namespace for the request.
`soapaction`	`""`	What to send in the request as the `SOAPAction` header.
`timeout`	`4`	How long to wait for a response from the remote server.
`trace`	`0`	Whether to save the text of the request and response for debugging.

The appropriate values for the `namespace` and `soapaction` options depend on the particular SOAP service you are using. Usually, you don't have to adjust the `timeout` value. However, if you're experiencing problems with a slow server, increasing `timeout` may help. Debugging with `trace` is explained in a few paragraphs.

Listing 7-6 shows, without WSDL, the earlier request you made to the ZIP code information service.

Listing 7-6. Another Request Without WSDL

```
require 'SOAP/Client.php';
$client = new SOAP_Client('http://webservices.instantlogic.com/zipcodes.ils');
$options = array('namespace' => 'http://www.instantlogic.com/');
$args = array('Zip' => '19096');
$ret = $client->call('ZipCodes',$args,$options);
```

Why does this request not require a namespace in the argument name? Because the person who wrote the Web service didn't specify that the `Zip` argument had to be

2. If you're using WSDL and want to set one of these options (such as attachments or trace), call the `setOpt()` method on the proxy object. For example: `$client->setOpt('trace', 1);`

in some special namespace. This can be a conscious decision on the part of the Web service author, an accidental error on the part of the Web service author, or a behavior enforced by the software the Web service author is using to serve SOAP requests. Without WSDL, you have to do some research about the Web service and discover exactly how you need to set up the arguments and options.

Listing 7-6 uses the simple form for the `$args` array passed to `call()`. Because you don't need to put `Zip` into a namespace, you can take advantage of PEAR SOAP's automatic type conversion. It turns the string `19096` into a `SOAP_Value` object with type `string`. Table 7-2 lists PHP types and the corresponding SOAP types to which they are automatically converted.

Table 7-2. Autoconversion Between PHP Types and SOAP Types

PHP Type	SOAP Type	Conversion Conditions
`object`	`struct`	A `SOAP_Value` object isn't converted to a `struct` but stays as the SOAP type to which the object is set.
`array`	`struct`	If it has any noninteger keys or more than one `SOAP_Value` object as a value.
`array`	`struct`	If its first two elements are `SOAP_Value` objects with different names.
`array`	`array`	If neither of the previous two conditions are met.
`integer`	`int`	Always.
`boolean`	`boolean`	Always.
`double`	`float`	Always.
`float`	`float`	Always.
`string`	`string`	Always.

To debug your WSDL-less SOAP requests, use the tracing feature of the `SOAP_Client` object. Include `trace` in the array of options passed to the `call()` method and then call the `__get_wire()` method to see what was sent to the SOAP server and what the SOAP server sent back. Listing 7-7 shows how to use tracing with a request.

Listing 7-7. Tracing a SOAP Request

```
require 'SOAP/Client.php';
$client = new SOAP_Client('http://webservices.instantlogic.com/zipcodes.ils');
$options = array('namespace' => 'http://www.instantlogic.com/',
                 'trace' => true);
```

```
$args = array('Zip' =>
              new SOAP_Value('Zip','string','19096'));
$ret = $client->call('ZipCodes',$args,$options);
print $client->__get_wire();
```

The string that `__get_wire()` returns is divided up into two parts. Under the `OUTGOING` heading is the header and body of the request that the `SOAP_Client` object sent to the remote server. Under the `INCOMING` heading is what the remote server sent back. This is what `__get_wire()` reports for the ZIP code lookup:

```
OUTGOING

POST /zipcodes.ils HTTP/1.0
User-Agent: PEAR-SOAP 0.8.0RC3-devel
Host: webservices.instantlogic.com
Content-Type: text/xml; charset=UTF-8
Content-Length: 529
SOAPAction: ""

<?xml version="1.0" encoding="UTF-8"?>

<SOAP-ENV:Envelope  xmlns:SOAP-ENV="http://schemas.xmlsoap.org/soap/envelope/"
 xmlns:xsd="http://www.w3.org/2001/XMLSchema"
 xmlns:xsi="http://www.w3.org/2001/XMLSchema-instance"
 xmlns:SOAP-ENC="http://schemas.xmlsoap.org/soap/encoding/"
 xmlns:ns4="http://www.instantlogic.com/"
 SOAP-ENV:encodingStyle="http://schemas.xmlsoap.org/soap/encoding/">
<SOAP-ENV:Body>

<ns4:ZipCodes>
<Zip xsi:type="xsd:string">19096</Zip></ns4:ZipCodes>
</SOAP-ENV:Body>
</SOAP-ENV:Envelope>


INCOMING

HTTP/1.1 200 OK
Server: Microsoft-IIS/5.0
Date: Fri, 19 Dec 2003 17:14:39 GMT
Content-Type: text/xml; charset="utf-8"
Content-Length: 777
```

```
<env:Envelope xmlns:env="http://schemas.xmlsoap.org/soap/envelope/"➥
xmlns:xsi="http://www.w3.org/2001/XMLSchema-instance"➥
xmlns:xsd="http://www.w3.org/2001/XMLSchema"➥
xmlns:s0="http://www.instantlogic.com/"➥
xmlns:soapenc="http://schemas.xmlsoap.org/soap/encoding/">
<env:Body env:encodingStyle="http://schemas.xmlsoap.org/soap/encoding/">
<s0:ZipCodesResponse>
<CITY xsi:type="xsd:string">WYNNEWOOD</CITY>
<COUNTY xsi:type="xsd:string">MONTGOMERY</COUNTY>
<LATITUDE xsi:type="xsd:string">+40.051411</LATITUDE>
<LONGITUDE xsi:type="xsd:string">-075.164822</LONGITUDE>
<STATE xsi:type="xsd:string">PA</STATE>
<ZIP xsi:type="xsd:string">19096</ZIP>
<ZIP_CLASS xsi:type="xsd:string">STANDARD</ZIP_CLASS>
<Error xsi:type="xsd:string">
</Error>
</s0:ZipCodesResponse>
</env:Body>
</env:Envelope>
```

In the `OUTGOING` section, pay special attention to the `SOAPAction` header and the namespaces defined in the `<SOAP-ENV:Envelope>` tag. If you are having a problem with a request, usually it is because these are not set properly. Also examine how namespace usage inside the `<SOAP-ENV:Body>` tag corresponds with the namespace definitions. For example, in the ZIP code lookup, the namespace `http://www.instantlogic.com/` is given the prefix `ns4` in the `<SOAP-ENV:Envelope>` tag. The `<ns4:ZipCodes>` tag in the body indicates that the request is calling the `ZipCodes` method in the `http://www.instantlogic.com/` namespace.

Handling Errors

When there's an error, a SOAP service returns a SOAP fault. This is a specially formatted response body that indicates there was an error processing the request. A returned SOAP fault message is turned into a `PEAR_Error` object so that you can use standard PEAR error-handling routines to deal with SOAP-related errors. Listing 7-8 accesses the WSDL-generating Web service defined later in the chapter in Listings 7-12, 7-21, and 7-23. Don't worry about the details of the server implementation for now. The important point of this example is that when a SOAP server (written in any language, not just PHP) returns a fault, you can take special steps to handle the error. Listing 7-8 assumes that the server is accessible at the URL `http://www.example.com/soap.php`. When passed an unknown flavor such as `Trout`, the server returns a fault.

Listing 7-8. Handling a SOAP Fault

```
require 'SOAP/Client.php';
$wsdl = new SOAP_WSDL('http://www.example.com/soap.php?wsdl');
$client = $wsdl->getProxy();
$ret = $client->getFlavor('Trout');
if (PEAR::isError($ret)) {
    print "Can't get flavor information: " . $ret->getMessage();
} else {
    print "Calories: $ret->calories, Price: $ret->price";
}
```

Because the SOAP server returns a fault in response to the `getFlavor()` request, `$ret` becomes a `PEAR_Error` object. The `PEAR::isError()` function then returns `true`. Listing 7-8 prints the following:

```
Can't get flavor information: Unknown Flavor
```

Fault handling doesn't change when you're not using WSDL. Without WSDL, the `call()` method returns a `PEAR_Error` object if the SOAP request returned a fault.

Using SOAP Headers

As you saw in the trace output at the end of the "Making Requests Without WSDL" section, data representing your SOAP method call and its arguments goes inside the `<SOAP-ENV:Body>` tag. This part of the SOAP message, not surprisingly, is called the *body*. A SOAP message can also have one or more *headers*. These are separate from the HTTP headers, such as `SOAPAction`, that accompany a SOAP message when it is transmitted over HTTP.

SOAP headers typically provide information that augments the message body but is not explicitly part of it. Authentication information such as username and password is a good candidate for a SOAP header. A service may require you to provide the authentication information with each request, but putting it in a SOAP header allows the service to process it separately.

To add a header to a SOAP request, create a new `SOAP_Header` object and pass it to the `addHeader()` method on your `SOAP_Client` object. The `SOAP_Header` constructor takes three mandatory arguments that are the same as the arguments to the `SOAP_Value` constructor: the name of the header (including any namespace), the type, and the value.[3]

---

3. You can also pass `1` as an optional fourth argument to set the header's `mustUnderstand` attribute to `1`. However, because you can't access the `mustUnderstand` attribute from a PEAR SOAP server, I won't go into detail about it. You can learn more about `mustUnderstand` at `http://www.w3.org/TR/soap12-part1/#soapmu`.

Listing 7-9 shows code for a SOAP client that accesses the header-aware server in Listing 7-24 and provides a proper header. The server in Listing 7-24 uses the token value in the header for authentication. Listing 7-9 assumes that the server is accessible at the URL `http://www.example.com/soap-2.php`.

Listing 7-9. Sending SOAP Headers

```
require 'SOAP/Client.php';
$wsdl = new SOAP_WSDL('http://www.example.com/soap-2.php?wsdl');
$client = $wsdl->getProxy();
$header = new SOAP_Header('{http://www.example.com/icecream/headers}token',
                          'string',
                          md5('secret token'));
$client->addHeader($header);
$ret = $client->getFlavor('Chocolate');
```

Like fault handling, adding a header to a request doesn't change if you are using WSDL. Without WSDL, call `addHeader()` on the `SOAP_Client` object you instantiate.

Using SOAP Attachments

Like an e-mail message, a SOAP message can have attachments. A map server that uses SOAP could accept a longitude and latitude as inputs in a request and attach an image file of a map in its response. A document storage system using SOAP could accept an attached document as an input and respond with the filename where the new document has been stored in the system.

An attachment is treated like a special argument to a SOAP method. Instead of a native PHP type or a `SOAP_Value` object, the attachment is provided as a `SOAP_Attachment` object. The `SOAP_Attachment` constructor takes two forms, depending on whether you're providing it a filename to use as the attachment or the contents of the attachment in a string. If you have a filename, the arguments are the name, the content type, and the filename. This code constructs an attachment named `mydocument` with the content type `application/x-msword` from the file `/home/parlor/icecream.doc`:

```
$attachment = new SOAP_Attachment('mydocument', 'application/x-msword',
                                  '/home/parlor/icecream.doc');
```

If, instead of a filename, you have the attachment contents in a string, the arguments are the name, the content type, `NULL`, and the string. This code constructs an attachment named `salesdata` with the content type `text/csv` from the contents of the variable `$sales_data`:

```
// A hypothetical function that returns a string of CSV data
$sales_data = generate_csv_sales_data();
$attachment = new SOAP_Attachment('salesdata','text/csv',NULL,$sales_data);
```

Once you've created the `SOAP_Attachment` object, pass it to the `SOAP_Client` object like any other argument. Listing 7-10 shows the code for a SOAP client that accesses the attachment-processing function in Listings 7-25 and 7-26. Don't worry about what the server actually does with the attachments for now. Listing 7-10 assumes that the server is accessible at the URL `http://www.example.com/soap-3.php`.

Listing 7-10. Sending a SOAP Attachment

```
require 'SOAP/Client.php';
$wsdl = new SOAP_WSDL('http://www.example.com/soap-3.php?wsdl');
$client = $wsdl->getProxy();
$file = '/home/parlor/chocolate.gif';
$attachment = new SOAP_Attachment('picture','image/gif',$file);
$ret = $client->updatePicture('chocolate.gif',$attachment);
```

By default, PEAR SOAP encodes attachments using a standard called DIME. This is similar to the familiar MIME standard used with e-mail but produces more compact attachments. Because DIME is newer than MIME, however, not all SOAP servers support it. To use MIME instead of DIME, set the `attachments` client option to `Mime`. Listing 7-11 does the same thing as Listing 7-10 but uses MIME instead of DIME.

Listing 7-11. Sending a MIME-Encoded SOAP Attachment

```
require 'SOAP/Client.php';
$wsdl = new SOAP_WSDL('http://www.example.com/soap-3.php?wsdl');
$client = $wsdl->getProxy();
$client->setOpt('attachments','Mime');
$file = '/home/parlor/chocolate.gif';
$attachment = new SOAP_Attachment('picture','image/gif',$file);
$ret = $client->updatePicture('chocolate.gif',$attachment);
```

Serving SOAP Requests

You can also use PEAR SOAP to serve SOAP requests. It provides classes to parse the incoming requests and format return values into SOAP messages. You supply a class with methods that do the actual work of the Web service, such as looking up a value in a database, checking authentication credentials, or generating a customized image.

As long as your Web server accepts SSL connections, you don't have to do anything special in your code to serve SOAP requests over an SSL connection. Just have clients connect to an `https://` URL instead of an `http://` URL.

Creating a SOAP Server

These are the minimum steps required to create a SOAP server:

1. Write a class that implements the Web services you want to serve.
2. Tell a `SOAP_Server` object about that class.
3. Tell the `SOAP_Server` object to process incoming HTTP POST data.

Listing 7-12 contains a simple SOAP server. The `IceCream_Server` class implements one method: `isFlavor()`. This method returns `true` or `false` depending on whether a valid flavor name is passed to it.

Listing 7-12. Simple SOAP Server

```
require 'SOAP/Server.php';
class IceCream_Server {
    var $flavors =
        array('Chocolate' => array('calories' => 10,
                                   'price' => 4.50),
              'Vanilla' => array('calories' => 20,
                                 'price' => 4.50),
              'Heavenly Hash' => array('calories' => 60,
                                       'price' => 5.95),
              'Diet Cardboard' => array('calories' => 0,
                                        'price' => 1.15));

    function isFlavor($flavor) {
        if (array_key_exists($flavor, $this->flavors)) {
            return true;
        } else {
            return false;
        }
    }
}
```

```
// Create a new SOAP_Server object
$server = new SOAP_Server;
// Tell the server about IceCream_Server and its namespace
$server->addObjectMap(new IceCream_Server,
                      'http://www.example.com/icecream');
// Tell the server to handle any incoming data
$server->service($HTTP_RAW_POST_DATA);
```

The `SOAP_Server` class is defined in the `SOAP/Server.php` file, so this file must be included in any SOAP server page. The `IceCream_Server` class holds information about flavors in the `$flavors` variable, and the `isFlavor()` method tests to see whether the flavor name passed in `$flavor` is a valid flavor name.

The lines at the end of Listing 7-12 implement the SOAP side of things. The `addObjectMap()` method takes two arguments: an object and a namespace. Calling `addObjectMap()` tells the SOAP server that the passed-in object is responsible for all methods in the given namespace. Strictly speaking, a namespace is optional, but it's good practice always to include one.

The `service()` method of the `SOAP_Server` object is what kicks off the processing of an incoming request. You must pass `$HTTP_RAW_POST_DATA` to `service()` so that the `SOAP_Server` object can parse the POST data for a valid SOAP request.[4]

Listing 7-13 shows the client to access the SOAP server in Listing 7-12. It assumes that the server is accessible at the URL `http://www.example.com/soap-4.php`.

Listing 7-13 Accessing the Simple SOAP Server

```
require 'SOAP/Client.php';
$client = new SOAP_Client('http://www.example.com/soap-4.php');
$options = array('namespace' => 'http://www.example.com/icecream');
$args = array('Chocolate');
if ($client->call('isFlavor',$args,$options)) {
    print "Chocolate is a valid flavor.";
} else {
    print "Chocolate is not a valid flavor.";
}
```

The `isFlavor()` method in Listing 7-13 returns a Boolean: `true` or `false`. The `SOAP_Server` object knows enough about PHP types to convert a PHP Boolean into the XML Schema built-in type `boolean`.[5] The `SOAP_Server` converts the types listed in

---

4. The `service()` method doesn't just use `$HTTP_RAW_POST_DATA` by default in order to let you specify other sources of data if you are using SOAP over SMTP or another protocol.

5. The built-in XML Schema types are enumerated at `http://www.w3.org/TR/xmlschema-2/#built-in-datatypes`.

Table 7-2 automatically, but if you want to force the return of a certain type, you must return a SOAP_Value object instead of a PHP type.

For example, to return a dateTime type, create a SOAP_Value object with the type dateTime:

```
function getTime() {
    return new SOAP_Value('now','dateTime',
                          gmstrftime('%Y-%m-%dT%H:%M:%SZ'));
}
```

Like in Listing 7-5, you must also use a SOAP_Value object if you want to specify a particular namespace for a return value. The getFlavor() function in Listing 7-14 returns a value named flavor containing appropriate information if the passed-in flavor is found. This value is marked as being in the http://www.example.com/icecream namespace.

Listing 7-14. Including a Namespace in a Returned Value

```
function getFlavor($flavor) {
     if ($this->isFlavor($flavor)) {
         return new SOAP_Value('{http://www.example.com/icecream}flavor',
                               'struct',
                               $this->flavors[$flavor]);
     } else {
         return false;
     }
}
```

Generating a WSDL Document

As you saw in the "Making SOAP Requests" section, life with SOAP is greatly simplified with WSDL. If you provide some hints to the SOAP_Server object about your methods and call a few code-generation methods, it can automatically generate a WSDL document that describes the methods available in your server. The hints go in two arrays: in a "dispatch map" that lists methods and the types of the methods' arguments and return values; and an optional "data type map" that describes any custom complex types used in your methods. The code-generation methods get called at the end of your server script. After the WSDL-capable server is laid out in the next group of code listings, there's a client example that accesses the server using WSDL.

These two arrays are variables in your server class. The dispatch map is called $__dispatch_map, and the data type map is called $__typedef. Listing 7-15 shows the IceCream_Server class from Listing 7-11 with two more methods and a dispatch map.

Listing 7-15. `IceCream_Server` *Class with Dispatch Map*

```
class IceCream_Server {
    var $flavors =
        array('Chocolate' => array('calories' => 10,
                                   'price' => 4.50),
              'Vanilla' => array('calories' => 20,
                                 'price' => 4.50),
              'Heavenly Hash' => array('calories' => 60,
                                       'price' => 5.95),
              'Diet Cardboard' => array('calories' => 0,
                                        'price' => 1.15));

    // Initialize the dispatch map in the constructor to
    // make the code easier to read
    var $__dispatch_map;

    function IceCream_Server() {
        $this->__dispatch_map['isFlavor'] =
            array('in' => array('flavor' => 'string'),
                  'out' => array('flavorstatus' => 'boolean'));
        $this->__dispatch_map['getFlavor'] =
            array('in' => array('flavor' => 'string'),
                  'out' => array('flavor' => 'struct'));
    }

    function isFlavor($flavor) {
        if (array_key_exists($flavor, $this->flavors)) {
            return true;
        } else {
            return false;
        }
    }

    function getFlavor($flavor) {
        if ($this->isFlavor($flavor)) {
            return new SOAP_Value('{http://www.example.com/icecream}flavor',
                                  'struct',
                                  $this->flavors[$flavor]);
        } else {
            return false;
        }
    }
}
```

The getFlavor() method in Listing 7-15 is the same as in Listing 7-14. The IceCream_Server() constructor method in Listing 7-15 initializes the dispatch map associative array. The element names in the dispatch map are method names. The values in the dispatch map array are arrays that describe the arguments to each method and return values from each method. The in subarray describes arguments, and the out subarray describes the return values.

The in and out subarrays are themselves associative arrays with argument/return value names as keys and types as values. The dispatch map in Listing 7-15 indicates that the isFlavor() method accepts a string argument named flavor and returns a boolean argument named flavorstatus. It also indicates that the getFlavor() method accepts a string argument named flavor and returns a struct named flavor.[6]

The SOAP_Server class doesn't do any checking to make sure that the argument names and types specified in the dispatch map match any argument names or types you use in SOAP_Value objects in your methods. You need to ensure that they match in your code.

If a method accepts or returns more than one argument or value, add each to the appropriate in or out subarray in the dispatch map. Listing 7-16 shows a method that takes the names of two flavors and returns the names sorted by price.

Listing 7-16. Multiple Arguments and Return Values

```
function comparePrices($flavor1, $flavor2) {
    if ($this->isFlavor($flavor1) && $this->isFlavor($flavor2)) {
        if ($this->flavors[$flavor1]['price'] <
            $this->flavors[$flavor2]['price']) {
            return array($flavor1, $flavor2);
        } else {
            return array($flavor2, $flavor1);
        }
    } else {
        return false;
    }
}
```

Listing 7-17 shows the lines that must be added to the IceCream_Server constructor and that insert the comparePrices() method into the dispatch map.

6. Don't worry that the getFlavor() method may sometimes return not a struct but a boolean if the passed-in flavor isn't found. The correct way to deal with that is not to return a boolean but a SOAP Fault. I'll cover this in the next section.

Listing 7-17. Multiple Arguments and Return Values in the Dispatch Map

```
$this->__dispatch_map['comparePrices'] =
        array('in' => array('flavor1' => 'string',
                            'flavor2' => 'string'),
              'out' => array('lessflavor' => 'string',
                             'moreflavor' => 'string'));
```

Use the data type map when you want a method to accept or return a value whose type is not one of the XML Schema built-in types. Describing the custom type in the data type includes the type's definition in the WSDL file that the server generates. Listing 7-18 shows a new constructor for `IceCream_Server` that defines a `flavorinfo` type in the data type map. This type, which has elements for the name, calories, and price of an ice cream flavor, is also listed in the `out` subarray for `getFlavor()` in the dispatch map. This indicates that `getFlavor()` returns a value of the type `flavorinfo`. Note that the full name of the `flavorinfo` type includes the `http://www.example.com/icecream` namespace. Custom types should always be created in an application-specific namespace.

Listing 7-18. Constructor with a Data Type Map

```
function IceCream_Server() {
        $this->__typedef['{http://www.example.com/icecream}flavorinfo'] =
            array('name' => 'string',
                  'calories' => 'int',
                  'price' => 'float');

        $this->__dispatch_map['isFlavor'] =
            array('in' => array('flavor' => 'string'),
                  'out' => array('flavorstatus' => 'boolean'));
        $this->__dispatch_map['getFlavor'] =
            array('in' => array('flavor' => 'string'),
                  'out' => array('flavor' =>
                           '{http://www.example.com/icecream}flavorinfo'));
        $this->__dispatch_map['comparePrices'] =
            array('in' => array('flavor1' => 'string',
                                'flavor2' => 'string'),
                  'out' => array('lessflavor' => 'string',
                                 'moreflavor' => 'string'));
    }
```

Listing 7-19 shows a modified `getFlavor()` function that returns a value of the type `flavorinfo`.

Listing 7-19. Returning a Custom Type

```
function getFlavor($flavor) {
    if ($this->isFlavor($flavor)) {
        $flavorinfo = $this->flavors[$flavor];
        // add name to flavorinfo array
        $flavorinfo['name'] = $flavor;
        return new SOAP_Value('{http://www.example.com/icecream}flavor',
                              '{http://www.example.com/icecream}flavorinfo',
                              $flavorinfo);
    } else {
        return false;
    }
}
```

The custom type that the `getFlavor()` function in Listing 7-19 returns becomes an object in the SOAP client that calls `getFlavor()`. Listing 7-20 calls `getFlavor()` and displays some of the results. It assumes that the SOAP server is at `http://www.example.com/soap-5.php`.

Listing 7-20. Calling a SOAP Method That Returns a Custom Type

```
require 'SOAP/Client.php';
$wsdl = new SOAP_WSDL('http://www.example.com/soap-5.php?wsdl');
$client = $wsdl->getProxy();
$ret = $client->getFlavor('Chocolate');
print "Chocolate has $ret->calories calories.";
```

Listing 7-20 prints the following:

```
Chocolate has 10 calories.
```

In addition to defining the dispatch map and, optionally, the data type map, you need to add code to your SOAP server page that calls the WSDL generation function when appropriate. Replace the call to `$server->service($HTTP_RAW_POST_DATA)` with the code in Listing 7-21.

Listing 7-21. WSDL and DISCO Generation Code

```
if (isset($_SERVER['REQUEST_METHOD']) &&
    $_SERVER['REQUEST_METHOD']=='POST') {
    $server->service($HTTP_RAW_POST_DATA);
```

```
} else {
    require_once 'SOAP/Disco.php';
    $disco = new SOAP_DISCO_Server($server,'IceCream_Server');
    header("Content-type: text/xml");
    if (isset($_SERVER['QUERY_STRING']) &&
       strcasecmp($_SERVER['QUERY_STRING'],'wsdl')==0) {
        echo $disco->getWSDL();
    } else {
        echo $disco->getDISCO();
    }
}
```

The first three lines of Listing 7-21 call the `service()` method if the SOAP server has been invoked with HTTP POST, just as it has been in all of the client examples in this chapter. This preserves the behavior of the server in Listing 7-12: If a SOAP client has POSTed a request, process it and print a response.

The rest of the code in Listing 7-21 generates WSDL or DISCO output as appropriate. A `SOAP_DISCO_Server` object generates this output, so the `SOAP/Disco.php` file is included and then a new `SOAP_DISCO_Server` object is created. The `SOAP_DISCO_Server` constructor takes two arguments: a `SOAP_Server` object and a service name. Use the name of your server class as the service name.

If the URL query string is `wsdl`, then the `getWSDL()` method is called. This prints a WSDL document describing all of the SOAP methods available from the `SOAP_Server` object. Otherwise, the `getDISCO()` method is called, which prints a DISCO document that indicates where to find the WSDL document that describes the available methods.

Having your SOAP server print a DISCO document when it can't do anything else (such as display WSDL or handle an SOAP method request) provides a way for other services to find your server's WSDL document and, through that, catalog what methods your server offers.

Listing 7-22 accesses the WSDL-generating server. It assumes that the server is available at `http://www.example.com/soap-6.php`.

Listing 7-22. Accessing the WSDL-Generating Server

```
require 'SOAP/Client.php';
$wsdl = new SOAP_WSDL('http://www.example.com/soap-6.php?wsdl');
$client = $wsdl->getProxy();
$flavors = $client->comparePrices('Heavenly Hash','Chocolate');
print "$flavors[0] costs less than $flavors[1].";
```

Because Heavenly Hash costs $5.95 and Chocolate costs $4.50, Listing 7-21 prints the following:

```
Chocolate costs less than Heavenly Hash.
```

Returning Faults

If a SOAP method encounters an error, it should return a SOAP fault. The getFlavor() and comparePrices() methods should return SOAP faults instead of false when they encounter an unknown flavor. Using a fault instead of an ad-hoc convention such as "false means error" prevents a method from returning different types (such as string versus boolean) and provides SOAP clients with a standard way to handle errors.

To return a SOAP fault from a method, instantiate and then return a SOAP_Fault object. The SOAP_Fault constructor takes two arguments: an error message and an error code. The error message is a string that describes what went wrong. The error code is either Client or Server. Set it to Client if the error is caused by something the SOAP client did, such as passing an invalid argument or formatting something incorrectly. Set it to Server if the error is caused by something that went wrong on the server, such as an inability to connect to a database or not enough disk space being available to complete a task. Listing 7-23 shows a rewritten getFlavor() method that indicates when an unknown flavor is supplied with a SOAP_Fault object. This is the server method used by the client in Listing 7-8 to demonstrate client handling of a SOAP fault.

Listing 7-23. Returning a SOAP_Fault

```
function getFlavor($flavor) {
    if ($this->isFlavor($flavor)) {
        return new SOAP_Value('{http://www.example.com/icecream}flavor',
                              'struct',
                              $this->flavors[$flavor]);
    } else {
        $fault = new SOAP_Fault('Unknown Flavor','Client');
        $fault->backtrace = null;
        return $fault;
    }
}
```

A SOAP_Fault object is a subclass of the PEAR_Error object. This means when you create a SOAP_Fault object using PHP 4.3.0 or later, the backtrace property of the object is populated with the results of calling debug_backtrace(). In a regular PHP program, this is helpful. But in a SOAP server, it causes the backtrace to be sent to the SOAP client. The backtrace includes filenames and line numbers that reveal the inner workings of your server. Setting $fault->backtrace to null shrinks the size of the response considerably by removing the sensitive backtrace information from the SOAP_Fault object.

An optional third argument to the SOAP_Fault constructor can contain a *fault actor*, which provides more information about the namespace in which the fault occurred. Specifying a fault actor is useful to distinguish between faults that happen when processing a SOAP header compared to processing the request body.

Handling Headers

Take the following steps so you can process headers in your SOAP server:

1. Write a class to handle the headers whose method names correspond to header names. These methods should return faults if the client requires them to process a header and they can't.

2. In the main server class constructor, create an instance of the header-handling class and call `addObjectMap()` with that instance and a headers-only namespace.

3. Make sure the client uses the correct namespace when sending headers to the server.

Listing 7-24 shows a server with code to process a header called `token`. The `IceCream_Header` class is devoted to header processing, and its `token()` method determines whether a supplied token is valid. If so, it sets the `$icecream_token` property to `true`. If not, it returns a fault. This is the server method used in Listing 7-9 to demonstrate adding headers in a SOAP client.

Listing 7-24. Processing Headers in a SOAP Server

```
require 'SOAP/Server.php';
class IceCream_Header {
    var $icecream_token = null;
    var $header_ns = 'http://www.example.com/icecream/headers';

    function token($client_token) {
        if ($client_token == md5('secret token')) {
            $this->icecream_token = true;
            return 'Valid Token';
        } else {
            $fault = new SOAP_Fault('Invalid Token',
                                    'Client',
                                    $this->header_ns);
            $fault->backtrace = null;
            return $fault;
        }
    }
}
```

```
class IceCream_Server {
    var $method_ns = 'http://www.example.com/icecream';
    var $headers;
    var $flavors =
        array('Chocolate' => array('calories' => 10,
                                   'price' => 4.50),
              'Vanilla' => array('calories' => 20,
                                 'price' => 4.50),
              'Heavenly Hash' => array('calories' => 60,
                                       'price' => 5.95),
              'Diet Cardboard' => array('calories' => 0,
                                        'price' => 1.15));
    function IceCream_Server() {
        $this->__dispatch_map['getFlavor'] =
            array('in' => array('flavor' => 'string'),
                  'out' => array('info' => 'array'));
        // create a header handler and add it to the server
        $this->headers = new IceCream_Header;
        global $server;
        $server->addObjectMap($this->headers, $this->headers->header_ns);
    }

    function getFlavor($flavor) {
        if (is_null($this->headers->icecream_token)) {
            $fault = new SOAP_Fault('No Token Header',
                                    'Client',
                                    $this->method_ns);
            $fault->backtrace = null;
            return $fault;
        } elseif (array_key_exists($flavor, $this->flavors)) {
            return new SOAP_Value('info', 'array',
                                  $this->flavors[$flavor]);
        } else {
            $fault = new SOAP_Fault('Unknown Flavor','Client');
            $fault->backtrace = null;
            return $fault;
        }
    }
}
```

The IceCream_Server class is also modified to accommodate header processing. In the IceCream_Server() constructor, an IceCream_Headers object is instantiated and assigned to the $headers property. Then, addObjectMap() is called on the global $server SOAP_Server object, with the $header_ns property of the IceCream_Headers class providing the appropriate namespace for the header-handling methods.

The getFlavor() method is modified to check whether the $icecream_token property of the headers object is set before it does anything else. If this property is not set, it means that a valid token hasn't been provided, so it returns a fault. The $method_ns property is used as the actor in this fault to distinguish header-generated faults from body-generated faults.

From within a header-handling function such as IceCream_Header::token(), there is currently no way to access the mustUnderstand value that the client specified with the header.

Handling Attachments

If a SOAP client supplies an attachment as an argument, then the attachment body is passed to the method as the value of the corresponding argument. From inside the server method, you have access only to the content of the attachment, not its content type. To have a server method that accepts an attachment as an argument, specify the argument's type as base64Binary in the dispatch map. Listing 7-25 shows the dispatch map settings for a function named updatePicture() that accepts a string and an attachment as arguments and that returns a string.

Listing 7-25. Dispatch Map with an Attachment

```
$this->__dispatch_map['updatePicture'] =
       array('in' => array('name' => 'string',
                           'picture' => 'base64Binary'),
             'out' => array('filename' => 'string'));
```

Listing 7-26 contains the code for the updatePicture() function. If an acceptable filename is provided, it writes the contents of the attachment to the file. If an unacceptable filename is provided or the function encounters problems writing the file, it returns a fault. Listing 7-10 contains the SOAP client code that accesses this SOAP server method.

Listing 7-26. Processing an Attachment in a Function

```
function updatePicture($name, $picture) {
     if (! preg_match('/^\w+\.\w{3}$/', $name)) {
         $f = new SOAP_Fault('Bad Name Format', 'Client');
         $f->backtrace = null;
         return $f;
```

```
        }
        $filename = '/usr/local/pictures/'.$name;
        if (! ($fh = fopen($filename,'wb'))) {
            $f = new SOAP_Fault("Can't open file for writing",'Server');
            $f->backtrace = null;
            return $f;
        }
        if (fwrite($fh,$picture) != strlen($picture)) {
            $f = new SOAP_Fault("Can't write all data",'Server');
            $f->backtrace = null;
            return $f;
        }
        if (! fclose($fh)) {
            $f = new SOAP_Fault("Can't close file",'Server');
            $f->backtrace = null;
            return $f;
        }
        // Everything succeeded, so return the new filename
        return $filename;
}
```

Just as a function can accept attachments as arguments, it can also return an attachment. Listing 7-27 shows the dispatch map for a `getPicture()` function that accepts a `string` argument and returns an attachment. The code for the `getPicture()` function, which sends back a previously uploaded picture, if available, is in Listing 7-28.

Listing 7-27. Dispatch Map with a Returned Attachment

```
$this->__dispatch_map['getPicture'] =
      array('in' => array('name' => 'string'),
            'out' => array('picture' => 'base64Binary'));
```

Listing 7-28. Returning an Attachment

```
function getPicture($name) {
        if (! preg_match('/^\w+\.\w{3}$/', $name)) {
            $f = new SOAP_Fault('Bad Name Format', 'Client');
            $f->backtrace = null;
            return $f;
        }
        $filename = '/tmp/'.$name;
```

```
        if (! is_readable($filename)) {
            $f = new SOAP_Fault("Can't read File",'Server');
            $f->backtrace = null;
        }
        $attachment = new SOAP_Attachment('picture',
                                          'application/octet-stream',
                                          $filename);
        return $attachment;
    }
```

As Listing 7-28 shows, returning a `SOAP_Attachment` object from a method causes the attachment to be sent to the SOAP client as the return value from the method. The code in Listing 7-28 uses the generic content type `application/octet-stream`. In your applications, however, it's best to return the most specific content type possible. A good practice is to examine the file's extension to figure out what an appropriate content type should be. If you are working with images, use the `exif_imagetype()` function to find out what kind of image a particular file is.

Exploring Further

You can learn more about SOAP from the official SOAP specification at `http://www.w3.org/TR/SOAP/`. As you might expect from SOAP's pickup truck nature, reading the specification is a long and involved activity. A gentler introduction to SOAP at `http://www.w3.org/TR/soap12-part0/` can also be a little rough going at times but is much friendlier than the specification.

SOAP has great promise as a cross-platform, language-neutral data exchange format, but it may be a little while longer before all of the dust settles from the many implementation-specific incompatibilities.

Software exists for languages such as C# and Java that ease or automate the process of exposing already written functions via SOAP with minimal or no modification. The flexible type conversion architecture makes that task somewhat more difficult in PHP but not impossible. However, as SOAP and PHP each become more popular, more tools to help you code SOAP-aware applications in PHP will be developed. SOAP's loosely coupled information exchange model combined with PHP's Web simplicity provides an exciting opportunity to build flexible, distributed applications.

CHAPTER 8

Performing Easier XML Parsing with SimpleXML

SIMPLEXML IS A BUILT-IN extension that uses new features of PHP 5 to provide an interface to reading and writing XML documents in which an XML document acts like a PHP object. By getting and setting properties of the object, you read and write elements of the XML document.

The increased convenience of easy access to XML elements and their contents via object property syntax comes with the trade-off of decreased XML manipulation power. SimpleXML lets you modify the existing elements of an XML document but not add new ones.

It's best for parsing and searching a relatively plain XML document that already exists, such as a blog's RSS syndication feed or a small purchase order. However, SimpleXML isn't the right tool to generate a new XML document or wade through a large or complex document. For that, check out PHP 5's revamped DOM extension.

Creating SimpleXML Objects

You can create a SimpleXML object from a string containing an XML fragment, an XML file, or a DOM object. Use the `simplexml_load_string()` function if your XML is stored in a string:

```
$icecream_xml =<<<XML
<icecream>
<flavor id="6">
 <name>Chocolate</name><calories>10</calories><price>4.50</price>
</flavor>
<flavor id="5">
 <name>Vanilla</name><calories>20</calories><price>4.50</price>
</flavor>
<flavor id="19">
 <name>Heavenly Hash</name><calories>60</calories><price>5.95</price>
</flavor>
```

```
<flavor id="12">
 <name>Diet Cardboard</name><calories>0</calories><price>1.15</price>
</flavor>
</icecream>
XML;
$sxe = simplexml_load_string($icecream);
```

Use `simplexml_load_file()` if your XML is stored in a file:

```
$sxe = simplexml_load_file('icecream.xml');
```

Use `simplexml_import_dom()` if your XML is in a DOM object:

```
$dom = new domDocument;
$root = $dom->appendChild(new domElement('flavor'));
$root->setAttribute('id',6);
$root->appendChild(new domElement('name','Chocolate'));
$root->appendChild(new domElement('calories',10));
$root->appendChild(new domElement('price','4.50'));
$sxe = simplexml_import_dom($dom);
```

To extract the XML from a SimpleXML object, use the `asXML()` method:

```
print $sxe->asXML();
```

With the previous `icecream.xml` example, this prints the following:

```
<?xml version="1.0"?>
<icecream>
<flavor id="6">
 <name>Chocolate</name><calories>10</calories><price>4.50</price>
</flavor>
<flavor id="5">
 <name>Vanilla</name><calories>20</calories><price>4.50</price>
</flavor>
<flavor id="19">
 <name>Heavenly Hash</name><calories>60</calories><price>5.95</price>
</flavor>
<flavor id="12">
 <name>Diet Cardboard</name><calories>0</calories><price>1.15</price>
</flavor>
</icecream>
```

You can also write the XML in a SimpleXML object directly to a file by passing a filename to asXML():

```
$sxe->asXML('my-icecream.xml');
```

Working with SimpleXML Objects

A SimpleXML object exposes the structure of the XML document in a few different ways. You access child elements as object properties and element attributes as array indices. Consider this XML fragment holding information about one ice cream flavor:

```
$xml = '<flavor id="6">
 <name>Chocolate</name>
 <calories>10</calories>
 <price>4.50</price>
</flavor>';
$sxe = simplexml_load_string($xml);
```

The $sxe variable is a SimpleXML object holding the <flavor> element with all its attributes and children. To access the name, calories, or price of the flavor, use the appropriate object property:

```
print "$sxe->name has $sxe->calories calories and costs ";
print '$' . $sxe->price . '.';
```

This prints the following:

```
Chocolate has 10 calories and costs $4.50.
```

To access an attribute, such as id, treat the SimpleXML object as an array and use the attribute name as an array index:

```
print "$sxe->name has flavor id $sxe[id].";
```

This prints the following:

```
Chocolate has flavor id 6.
```

If child elements have attributes, access them with the same array element notation. In this XML, the <calories> element has a source attribute:

```
$xml = '<flavor id="6">
 <name>Chocolate</name>
```

```
 <calories source="fat and carbs">10</calories>
 <price>4.50</price>
</flavor>';
$sxe = simplexml_load_string($xml);
```

This code accesses the <calories> element and its source attribute:

```
print "The $sxe->calories calories come from ";
print $sxe->calories['source'] . '.';
```

The code prints the following:

```
The 10 calories come from fat and carbs.
```

If a child element is not just plain text but itself contains child elements, then accessing it doesn't return a string but another SimpleXML object. Consider the following XML, in which the calories are broken down into calories from fat and calories from everything else:

```
$xml = '<flavor id="6">
 <name>Chocolate</name>
 <calories>
  <fat>6</fat>
  <other>4</other>
 </calories>
 <price>4.50</price>
</flavor>';
$sxe = simplexml_load_string($xml);
```

Now, $sxe->calories is not a string but a SimpleXML object. The properties of this object are the names of the child elements of the <calories> XML tag: fat and other. To print a calorie breakdown, access those properties:

```
print "$sxe->name has {$sxe->calories->fat} fat calories and ";
print "{$sxe->calories->other} non-fat calories.";
```

This prints the following:

```
Chocolate has 6 fat calories and 4 non-fat calories.
```

The curly braces are necessary when interpolating expressions such as $sxe->calories->fat in a double-quoted string so that PHP knows you mean "the fat property of the $sxe->calories object" and not "the $sxe->calories object followed by a literal ->fat."

If an element has multiple child elements each with the same name, then the object property representing the child elements is an array instead of a string. Each array element holds one child element. Consider again the example from the beginning of the chapter:

```
$icecream_xml =<<<XML
<icecream>
<flavor id="6">
 <name>Chocolate</name><calories>10</calories><price>4.50</price>
</flavor>
<flavor id="5">
 <name>Vanilla</name><calories>20</calories><price>4.50</price>
</flavor>
<flavor id="19">
 <name>Heavenly Hash</name><calories>60</calories><price>5.95</price>
</flavor>
<flavor id="12">
 <name>Diet Cardboard</name><calories>0</calories><price>1.15</price>
</flavor>
</icecream>
XML;
$sxe = simplexml_load_string($icecream_xml);
```

Because there are four `<flavor>` elements, the `$sxe->flavor` property is an array. Each flavor can be accessed as an element of `$sxe->flavor`:

```
print $sxe->flavor[0]->name . ' has ';
print $sxe->flavor[0]->calories . ' calories, but ';
print $sxe->flavor[3]->name . ' (id=' . $sxe->flavor[3]['id'] . ') ';
print 'only has ' . $sxe->flavor[3]->calories . '.';
```

This prints the following:

```
Chocolate has 10 calories, but Diet Cardboard (id=12) only has 0.
```

A SimpleXML object implements the Iterator interface, so you can loop through all of the child elements in an object with `foreach`. Keys are child element names, and values are SimpleXML objects for each child element. For example:

```
$xml = '<flavor id="6">
 <name>Chocolate</name>
 <calories>10</calories>
 <price>4.50</price>
</flavor>';
```

```
$sxe = simplexml_load_string($xml);
foreach ($sxe as $element_name => $element) {
    print "$element_name is $element\n";
}
```

This prints the following:

```
name is Chocolate
calories is 10
price is 4.50
```

Working with Namespaces

When your document contains elements in different namespaces, you need to tell SimpleXML which namespace an element lives in so it can access the element. Consider the following XML document, in which the chocolate and vanilla flavors are in a namespace, but the lemon and tangerine flavors are not. The code following the XML iterates through each element:

```
$xml = '
<dessert xmlns:ic="http://www.example.com/ns/icecream">
<ic:flavor id="6">
 <ic:name>Chocolate</ic:name>
 <ic:calories>10</ic:calories>
 <ic:price>4.50</ic:price>
</ic:flavor>
<ic:flavor id="5">
 <ic:name>Vanilla</ic:name>
 <ic:calories>20</ic:calories>
 <ic:price>4.50</ic:price>
</ic:flavor>
<flavor id="19">
 <name>Lemon</name><calories>60</calories><price>5.95</price>
</flavor>
<flavor id="12">
 <name>Tangerine</name><calories>0</calories><price>1.15</price>
</flavor>
</dessert>';

$sxe = simplexml_load_string($xml);
foreach ($sxe as $element_name => $element) {
    print "$element_name $element->name has $element->calories calories.\n";
}
```

The code prints the following:

```
flavor Lemon has 60 calories.
flavor Tangerine has 0 calories.
```

The iteration finds only lemon and tangerine because chocolate and vanilla are inside a namespace. To iterate over the elements in the namespace, you must access them with the `children()` method. This method accepts a namespace as an argument and returns the elements in that namespace. The code that follows demonstrates the `children()` method:

```
$flavors = $sxe->children('http://www.example.com/ns/icecream');
foreach ($flavors as $element_name => $element) {
    $children = $element->children('http://www.example.com/ns/icecream');
    print "$element_name $children->name has $children->calories calories.\n";
}
```

The code prints the following:

```
flavor Chocolate has 10 calories.
flavor Vanilla has 20 calories.
```

You need to use `children()` to get the initial list of flavors and to retrieve the child elements of each flavor because the child elements are also in the `http://www.example.com/ns/icecream` namespace.

Searching with XPath

If you know the name of a child element you're looking for and the names of all its parents, then you can find it with the standard `$sxe->property` syntax. For more flexible and powerful searching of the elements in a SimpleXML object, use the `xpath()` method. This performs an XPath query against a SimpleXML object and returns an array that holds all matching elements. For example, to find all of the flavors with fewer than 20 calories, use this:

```
$diet_flavors = $sxe->xpath('flavor[calories < 20]');
foreach ($diet_flavors as $f) {
    print "$f->name (id $f[id]) only has $f->calories calories.\n";
}
```

Because only chocolate and diet cardboard have fewer than 20 calories, this example prints the following:

```
Chocolate (id 6) only has 10 calories.
Diet Cardboard (id 12) only has 0 calories.
```

When the `xpath()` method doesn't find any elements that match the given XPath expression, it returns `false`.

If your document uses namespaces, be sure to include the namespace in the XPath query to get the correct results. For example, this XML puts the flavors in an ic namespace:

```
$xml = '<icecream xmlns:ic="http://www.example.com/ns/icecream">
<ic:flavor id="6">
 <ic:name>Chocolate</ic:name><ic:calories>10</ic:calories>
 <ic:price>4.50</ic:price>
</ic:flavor>
<ic:flavor id="5">
 <ic:name>Vanilla</ic:name><ic:calories>20</ic:calories>
 <ic:price>4.50</ic:price>
</ic:flavor>
<ic:flavor id="19">
 <ic:name>Heavenly Hash</ic:name><ic:calories>60</ic:calories>
 <ic:price>5.95</ic:price>
</ic:flavor>
<ic:flavor id="12">
 <ic:name>Diet Cardboard</ic:name><ic:calories>0</ic:calories>
 <ic:price>1.15</ic:price>
</ic:flavor>
</icecream>';
$sxe = simplexml_load_string($xml);
```

The corresponding XPath query must include the `ic:` namespace prefix before element names:

```
$diet_flavors = $sxe->xpath('ic:flavor[ic:calories < 20]');
```

Part Four

Networking

CHAPTER 9

Sending Mail

WEB SITES DON'T JUST display Web pages. Often, they also send e-mail messages. For example, sending a confirmation message to a user after he creates an account, changes a password, or places an order is a common practice. Many Web sites also send periodic e-mail newsletters containing new headlines or information about recent site updates. The PEAR Mail and Mail_mime modules provide a flexible, robust way to send e-mail messages from your PHP programs.

This chapter discusses PEAR Mail 1.1.2 and Mail_mime 1.2.1. With the PEAR Mail module, you have more control over how your e-mail messages are sent than if you just use PHP's built-in `mail()` function. The Mail_mime module supplies a way to send messages that are more complicated than plain-text ones—messages with attachments, HTML, and embedded images.

Sending Plain-Text Mail Messages with PEAR Mail

The PEAR Mail module sends e-mail messages and lets you switch easily between using a local or remote method to send your message and piggybacking on PHP's built-in `mail()` function. PEAR Mail also automatically takes care of platform dependencies such as line endings.

To send a message, create a new `Mail` object using the `Mail::factory()` method and then call the `send()` method on that object, passing it the recipient's address, message body, and headers. Listing 9-1 demonstrates sending a message with the Mail module.

Listing 9-1. Sending an E-mail Message

```
require 'Mail.php';
$mailer =& Mail::factory('mail');
$to = 'destination@example.com';
$headers = array('Subject' => 'Hungry?',
                 'Cc: other-destination@example.com');
$body=<<<_MSG_
Are you hungry? Wouldn't you like a cold, sweet ice cream cone?
Why not stop by your local ice cream parlor today for a few
scoops of Guava Mint Bouillon?

Sincerely,
Your local ice cream booster
```

```
_MSG_;
$res = $mailer->send($to, $headers, $body);
// If the message can't be sent, send() returns a
// PEAR::Error object
if (PEAR::isError($res)) {
   print "Couldn't send message: " . $res->getMessage();
}
```

The first argument to `Mail::factory()` is which driver to use. The driver controls how the `Mail` object sends the message. Your driver choices are `mail`, `smtp`, and `sendmail`. The `mail` driver uses PHP's built-in `mail()` function, and the `smtp` driver uses an SMTP server. If you have Sendmail or a similar mailer program installed, you can use the `sendmail` driver as well.

Because the `mail` driver sends messages with PHP's built-in `mail()` function, it relies on the mail-related PHP configuration settings: `sendmail_path` and, on Windows, `sendmail_from`. The `sendmail_path` configuration setting should be set to the path of an external mailer program and any arguments you want to pass to the program. If you're using Sendmail on Unix, its path is probably `/usr/sbin/sendmail` or `/usr/lib/sendmail`. When you build and install PHP, the `configure` script looks for Sendmail and sets the configuration setting appropriately.

If you are using a mailer program other than Sendmail, set `sendmail_path` to the location of a Sendmail-compatible mail program that may have been supplied with your mailer software. For example, use the `sendmail` wrapper program that comes with qmail or the regular `exim` binary for Exim.

PHP 5 supports another mail-related configuration setting: `mail_force_extra_parameters`. The value of this setting is tacked onto the end of the command line when the `mail()` function runs Sendmail. You can use `mail_force_extra_parameters` to pass arguments to Sendmail.

Windows doesn't come with a built-in mailer program, but you can instruct the `mail()` function to send mail via an SMTP server with the `SMTP` and `smtp_port` configuration settings. Set `SMTP` to the name of the SMTP server you want to use, and, if the SMTP server uses a port other than 25 (the default SMTP port), set `smtp_port` to that alternative port number. With `SMTP` set and `sendmail_path` not set, the `mail()` function connects to the server defined by `SMTP` and relays the message through that server.

On any platform, you can bypass the `mail()` function and the intricacies of its configuration directives with the `smtp` driver. However, this driver requires that the Net_SMTP and Net_Socket PEAR modules be installed. Listing 9-2 shows how to send a message with the `smtp` driver.

Listing 9-2. Sending a Message with the `smtp` *Driver*

```
require 'Mail.php';
$params = array('host' => 'smtp-server.example.com',
                'port' => '25');
```

```
$mailer =& Mail::factory('smtp',$params);
$to = 'destination@example.com';
$headers = array('From' => 'icecream@example.com',
                 'Subject' => 'Hungry?',
                 'Cc' => 'other-destination@example.com');
$body=<<<_MSG_
Are you hungry? Wouldn't you like a cold, sweet ice cream cone?
Why not stop by your local ice cream parlor today for a few
scoops of Guava Mint Bouillon?

Sincerely,
Your local ice cream booster
_MSG_;

$res = $mailer->send($to, $headers, $body);

// If the message can't be sent, send() returns a
// PEAR::Error object
if (PEAR::isError($res)) {
   print "Couldn't send message: " . $res->getMessage();
}
```

Two differences exist between the code that uses the `smtp` driver and the code that uses the `mail` driver. First, when the `smtp` driver is specified, the `Mail::factory()` method can take a second argument, an array of parameters. Second, the `smtp` driver requires that a `From` address is specified in the message headers. This can be with a `From` header, as shown in Listing 9-2, or with a `Return-Path` header. Table 9-1 shows the complete list of the parameters that the `smtp` driver accepts.

Table 9-1. Options for the `smtp` *Driver*

Option	**Description**	**Default**
`host`	Hostname of an SMTP server to connect to	`localhost`
`port`	Port on the SMTP server to connect to	`25`
`auth`	Whether to use SMTP authentication	`false`
`username`	Username for authentication	
`password`	Password for authentication	
`localhost`	How the connecting host identifies itself to the remote SMTP server	`localhost`

The Net_SMTP module, used by the Mail module, can handle four SMTP authentication methods: DIGEST-MD5, CRAM-MD5, LOGIN, and PLAIN.[1] If you choose to use SMTP authentication, Net_SMTP asks the SMTP server what kind of authentication it knows about and then chooses a method that both it and the server support, preferring DIGEST-MD5 to CRAM-MD5, CRAM-MD5 to LOGIN, and LOGIN to PLAIN.

In addition to the `mail` and `smtp` drivers, Mail also has a `sendmail` driver. This driver runs a local Sendmail program (or a similarly behaving program from another mailer) to send a message. If you want to use a local mailer program but can't alter the `sendmail_path` configuration setting because of how your PHP installation is set up, this driver is a good choice. Listing 9-3 demonstrates how to send a message with the `sendmail` driver.

Listing 9-3. Sending a Message with the `sendmail` *Driver*

```
require 'Mail.php';
$params = array('sendmail_path' =>'/usr/lib/sendmail',
                'sendmail_args' => '-i');
$mailer =& Mail::factory('sendmail',$params);
$to = 'destination@example.com';
$headers = array('From' => 'icecream@example.com',
                 'Subject' => 'Hungry?',
                 'Cc' => 'other-destination@example.com');
$body=<<<_MSG_
Are you hungry? Wouldn't you like a cold, sweet ice cream cone?
Why not stop by your local ice cream parlor today for a few
scoops of Guava Mint Bouillon?

Sincerely,
Your local ice cream booster
_MSG_;

$res = $mailer->send($to, $headers, $body);

// If the message can't be sent, send() returns a
// PEAR::Error object
if (PEAR::isError($res)) {
   print "Couldn't send message: " . $res->getMessage();
}
```

1. To use the DIGEST-MD5 or CRAM-MD5 methods, you must have the PEAR Auth_SASL module installed.

The sendmail driver requires you to set a From address in the message headers. When it runs the Sendmail program, specified in the sendmail_path parameter, it adds a -f argument including the From address to the command line. Any other arguments specified in the sendmail_args parameter are also added to the Sendmail command line. The -i argument is useful because without it Sendmail considers a period by itself on a line as the end of the message. Be careful not to include any external input that could contain shell metacharacters in the sendmail_args parameter—this data ends up being passed to the shell for execution. The sendmail_path and sendmail_args parameters are the only two parameters that the sendmail driver understands.

Sending MIME Mail Messages with Mail_mime

When SMTP servers exchange messages, they expect those messages to consist of plain ASCII text. No binary data or control characters are allowed. MIME is a way to get around that limitation. The MIME standard defines two things that are useful when sending e-mail messages: how to represent documents such as images or PDFs as plain text and how to package multiple documents in one message.

Every kind of document has a MIME media type, which is divided into two parts. The first part, the *type*, tells what kind of general category a document falls into (for example, image, video, or text). The second part of a media type, the *subtype*, describes the kind of document more specifically (for example, jpeg, mpeg, or html). A MIME media type is represented with the type and subtype joined by a slash: image/jpeg, video/mpeg, or text/html. Table 9-2 lists some common MIME media types. A directory of official MIME media types is available at http://www.iana.org/assignments/media-types/index.html.

Table 9-2. Some Common MIME Media Types

Media Type	Description
text/plain	ASCII text without markup or special formatting
text/html	HTML
text/csv	Tabular comma-separated value data
image/jpeg	JPEG image
image/gif	GIF image
image/png	PNG image
audio/wav	WAV sound
audio/mpeg	MP3 sound file

Table 9-2. Some Common MIME Media Types (continued)

Media Type	Description
video/mpeg	MPEG video
video/quicktime	QuickTime video
application/msword	Microsoft Word document

In addition to the MIME media types that describe individual documents, there are a set of media types called *composite types*, such as `multipart/alternative` and `multipart/mixed`. A document with a composite type holds inside it one or more other documents.

For example, an e-mail message with attachments has the media type `multipart/mixed`. Inside the `multipart/mixed` document are sections for the message body and each attachment. Each of these sections has its own media type.

Attachments

Although constructing documents with the right media type and the correct encoding of binary data can be a hassle, the PEAR Mail_mime module makes it a snap. It provides methods that produce the proper message headers and body, which can be passed to the Mail module's `send()` method for delivery. Listing 9-4 shows how to use Mail_mime to send a message with an attachment.

Listing 9-4. Sending an E-mail Message with an Attachment

```
require 'Mail.php';
require 'Mail/mime.php';
$to = 'destination@example.com';
$headers = array('From' => 'icecream@example.com',
                 'Subject' => 'Hungry?',
                 'Cc' => 'other-destination@example.com');
$body=<<<_MSG_
Why not stop by your local ice cream parlor today for a few
scoops of Guava Mint Bouillon? The attached document lists
the numerous health benefits of this delicious flavor.

Sincerely,
Your local ice cream booster
_MSG_;
```

```
$mime = new Mail_mime();
$mime->setTXTBody($body);
$mime->addAttachment('/home/icecream/guava-health.doc','application/msword');
$body = $mime->get();
$headers = $mime->headers($headers);
$mailer =& Mail::factory('mail');
$mailer->send($to,$headers,$body);
```

The setTXTBody() method sets the body of the message to the text in $body. You can also give setTXTBody() a filename to use the contents of a file as the body of the message. Pass the filename as the first argument and true as the second argument:

```
// Uses the contents of /home/icecream/healthy.txt as the message body
$mime->setTXTBody('/home/icecream/healthy.txt', true);
```

The setTXTBody() method also supports creating the body incrementally. When you pass true as a third argument, setTXTBody() appends the new content to the message body. You can combine data in a variable and the contents of a file with multiple calls to setTXTBody():

```
// Start off with the contents of a file
$mime->setTXTBody('/home/icecream/header.txt', true);
// Append a string
$mime->setTXTBody('The date today is ' . strftime('%c') . "\n\n", false, true);
// Append a file
$mime->setTXTBody('/home/icecream/healthy.txt', true, true);
// Append another file
$mime->setTXTBody('/home/icecream/footer.txt', true, true);
```

The addAttachment() method adds an attachment to the message. To add a file as an attachment, you need to pass addAttachment() two arguments: the filename and the MIME media type of the file. In Listing 9-4, the media type is application/msword because guava-health.doc is a Microsoft Word document.

The get() method of the Mail_mime object returns the body of the entire message, attachments and all, properly encoded as plain text. The headers() method returns an array of headers. You pass headers() an array containing any headers you want to add, and it returns a new array that contains the passed-in headers along with the additional headers required for the MIME encoding of the message. You must call get() before headers() because get() computes information about the content of the message that headers() needs to function properly. The return values from get() and headers() are formatted such that you can pass them directly to the Mail object's send() method.

Instead of passing a filename to addAttachment(), you can provide it with a variable that contains data you want to use as an attachment. You must supply a filename for the attachment to be known as in the third argument. Passing false as the fourth argument tells addAttachment() that its first argument holds the content of the attachment, not a filename. Listing 9-5 demonstrates sending a CSV file as a dynamic attachment.

Listing 9-5. Sending a Dynamic Attachment

```
require 'Mail.php';
require 'Mail/mime.php';
require 'DB.php';
$dbh = DB::connect('mysql://phpgems:phpgems1@localhost/phpgems');
$flavors = $dbh->getAll('SELECT * FROM ice_cream');
// The tocsv() function, defined below, turns an array of arrays
// into a string holding CSV data
$flavors_csv = tocsv($flavors);
$headers = array('From' => 'flavordept@example.com',
                 'Subject' => 'Flavor Matrix');
$to = 'flavor-summit-list@example.com';
$body=<<<_MSG_
The attached spreadsheet contains the current flavor matrix.
Please review it in detail before the flavor summit meeting tomorrow.

Sincerely,
The flavor department
_MSG_;

$mime = new Mail_mime();
$mime->setTXTBody($body);
// Since $flavors_csv holds the attachment data, we must supply a filename
// for the e-mail client to use and tell addAttachment() that the first
// argument holds data, not a filename
$mime->addAttachment($flavors_csv,'text/csv', 'flavors.csv',false);
$body = $mime->get();
$headers = $mime->headers($headers);
$mailer =& Mail::factory('mail');
$mailer->send($to,$headers,$body);
// The utility function to CSV-format an array of arrays
```

```
function tocsv($ar) {
    $s = '';
    foreach ($ar as $row) {
        $out = array();
        foreach ($row as $cell) {
            $quote = false;
            // double any double quotes, and quote the cell
            if (false !== strpos($cell,'"')) {
                $cell = str_replace('"','""',$cell);
                $quote = true;
            }
            // also quote the cell if there is an embedded
            // newline, comma, or the cell begins or ends
            // with whitespace
            elseif ((false !== strpos($cell,"\n")) ||
                    (false !== strpos($cell,"\r")) ||
                    (false !== strpos($cell,",")) ||
                    preg_match('/^\s/',$cell) ||
                    preg_match('/\s$/',$cell)) {
                $quote = true;
            }
            // add the cell, with optional quoting, to $out
            $out[] = $quote ? '"'.$cell.'"' : $cell;
        }
        // add the whole line, joined by commas, to $s
        $s .= join(',',$out)."\n";
    }
    return $s;
}
```

HTML Message Bodies

A message with attachments has a one main body and then one or more attachments. It is also possible to send a message with two main bodies—one that is plain text and one that is HTML. This is called a `multipart/alternative` message. The e-mail client decides which message body to display based on its capabilities. A text-based mail reader such as Pine or Mutt displays the plain-text message body, and a graphical mail reader such as Outlook or Eudora displays the HTML body. Sending a message with both plain-text and HTML bodies lets you offer a more fancily formatted version to users with capable mail readers but also accommodates people who can't (or don't like to) have their e-mail jazzed up by HTML. To include text and HTML alternatives, call both `setTXTBody()` and setHTMLBody() on the Mail_mime object. Listing 9-6 shows how send a message with both text and HTML bodies.

Listing 9-6. Sending a Message with Text and HTML Bodies

```
require 'Mail.php';
require 'Mail/mime.php';
$to = 'destination@example.com';
$headers = array('From' => 'icecream@example.com',
                 'Subject' => 'Hungry?',
                 'Cc' => 'other-destination@example.com');
$text_body=<<<_MSG_
Are you hungry? Wouldn't you like a cold, sweet ice cream cone?
Why not stop by your local ice cream parlor today for a few
scoops of Guava Mint Bouillon?

Sincerely,
Your local ice cream booster
_MSG_;

$html_body=<<<_HTML_
<p>Are you <i>hungry?</i> Wouldn't you like a <b>cold</b>, <b>sweet</b>
ice cream cone? Why not stop by your local ice cream parlor today for
a few scoops of <font size="+1">Guava Mint Bouillon</font>?</p>

<p><a href="http://coupons.example.com/">Click Here</a> for a coupon.</p>

<p>Sincerely, <br/>
Your local ice cream booster</p>
_HTML_;

$mime = new Mail_mime();
$mime->setTXTBody($text_body);
$mime->setHTMLBody($html_body);
$body = $mime->get();
$headers = $mime->headers($headers);
$mailer =& Mail::factory('mail');
$res = $mailer->send($to, $headers, $body);

// If the message can't be sent, send() returns a
// PEAR::Error object
if (PEAR::isError($res)) {
   print "Couldn't send message: " . $res->getMessage();
}
```

Figure 9-1 shows what the message from Listing 9-6 looks like in Mutt, which displays the text body. Figure 9-2 shows how Outlook displays the HTML body.

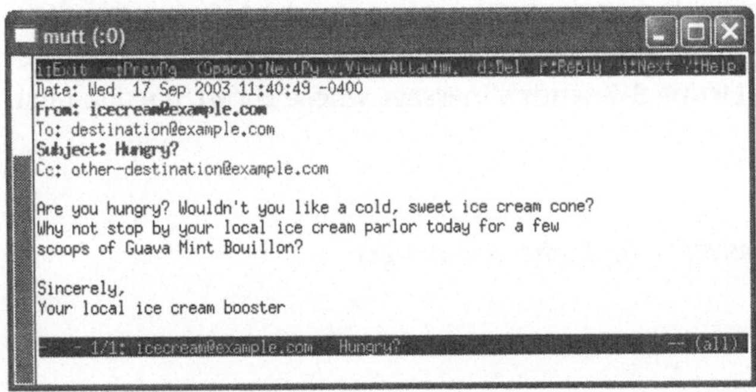

Figure 9-1. Mutt displays the text part of a `multipart/alternative` *message.*

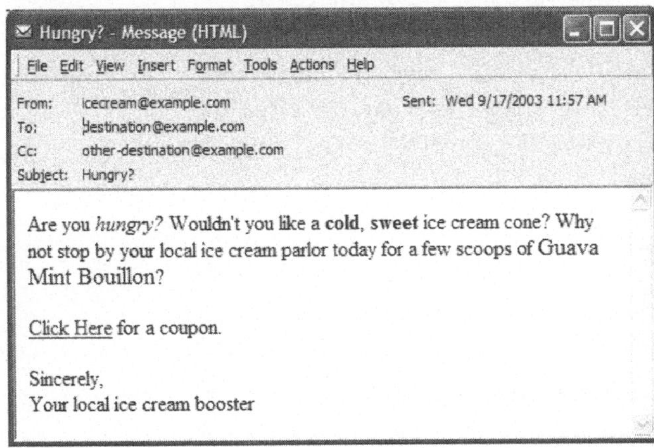

Figure 9-2. Outlook displays the HTML part of a `multipart/alternative` *message.*

The `setHTMLBody()` method supports the same syntax as `setTXTBody()` to specify content in a file instead of in a variable:

```
// Use the contents of /home/icecream/healthy.html as the HTML body
// of the message
$mime->setHTMLBody('/home/icecream/healthy.html', true);
```

Unlike `setTXTBody()`, however, you cannot append content with multiple calls to `setHTMLBody()`. If you call `setHTMLBody()` twice, the content from the second call replaces the content from the first.

Embedded Images

A message with an HTML body can include embedded images. To embed an image in an e-mail message, link to the image with a standard `<img>` tag in the HTML portion of the message and then add the image to the message with the `addHTMLImage()` method. Listing 9-7 sends a message whose HTML portion references two images.

Listing 9-7. Sending a Message with Embedded Images

```
require 'Mail.php';
require 'Mail/mime.php';
$to = 'destination@example.com';
$headers = array('Subject' => 'Hungry?', 'From' => 'icecream@example.com',
                 'Cc' => 'other-destination@example.com');
$text_body=<<<_MSG_
Are you hungry? Wouldn't you like a cold, sweet ice cream cone?
Why not stop by your local ice cream parlor today for a few
scoops of Guava Mint Bouillon?

Sincerely,
Your local ice cream booster
_MSG_;

$html_body=<<<_HTML_
<img src="header.gif" width="250" height="20"/>
<br clear="all"/>
<p>Are you <i>hungry?</i> Wouldn't you like a <b>cold</b>, <b>sweet</b>
ice cream cone? Why not stop by your local ice cream parlor today for
a few scoops of <font size="+1">Guava Mint Bouillon</font>?</p>

<p>Print out this coupon for 50% off a large cone:</p>
<img src="coupon.jpg"/>

<p>Sincerely, <br/>
Your local ice cream booster</p>
_HTML_;

$mime = new Mail_mime();
$mime->setTXTBody($text_body);
$mime->setHTMLBody($html_body);
$mime->addHTMLImage('/usr/local/images/header.gif','image/gif');
$mime->addHTMLImage('/usr/local/images/coupon.jpg','image/jpeg');
$body = $mime->get();
```

```
$headers = $mime->headers($headers);
$mailer =& Mail::factory('mail');
$res = $mailer->send($to, $headers, $body);

// If the message can't be sent, send() returns a
// PEAR::Error object
if (PEAR::isError($res)) {
   print "Couldn't send message: " . $res->getMessage();
}
```

The two required arguments to addHTMLImage() are the filename of the image to add to the message and the MIME media type of the image. For each image added to the message, Mail_mime does two things. First, it adds a new section containing the image to the message. This section has appropriate headers that identify the image's MIME media type and filename. The image section also gets a Content-ID header, which is a unique string to identify the section. The second thing that happens is that any instances of the image's filename in the HTML message body are replaced with the Content-ID value for the image. For example, `<img src="header.gif" width="250" height="20"/>` becomes `<img src="cid:5e74ee95a04dc3d3c740af4f677f0dc7" width="250" height="20"/>`. This new src attribute for the <img> tag tells a mail reader such as Outlook where in the MIME-encoded message it can find the appropriate image to display. Image filenames aren't just replaced inside <img> tags, however, but anywhere in the HTML message body. If you refer to images by filename elsewhere in your HTML, those references change as well.

When you add an image to a message with addHTMLImage(), only the filename portion of the path is preserved. This means you shouldn't add two images with the same name that are in different directories to the same message, for example, /usr/local/images/header.gif and /usr/local/images/sports/header.gif.

An HTML message body can also include references to images that are hosted on a remote server. Instead of sending header.gif along with the message, you can have an <img> tag that retrieves header.gif from your Web server: `<img src="http://images.example.com/mail/header.gif" width="250" height="20"/>`. To see this image, however, a user must be online when he views the message. Additionally, many people bristle at the privacy implications of alerting a remote server (by downloading an image) that they are looking at an e-mail message. This situation is compounded when image URLs include query string information that uniquely identifies a user. On the other hand, messages that reference external URLs are much smaller because they don't include copies of image data.

Whether you use external images or not, it's always a good idea to include a plain-text message body when you include an HTML message body. Even if the plain-text message body contains only a short explanation that the main thrust of the message is located in the HTML section, it makes things much clearer for users who can't see the HTML. If you're sending out a newsletter that can be delivered in either plain text or HTML, a good solution is to ask users when they sign up for the newsletter whether they would like to receive the plain-text or HTML version. Send a regular non-MIME-encoded plain-text message to users who opt for plain text. To users who opt for HTML, send a message with the newsletter content in the HTML body and a short text body telling them what URL to visit if they want to change their subscription to plain text. This saves bandwidth because you don't have to send every user both the text and HTML copies of the message.

Like the `addAttachment()` method, `addHTMLImage()` also accommodates image data stored in a variable instead of a file. This is good for generating an image dynamically and then embedding it in a message.

Listing 9-8 shows how to generate an embedded image with functions from the GD graphics drawing extension to send a registration confirmation code in an e-mail message. Sending the code in an image instead of as plain text thwarts many programs that could otherwise parse the message and automatically complete the registration.

Listing 9-8. Sending a Dynamic Image

```
require 'Mail.php';
require 'Mail/mime.php';
$to = 'destination@example.com';
$headers = array('Subject' => 'Thanks!',
                 'From' => 'icecream@example.com',
                 'Cc' => 'other-destination@example.com');

$text_body=<<<_MSG_
Your confirmation code is listed in the HTML portion of this message.
_MSG_;
$html_body=<<<_HTML_
<p>Thanks for signing up with the Free Ice Cream Club. To prevent
automated registrations, please visit the confirmation URL and
enter the confirmation code displayed in the image below:</p>
<img src="conf-code.png"/>
<br clear="all"/>
<p>The confirmation URL is:</p>
<p><b><a href="http://icecream.example.com/confirm.php">
http://icecream.example.com/confirm.php</a></b></p>
_HTML_;

// Create the confirmation code as three sets of five letters,
// separated by hyphens
$code = ''; $code_length = 15;
while ($code_length--) { $code.= chr(65+mt_rand(0,25)); }
$code = substr($code,0,5) . '-' . substr($code,5,5) . '-' . substr($code,10,5);
```

```
// Use GD to create a 200x50 image with the confirmation code
// in the middle of it. The imagecreatetruecolor() function
// is for GD 2.0.1 or later. Use imagecreate() if you have
// an earlier version of GD.
$im = imagecreatetruecolor(200,50);
$bg_color = imagecolorallocate($im, 0xff, 0xff, 0xff);
$text_color = imagecolorallocate($im, 102, 153, 0);
imagefill($im, 0, 0, $bg_color);
imagestring($im, 5, 23, 15, $code, $text_color);

// GD has no way to put the image data directly into a string, so we use
// output buffering to capture what GD would otherwise send to the browser
ob_start();
imagepng($im);
$image_data = ob_get_contents ();
ob_end_clean();
imagedestroy($im);

// Adding the dynamic image to the message is like adding an image file, but
// with two more arguments to addHTMLImage()
$mime = new Mail_mime();
$mime->setTXTBody($text_body);
$mime->setHTMLBody($html_body);
$mime->addHTMLImage($image_data,'image/png','conf-code.png',false);
$body = $mime->get();
$headers = $mime->headers($headers);
$mailer =& Mail::factory('mail');
$res = $mailer->send($to, $headers, $body);

// If the message can't be sent, send() returns a
// PEAR::Error object
if (PEAR::isError($res)) {
   print "Couldn't send message: " . $res->getMessage();
}
```

When adding a dynamic image with `addHTMLImage()`, four arguments are required. The first argument is the variable holding the image data, and the second argument is the MIME media type of the image. The third argument is the filename to use inside the message for the image. In Listing 9-8, the filename is `conf-code.png` to match the filename in the `src` attribute of the `<img>` tag in the HTML message body. The last argument, `true`, tells `addHTMLImage()` that the first argument holds image data, not the filename of an image. Figure 9-3 shows what the message generated by Listing 9-8 looks like in a text-based e-mail client, and Figure 9-4 shows the message in a graphical e-mail client.

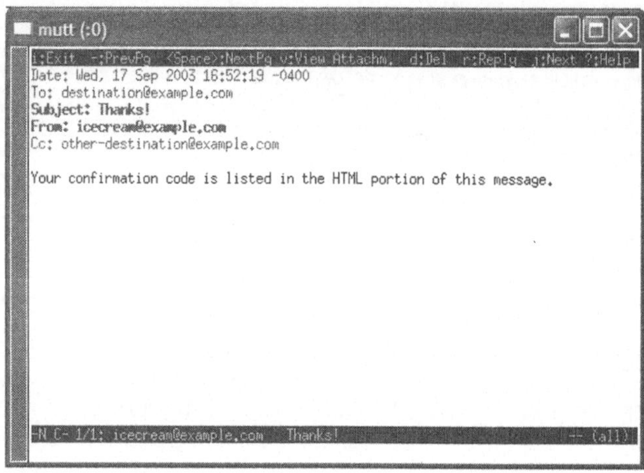

Figure 9-3. Mutt displays the text part of the message.

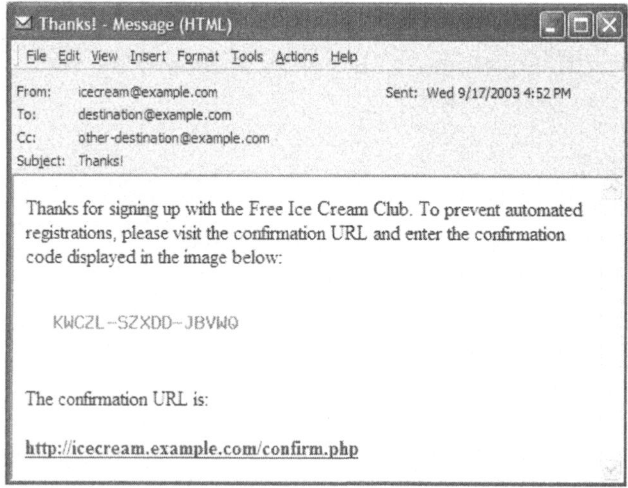

Figure 9-4. Outlook displays the HTML part of the message, including the dynamic image.

A confirmation code embedded in an image is harder for an automated program to process than a plain-text confirmation code, but not impossible.

For more information about distorted embedded text and other mechanisms that are more difficult for computers to parse, visit the CAPTCHA project at `http://www.captcha.net/`.

CHAPTER 10

Working with Authentication, Users, and Passwords

AUTHENTICATION PROVIDES a way to track user behavior on your Web site. Once a user logs in, you can attach their name to a particular message in a forum or other uploaded content. Plus, authentication is a way to restrict access to parts of your site. Making users log in with a username and password prevents random surfers from stumbling upon sensitive data.

This chapter talks about Auth 1.2.2 and Auth_HTTP 2.0. With these modules, you can require users to enter a username and password before accessing certain pages on your site or your entire site. Because these modules build on PHP's built-in session capabilities, they work with or without cookies.

Use Auth when you want to display an HTML-based login form in a page. Use Auth_HTTP when you want to display a browser-based login dialog box. Both modules support a number of back ends for authentication data storage, including databases, flat files, LDAP servers, POP servers, and IMAP servers.

Using the Auth Module

The Auth module handles displaying a login form, managing sessions and expiration times, and verifying passwords. You interact with the Auth module through the methods and properties of the Auth object. When you create a new Auth object, you specify the storage container you want to use. This determines where and how Auth looks for usernames and passwords to match against user input. Table 10-1 lists the storage containers Auth supports.

Table 10-1. Storage Containers for Auth

Name	Description	Additional Module or Extension Dependencies
DB	SQL database via PEAR DB	DB
File	/etc/passwd-style file	File_Passwd
IMAP	Accounts on an IMAP server	imap extension
LDAP	LDAP server	ldap extension
MDB	SQL database via PEAR MDB	MDB
POP3	Accounts on a POP server	Net_POP3
RADIUS	RADIUS server	Auth_Radius, Crypt_CHAP
SMBPasswd	Local Samba password file	File_SMBPasswd
SOAP	SOAP method	SOAP
vpopmail	vpopmail server	vpopmail extension

Calling the Auth constructor is the only time you have to be concerned about the details of how your usernames and passwords are stored. The syntax for displaying a login form, forcing a user to log out, checking what user is logged in, or performing other Auth-related actions is the same no matter what storage container you use. So, although most of the examples in this chapter use the DB storage container, they work with the other containers, too. The section "Using Different Storage Containers" explains how to pass the appropriate information to the Auth constructor to use the other storage containers.

Requiring Login

The most basic operation with Auth is requiring a user to enter a username and password to look at a particular Web page. At a minimum, this operation has four steps:

1. Load the `Auth/Auth.php` file.
2. Instantiate a new Auth object.
3. Call the `start()` method on the Auth object.
4. Call the `getAuth()` method on the Auth object to determine if a user is logged in.

Later in the chapter, you'll see how to modify the behavior of the Auth object by calling various methods between step 2 (instantiating a new Auth object) and step 3 (calling the `start()` method). For now, though, you need only these four steps to make a user log in. Listing 10-1 shows how to require login using the DB storage container.

Listing 10-1. Requiring Login with Auth

```
require 'Auth/Auth.php';
$opts = array('table' => 'users',
              'dsn' => 'mysql://phpgems:phpgems1@localhost/phpgems');
$a = new Auth('DB',$opts);
$a->start();
if (! $a->getAuth()) {
    // the user isn't logged in, so don't show them anything else
    exit();
}
// Anything past here is shown to only those users who are successfully logged in
```

If a user is not logged in, then calling `start()` displays the login form. Figure 10-1 shows the default form. The "Customizing the Login Form" section of this chapter explains how to do just that. The `getAuth()` method returns `true` if a user is logged in and `false` if not. Listing 10-1 uses `getAuth()` to exit if a user is not logged in. If you want to display different information to logged-in and not-logged-in users, use the result of `getAuth()` to control what is displayed.

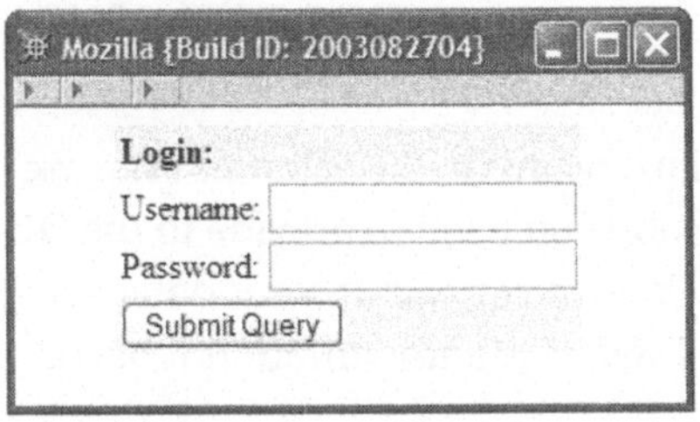

Figure 10-1. The default login form

The Auth module uses PHP's built-in session support. When you use Auth, each visitor to your Web site is assigned a `PHPSESSID` cookie that associates him with a particular session. Auth stores details about the user such as their username and when their login expires in an associative array called `auth` inside the session.

Using Different Storage Containers

This section provides details on five of the most popular storage containers for Auth: DB, MDB, File, SMBPasswd, and SOAP.

DB and MDB

The DB and MDB containers offer access to authentication information stored in a database. The DB container uses the PEAR DB abstraction layer, and the MDB container uses the MDB abstraction layer. Table 10-2 lists the options that these containers accept.

Table 10-2. Options for DB and MDB

Name	Default	Description
table	auth	The table that holds the authentication information
usernamecol	username	The column in table that holds the username
passwordcol	password	The column in table that holds the password
dsn		The DSN for the database that table is in
db_fields		Additional columns other than usernamecol and passwordcol to retrieve
cryptType	md5	How the passwords in passwordcol are encrypted

If you store usernames and MD5-encrypted passwords in the columns username and password in a table called auth, the only option you need to provide to the DB or MDB storage container is a DSN describing how to connect to your database. Use the standard DB and MDB syntax for the DSN. If you use different table or column names, specify those options as well.

Aside from md5, you can use crypt for the cryptType option, which tells Auth that stored passwords are encrypted with PHP's crypt() function. If you specify cryptType as none, then Auth assumes that the stored passwords are not encrypted. Any other value for cryptType is treated as the name of a function that accepts a plain-text password as an argument and returns an encrypted password. For example, to use PHP's built-in sha1() function to encrypt passwords, pass sha1 for cryptType.

The DB and MDB containers can retrieve information other than usernames and passwords from the database and store that information in the authentication session, as shown in the "Accessing Session Data" section. Don't use unchecked external input for the db_fields value because it is inserted without modification into the SQL query that retrieves the authentication information from the database.

At a minimum, the SQL to create a user table is as follows:

```
CREATE TABLE users (
    username varchar(255) NOT NULL,
    password varchar(32) NOT NULL,
    PRIMARY KEY(username)
);
```

You can make the username column shorter than 255 characters if you'd like to limit what users can enter. The password column must be 32 characters to accommodate the 32 character strings that md5(), the default encryption function, generates.

File and SMBPasswd

The File and SMBPasswd containers are for authentication information stored in a Unix /etc/passwd-style file (File) or a Samba password file (SMBPasswd). To use the File container, you must have the File_Passwd PEAR module installed. To use the SMBPasswd container, you must have the File_SMBPasswd PEAR module installed.[1] The File container also works with the password files generated by Apache's htpasswd utility, as long as the passwords in it have been encrypted with the default crypt method.

Both containers accept only one option: the filename to look in for usernames and passwords. This filename should be passed to the Auth constructor instead of an options array. For example:

```
// Use /etc/passwd for authentication
$a = new Auth('File','/etc/passwd');
// Use /etc/samba/smbusers for authentication
$a = new Auth('SMBPasswd','/etc/samba/smbusers');
```

You can't use the File container with /etc/passwd if you are also using shadow password files. This is a limitation of the File_Passwd module on which the File container depends.

SOAP

The SOAP container retrieves authentication information from a SOAP method. Table 10-3 lists the options for this container.

---

1. The File_SMBPasswd PEAR module in turn requires the mhash PHP extension and the Crypt_CHAP PEAR module.

Table 10-3. Options for SOAP

Name	Default	Description
endpoint		The SOAP endpoint to connect to
namespace		The namespace for the authentication method
method		The SOAP method to execute
encoding		The character encoding to use
usernamefield		The name of the parameter to method that contains the username
passwordfield		The name of the parameter to method that contains the password
matchpasswords	true	Should the container match the supplied password with one returned from method
_features		An optional array of additional parameters for method

Listing 10-2 provides an example of how to use the SOAP container.

Listing 10-2. Authentication with the SOAP Container

```
require 'Auth/Auth.php';
$opts = array('endpoint' => 'http://www.example.com/soap-auth-server.php',
              'namespace' => 'urn:Auth_Server',
              'method' => 'verify_user',
              'encoding' => 'utf-8',
              'usernamefield' => 'username',
              'passwordfield' => 'password',
              'matchpasswords' => false);
$a = new Auth('SOAP',$opts);
$a->start();
if (! $a->getAuth()) {
    // the user isn't logged in, so don't show them anything else
        exit();
}
// Anything past here is shown to only those users who are successfully
// logged in
```

The code in Listing 10-2 tells Auth to call a method named `verify_user()` at the endpoint `http://www.example.com/soap-auth-server.php` and to supply the username to `verify_user()` in a string parameter called `username` and the password in a string parameter called `password`. Setting the `matchpasswords` parameter to false means that Auth expects the verify_user() method to compare the supplied password to the stored password and return a SOAP fault if they don't match. Any value can be returned if the passwords match. Auth ignores the actual value—if a SOAP fault isn't returned, Auth considers the username and password as valid. Listing 10-3 shows the code that implements the SOAP server called in Listing 10-2.

Listing 10-3. SOAP Authentication Server

```
require 'SOAP/Server.php';
// A real authentication server wouldn't use a hard-coded
// list of users and passwords like this, but instead get
// the info from an external source like a database
$users = array('funes'  => '7asdfh23',
               'bioy'   => 'J2hy287',
               'jvmoon' => '&#b12y',
               'villar' => 'ju@^216');
class Auth_Server {
    var $__dispatch_map = array();
    function Auth_Server() {
        // verify_user() takes the username and password as
        // arguments and returns an int if the password is OK.
        // Otherwise, it returns a fault
        $this->__dispatch_map['verify_user'] =
            array('in' => array('username' => 'string',
                                'password' => 'string'),
                  'out' => array('is_ok' => 'int'));
        // get_password() returns a struct containing the
        // stored password
        $this->__dispatch_map['get_password'] =
            array('in' => array('username' => 'string',
                                'password' => 'string'),
                  'out' => array('password_struct' => 'struct'));
    }
    // Compare the supplied password to the stored password
    // for $username and return a SOAP_Value or a SOAP_Fault
    function verify_user($username, $password) {
        if (isset($GLOBALS['users'][$username]) &&
            $GLOBALS['users'][$username] == $password) {
            return new SOAP_Value('is_ok','int',1);
        } else {
            return new SOAP_Fault('Bad username/password','Client');
        }
    }
    // If the supplied user exists, return the stored password
    // The SOAP Auth container expects the password to be in
```

```
    // a struct element called "password," not just in a plain string
    function get_password($username,$password) {
        if (isset($GLOBALS['users'][$username])) {
            $s = new SOAP_Value('password','string',
                                $GLOBALS['users'][$username]);
            return new SOAP_Value('password_struct', 'struct',
                                  array('password' => $s));
        } else {
            return SOAP_Fault('No such user','Client');
        }
    }
}
// The standard server setup stuff
$server = new SOAP_Server;
$soapclass = new Auth_Server;
$server->addObjectMap($soapclass,'urn:Auth_Server');
if (isset($_SERVER['REQUEST_METHOD']) &&
    $_SERVER['REQUEST_METHOD']=='POST') {
    $server->service($HTTP_RAW_POST_DATA);
} else {
    require_once 'SOAP/Disco.php';
    $disco = new SOAP_DISCO_Server($server,'Auth_Server');
    header("Content-type: text/xml");
    if (isset($_SERVER['QUERY_STRING']) &&
       strcasecmp($_SERVER['QUERY_STRING'],'wsdl')==0) {
        echo $disco->getWSDL();
    } else {
        echo $disco->getDISCO();
    }
    exit;
}
```

In addition to verify_user(), Listing 10-3 also implements a method called get_password(), which can be used with the SOAP container when matchpasswords is true. If get_password() finds a password for the provided user, it returns it in a struct member named password. After retrieving the password, the SOAP container compares it to the one provided by the user and reports success or failure based on that comparison.

Customizing the Login Page

The default login form that Auth displays is too generic for most situations. The Auth module makes it easy, however, for you to display a custom login form.

Define a function that prints your login form and pass its name as the third argument to the Auth constructor. In Listing 10-4, the `custom_login()` function displays the login form.

Listing 10-4. Using a Customized Login Page

```
require 'Auth/Auth.php';
$opts = array('table' => 'users',
              'dsn' => 'mysql://phpgems:phpgems1@localhost/phpgems');
// define the function to print the login page
function custom_login() {
print<<<_HTML_
<form method="POST" action="$_SERVER[PHP_SELF]">
<table>
<tr bgcolor="#cccccc"><td colspan="2" align="center">Please Log In</td></tr>
<tr><td>Username: </td>
    <td><input type="text" name="username" size="20"/></td></tr>
<tr><td>Password: </td>
        <td><input type="password" name="password" size="20"/></td></tr>
        <tr bgcolor="#cccccc"><td colspan="2" align="center">
        <input type="submit" value="Log In"/></td></tr>
</table>
</form>
_HTML_;
}
// The name of the function that prints the login form is passed to the
// Auth constructor as the third argument
$a = new Auth('DB',$opts,'custom_login');
$a->start();
if (! $a->getAuth()) {
    // the user isn't logged in, so don't show them anything else
    exit();
}
// Anything past here is shown to only those users who are successfully
// logged in
```

Figure 10-2 shows the login form that Listing 10-4 displays. This particular form isn't going to win any Web design awards, but it illustrates how you can tailor the login form display to meet your needs. Two things you can't customize, however, are the form method and the field names. The Auth module looks for the submitted username and password in POST variables called `username` and `password`. If you use a different form method or change the name of the fields, then Auth can't find the data. You can add additional fields to the form, but you must have the `username` and `password` fields.

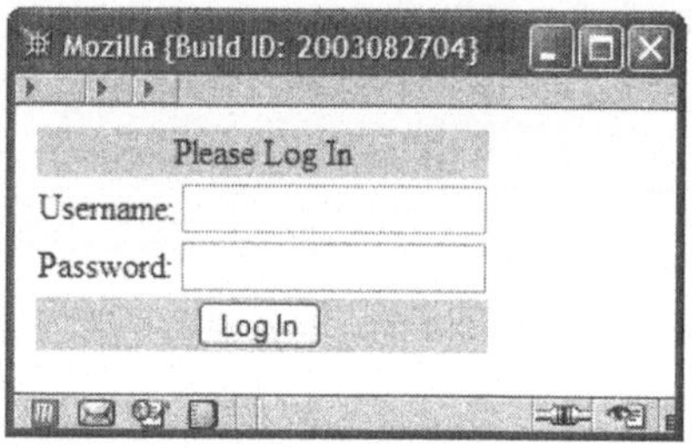

Figure 10-2. A customized login form

Using the customized login form in Listing 10-4, if you enter an invalid username or password, the form is redisplayed with no error message or other indication of what went wrong. You can make your customized login forms slightly more complicated to remedy this absence. The login form function takes two optional arguments. The first is a username, if available, and the second is a login status. Auth passes the username to a custom login function after an unsuccessful login attempt if the username is valid but the password that was entered is not valid. The status passed to the custom login function is one of three constants: `AUTH_IDLED`, `AUTH_EXPIRED`, or `AUTH_WRONG_LOGIN`. The `AUTH_IDLED` constant means that the user is being forced to log in because he has been idle too long, the `AUTH_EXPIRED` constant means that the user is being forced to log in because his session is too old, and the `AUTH_WRONG_LOGIN` constant means that the username and password supplied weren't a valid pair—in other words, the username doesn't exist or the password doesn't match the username. Listing 10-5 shows a custom login function that uses the optional username and status arguments.

Listing 10-5. A Custom Login Function with Username and Status Display

```
require 'Auth/Auth.php';
$opts = array('table' => 'users',
              'dsn' => 'mysql://phpgems:phpgems1@localhost/phpgems');
function custom_login($username = null,$status = null) {
    // If a username was passed in, encode any special
    // characters to prevent a cross-site scripting attack
    if (! is_null($username)) { $username = htmlspecialchars($username); }
    // Create a status message if $status is set
    if (! is_null($status)) {
        if ($status == AUTH_WRONG_LOGIN) {
            $status_msg = 'Incorrect username or password.';
        } elseif ($status == AUTH_IDLED) {
            $status_msg = 'You have been idle too long.';
```

```
        } elseif ($status == AUTH_EXPIRED) {
            $status_msg = 'Your session has expired.';
        }
    } else {
        $status_msg = '';
    }
    // Display the beginning of the form
    print<<<_HTML_
<form method="POST" action="$_SERVER[PHP_SELF]">
<table>
<tr bgcolor="#cccccc"><td colspan="2" align="center">Please Log In</td></tr>
_HTML_;
    // Display a status message if there is one
    if ($status_msg) {
        print '<tr><td colspan="2" align="center"><font color="#ff0000">' .
            $status_msg . '</font></td></tr>';
    }
    // Display the rest of the form
    print<<<_HTML_
<tr><td>Username: </td>
    <td><input type="text" name="username" size="20" value="$username"/>
</td></tr>
<tr><td>Password: </td>
        <td><input type="password" name="password" size="20"/></td></tr>
        <tr bgcolor="#cccccc"><td colspan="2" align="center">
<input type="submit" value="Log In"/></td></tr>
</table>
</form>
_HTML_;
}
$a = new Auth('DB',$opts,'custom_login');
$a->start();
if (! $a->getAuth()) {
    // the user isn't logged in, so don't show them anything else
    exit();
}
// Anything past here is shown only to those users who are successfully
// logged in
```

Figure 10-3 shows the custom login form from Listing 10-5 after it is submitted with the username funes and an incorrect password.

Figure 10-3. A custom login form with an error message

The username and status variables let you present a form with helpful context if a user enters an incorrect username and password. One other important element in custom login forms is the preservation of other form variables. Form variables are passed to a page that doesn't require login with no interference. When the page requires login, however, the login form jumps in before the rest of the page can be processed. When the login form is submitted successfully, the page processing can continue. That page processing needs the original non-login-related form variables to work properly, though. So any non-login-related form variables need to go along for the ride as hidden elements in the login form. Use the `print_hidden_vars()` function defined in Listing 10-6 to include the appropriate hidden elements in the custom login form.

Listing 10-6. A Function to Include Hidden Elements in a Form

```
function print_hidden_vars($ar, $prefix = null) {
    // If an array prefix is passed in, format it properly
    // for hidden element naming and set $suffix
    if (! is_null($prefix)) {
        $prefix = htmlentities($prefix) . '[';
        $suffix = ']';
    } else {
        $prefix = $suffix = null;
    }
    // Iterate through the array
    foreach ($ar as $key => $value) {
        // Skip this array element if we're not iterating through a
        // subarray (i.e. we're in $_GET or $_POST) and the element name
        // is "username" or "password"
        if (is_null($prefix) && (($key === 'username') ||
                                 ($key === 'password'))) {
            continue;
```

```
        }
        // If this array element is itself an array, recurse into it with
        // a proper hidden element name prefix
        if (is_array($value)) {
            print_hidden_vars($value, $prefix . htmlentities($key) . $suffix);
        } else {
            // If this array element is not an array, print out a hidden
            // element form tag with the appropriate name and value
            print '<input type="hidden" name="' .
                $prefix . $key . $suffix . '" value="' .
                htmlentities($value) . '"/>';
        }
    }
}
```

The `print_hidden_vars()` function should be called from the custom login form function once for GET variables and once for POST variables. Listing 10-7 shows the `custom_login()` function from Listing 10-5, slightly modified at the end to call `print_hidden_vars()`.

Listing 10-7. A Custom Login Function That Preserves Form Variables

```
function custom_login($username = null,$status = null) {
    // If a username was passed in, encode any special
    // characters to prevent a cross-site scripting attack
    if (! is_null($username)) { $username = htmlspecialchars($username); }
    // Create a status message if $status is set
    if (! is_null($status)) {
        if ($status == AUTH_WRONG_LOGIN) {
            $status_msg = 'Incorrect username or password.';
        } elseif ($status == AUTH_IDLED) {
            $status_msg = 'You have been idle too long.';
        } elseif ($status == AUTH_EXPIRED) {
            $status_msg = 'Your session has expired.';
        }
    } else {
        $status_msg = '';
    }
    // Display the beginning of the form
    print<<<_HTML_
<form method="POST" action="$_SERVER[PHP_SELF]">
<table>
<tr bgcolor="#cccccc"><td colspan="2" align="center">Please Log In</td></tr>
```

```
_HTML_;
    // Display a status message if there is one
    if ($status_msg) {
        print '<tr><td colspan="2" align="center"><font color="#ff0000">' .
            $status_msg . '</font></td></tr>';
    }
    // Display the rest of the form
    print<<<_HTML_
<tr><td>Username: </td>
    <td><input type="text" name="username" size="20" value="$username"/>
</td></tr>
<tr><td>Password: </td>
        <td><input type="password" name="password" size="20"/></td></tr>
        <tr bgcolor="#cccccc"><td colspan="2" align="center">
<input type="submit" value="Log In"/></td></tr>
</table>
_HTML_;
    print_hidden_vars($_GET);
    print_hidden_vars($_POST);
    print '</form>';
}
```

Making Login Optional

When you call start(), Auth displays the login form if a user isn't already logged in. This is ideal for pages that require login but not for pages where login is optional. For example, on a message board page, you could display messages to all users, logged in or not, but only include a Post a Message button if a user is logged in.

You can make login optional with an additional step before calling Auth's start() method. Call setShowLogin() with an argument of false. Then, after calling start(), use getAuth() to determine if a user is logged in. This method returns true when a user is logged in and false otherwise. Listing 10-8 demonstrates a page with optional login that displays different information to logged-in and not-logged-in users.

Listing 10-8. Optional Login

```
require 'Auth/Auth.php';
$opts = array('table' => 'users',
              'dsn' => 'mysql://phpgems:phpgems1@localhost/phpgems');
$a = new Auth('DB',$opts);
$a->setShowLogin(false);
$a->start();
```

```
// Everyone gets welcomed
print "Welcome, ";
// Greet the user appropriately
if ($a->getAuth()) {
    print "logged-in user!";
} else {
    print "guest.";
}
```

When a logged-in user accesses the page in Listing 10-8, he sees a "Welcome, logged-in user!" message. When a not-logged-in user accesses the page, he sees a "Welcome, guest!" message. In the "Accessing Session Data" section later in the chapter, you'll see how to display information such as a username that changes based on which user is logged in.

Forcing Logout

To log out a user, call the `logout()` method after calling `start()`. When using `logout()`, you should also call `setShowLogin(false)`. This prevents displaying the login form if you attempt to log out a non-logged-in user. Listing 10-9 shows how to log out a user.

Listing 10-9. Forcing Logout

```
require 'Auth/Auth.php';
$opts = array('table' => 'users',
              'dsn' => 'mysql://phpgems:phpgems1@localhost/phpgems');
$a = new Auth('DB',$opts);
$a->setShowLogin(false);
$a->start();
$a->logout();
print "You are now logged out.";
```

Understanding Expiration and Idle Time

An authentication session has an expiration time and a maximum allowable idle time. The expiration time is the number of seconds, counting from when a user logs in successfully, that her authentication session lasts. If that expiration time is 3,600 seconds (1 hour), then after an hour, the user is automatically logged out and she must log in again. The maximum allowable idle time is the amount of time that Auth allows to elapse between requests without logging out the user.

If the idle time is 1,800 seconds (30 minutes), then a user can log in at noon, request a page at 12:15, 12:44, and 1:09, and never have to log in again because there are fewer than 30 minutes between each request. But if the user logs in at noon, requests pages at 12:01, 12:02, and then at 12:33, she is presented with a login form on the last request because more than 30 minutes have elapsed since her previous request.

The expiration time and maximum allowable idle time both default to zero, which means that authentication sessions never expire and any amount of idle time is allowable.[2]

To change the expiration time, call `setExpire()`. To change the maximum allowable idle time, call `setIdle()`. Call these methods before you call `start()` for them to have the appropriate effect:

```
require 'Auth/Auth.php';
$opts = array('table' => 'users',
              'dsn' => 'mysql://phpgems:phpgems1@localhost/phpgems');
$a = new Auth('DB',$opts);
// This auth session lasts one day from when the user logs in
$a->setExpire(86400);
// The user can't be idle for more than an hour
$a->setIdle(3600);
$a->start();
```

The `setExpire()` and `setIdle()` methods also accept an optional second argument. When this argument is `true`, then the expiration time or idle time in the first argument is added to the existing expiration time or idle time. For example, to increment the expiration time by one hour and the idle time by two hours, use this:

```
$a->setExpire(3600, true);
$a->setIdle(7200, true);
```

You can pass negative numbers to decrease expiration time or idle time, but these methods don't do any checking to prevent you from setting either value to something less than zero.

---

2. The authentication session expiration time is separate from the underlying session module garbage collection lifetime set by the `session.gc_maxlifetime` configuration setting. The `session.gc_maxlifetime` setting controls how often the session module deletes (or *garbage collects*) old sessions. Make sure `session.gc_maxlifetime` is set to a larger value than your authentication session expiration time or maximum allowed idle time. If you set authentication session expiration time and maximum idle time to `0`, set `session.gc_probability` to `0` to prevent the underlying session module from ever garbage collecting sessions.

Accessing Session Data

The getUsername() method returns the username of the currently logged-in user. The username is good for personalizing pages and making it obvious to a logged-in user that they are indeed logged in. Listing 10-10 updates Listing 10-8 by changing the message for a logged-in user to include the username.

Listing 10-10. Displaying a Username

```
require 'Auth/Auth.php';
$opts = array('table' => 'users',
              'dsn' => 'mysql://phpgems:phpgems1@localhost/phpgems');
$a = new Auth('DB',$opts);
$a->setShowLogin(false);
$a->start();
// Everyone gets welcomed
print "Welcome, ";
// Greet the user appropriately
if ($a->getAuth()) {
    print $a->getUsername() . '!';
} else {
    print "guest.";
}
```

When user funes retrieves the page in Listing 10-10, he sees a "Welcome, funes!" message.

The DB and MDB storage containers also provide a way to include arbitrary additional information about a user in a session. Specify a comma-separated list of field names in the db_fields option to the storage container, and those fields are retrieved from the database when the user logs in. The fields are available through the getAuthData() method. Listing 10-11 demonstrates this with two additional fields, full_name and job. These fields are in the users table of the database from which the username and password are also retrieved.

Listing 10-11. Accessing Additional Session Data

```
require 'Auth/Auth.php';
$opts = array('table' => 'users',
              'db_fields' => 'full_name,job',
              'dsn' => 'mysql://phpgems:phpgems1@localhost/phpgems');
$a = new Auth('DB',$opts);
$a->start();
```

```
if (! $a->getAuth()) {
    // the user isn't logged in, so don't show them anything else
    exit();
}
// Anything past here is shown to only those users who are successfully
// logged in
print 'Hello, ' . $a->getAuthData('full_name') . '. ';
print 'Do you like working as a ' . $a->getAuthData('job') . '?';
```

Adding and Removing Users

The DB, MDB, File, and SMBPasswd containers provide methods to add and remove users from the storage container. These methods are called `addUser()` and `removeUser()`. To add a user, pass `addUser()` the username and plain-text password to add. This code adds a user with the username `funes` and password `forking!path`:

```
require 'Auth/Auth.php';
$opts = array('table' => 'users',
              'dsn' => 'mysql://phpgems:phpgems1@localhost/phpgems');
$a = new Auth('DB',$opts);
$a->addUser('funes','forking!path');
```

The `addUser()` method also supports creating accounts with information in addition to the username and password. For the DB and MDB containers, pass the additional fields and values in an associative array as the third parameter to `addUser()`. For example, this code adds the user `funes` with values for the `full_name` and `job` database fields:

```
require 'Auth/Auth.php';
$opts = array('table' => 'users',
              'dsn' => 'mysql://phpgems:phpgems1@localhost/phpgems');
$a = new Auth('DB',$opts);
$a->addUser('funes','forking!path', array('full_name' => 'Ireneo Funes',
                                          'job' => 'Plumber'));
```

For the File container, you can specify a string that is written to the end of a new line in the password file. In a standard Unix password file, this is colon-delimited string of user ID, group ID, full name, home directory, and shell. For example:

```
require 'Auth/Auth.php';
$a = new Auth('File','/etc/passwd');
$a->addUser('funes','forking!path',
            '500:500:Ireneo Funes:/home/funes:/bin/bash');
```

This creates a new line in the password file that looks like this:

```
funes:$1$i6kNxuqk$CFhvp1cDUJj/XQo23CKOu/:500:500:Ireneo Funes:/home/funes:/bin/bash
```

Alternatively, you can specify a CVS user ID in the cvsuser element of the associative array. This is useful for CVS pserver-style password files:

```
require 'Auth/Auth.php';
$a = new Auth('File','/etc/passwd');
$a->addUser('funes','forking!path', array('cvsuser' => 'villar'));
```

This creates a line in the password file that looks like this:

```
funes:$1$tsoKnNLp$Ely6jDyESFK/DOeNZWDuR/:villar
```

With the SMBPasswd container, the only additional information you can specify is a numeric user ID in the userid element of the associative array:

```
require 'Auth/Auth.php';
$a = new Auth('SMBPasswd','/etc/smbpasswd');
$a->addUser('funes','forking!path', array('userid' => 27));
```

To remove a user, pass removeUser() the username to remove. This code removes the user funes:

```
require 'Auth/Auth.php';
$opts = array('table' => 'users',
              'dsn' => 'mysql://phpgems:phpgems1@localhost/phpgems');
$a = new Auth('DB',$opts);
$a->removeUser('funes');
```

The addUser() and removeUser() methods require the appropriate permission to write to the storage container. For the DB and MDB containers, this means that the database user specified in the DSN must have database INSERT permission to add a user and database DELETE permission to remove a user. For the File and SMBPasswd containers, this means that the user your Web server is running as needs write access to the password file. The File container also requires write access to the directory the running script is in for a temporary lockfile.

Auth_HTTP

The Auth_HTTP module builds on Auth to offer browser-based HTTP Basic authentication. Instead of displaying an HTML login form for login, Auth_HTTP sends headers that tell your browser to pop up an authentication dialog box like the one pictured in Figure 10-4.

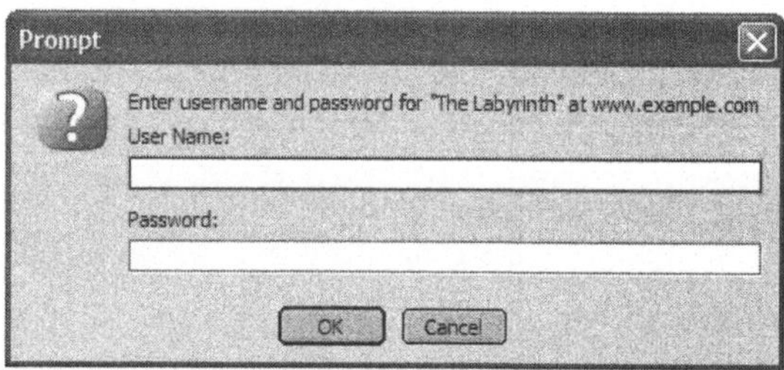

Figure 10-4. A browser-based authentication dialog box

Using the Auth_HTTP module is similar to using the Auth module. Listing 10-12 shows how to require login using Auth_HTTP.

Listing 10-12. HTTP-Based Login

```
require 'Auth/HTTP.php';
$opts = array('table' => 'users',
              'dsn' => 'mysql://phpgems:phpgems1@localhost.home/phpgems');
$a = new Auth_HTTP('DB',$opts);
$a->setRealm('The Labyrinth');
$a->start();
if (! $a->getAuth()) {
    // the user isn't logged in, so don't show them anything else
    exit();
}
// Anything past here is shown only to those users who are successfully
// logged in
```

There are three differences between Listing 10-12 and the basic Auth example in Listing 10-1:

- The `require` statement loads the file `Auth/HTTP.php` instead of `Auth/Auth.php`.
- The variable `$a` is instantiated as a new `Auth_HTTP` object instead of an Auth object.
- The `setRealm()` method is called.

A *realm* is a name for a section of your Web site protected by HTTP authentication. If you require separate logins for two sections of your site, use different realm names for each. The realm also appears in the browser authentication dialog box. Figure 10-4 is a result of the code in Listing 10-12. The code calls `setRealm('The Labyrinth')`, so the dialog box asks, "Enter username and password for 'The Labyrinth.'"

The `Auth_HTTP` class also has a `setCancelText()` method, which sets what the user sees if he hits Cancel in the authentication dialog box or otherwise refuses to present valid authentication credentials. The default cancel text is "Error 401 - Access denied," which you may want to change to something more appropriate for your application.

Using Auth_HTTP provides a good alternative to Auth when you don't want to embed a login form in a page. However, the only reliable method for users to log out of browser-based authentication is to quit their browsers. Different Web browsers cache authentication credentials in different ways, so there is no standard method to tell a browser to forget about a username and password for a particular realm.

Part Five

Debugging, Caching, and Optimizing

CHAPTER 11

Understanding PHP Internals

TO GET THE MOST out of the debugger and code cache chapters that follow, you should understand what happens under the hood when a PHP program runs and generates a Web page. This chapter provides a look inside PHP and explains what happens when a PHP script executes.

Strictly speaking, this chapter is mostly about a piece of software called the Zend Engine that forms the core of PHP. The Zend Engine takes care of the structure of the language—the fact that you enclose a function body in curly braces, that semicolons end each line, and that keywords such as `foreach`, `while`, and `else` have special meanings. Sitting on top of the Zend Engine are the libraries of PHP functions that do everything from generate dynamic images to encode special characters in URLs.

The Zend Engine sets the grammar rules, and PHP provides the vocabulary for your programs. The engine defines the language syntax, and PHP defines the semantics. The engine is responsible for you writing this:

```
function encode_and_reverse($s) {
     return strrev(urlencode($s));
}
```

instead of, for example, this:

```
sub encode_and_reverse() {
     strrev(urlencode($_));
}
```

But the fact that the `strrev()` function reverses a string and the `urlencode()` function hex-encodes special characters in a string is outside the Zend Engine's scope of responsibility. The engine simply sets out the rules for how to define a function and how to call a function, but it doesn't have anything to say about the code that implements a particular function.[1]

1. However, some low-level functions, such as printing and arithmetic, are part of the engine itself.

Going from Source File to Output

There is a furious amount of activity between the time a Web server receives a request for a PHP page and the time it returns the generated output back to the client. Usually, all of the processing happens so quickly, though, that it's hard to believe there's so much going on. Figure 11-1 shows the three major steps involved in running a PHP script.

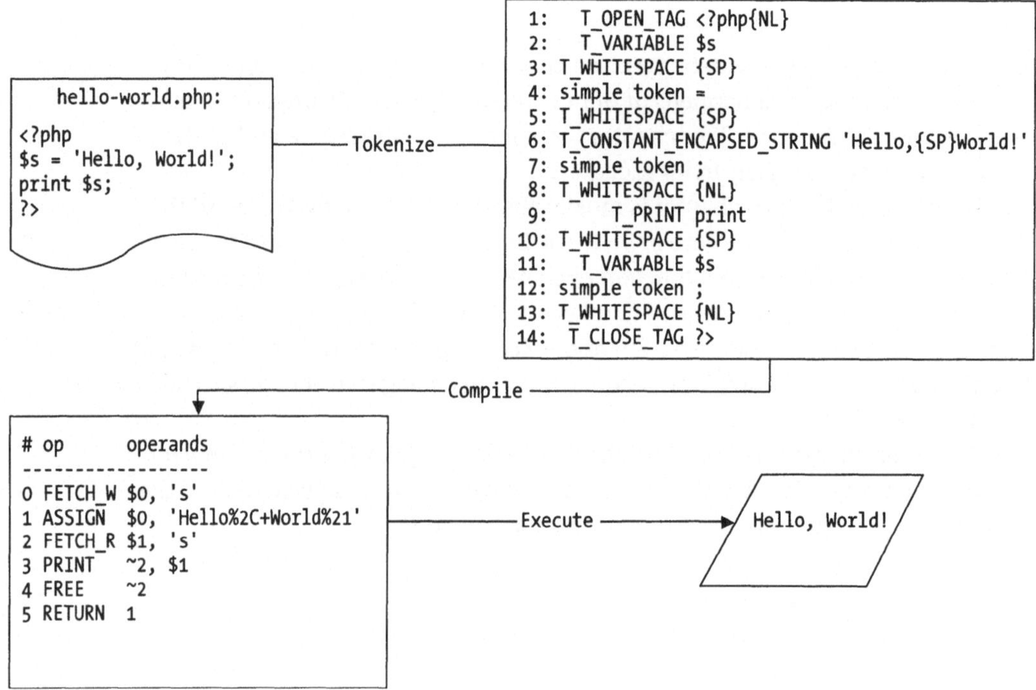

Figure 11-1. The steps from a PHP source file to output

The three steps in Figure 11-1 are tokenize, compile, and execute:

- **Tokenize**: This standardizes the potentially messy text of a PHP file into a regularized series of symbols, called *tokens*, that are easier for the Zend Engine to process.
- **Compile**: This turns the list of tokens into instructions, called *opcodes*, for the Zend Engine. Each opcode tells the Zend Engine to take a particular action, such as adding two numbers or printing a string.
- **Execute**: The Zend Engine follows the instructions of the opcodes, producing whatever result the script is supposed to, such as displaying text or accessing a database.

Initially, the Zend Engine reads a file from disk and tokenizes it. *Tokenizing* is the process of scanning through the entire file and turning the plain text of `hello-world.php` into a series of language tokens. This is sort of like the sentence diagramming you might have learned in junior high school English class. For example, the Zend Engine turns the PHP code `$monkeys+=12` into the tokens `T_VARIABLE`, `T_PLUS_EQUAL`, and `T_LNUMBER`.[2]

Syntax errors in the source file are found during the tokenizing process. Listing 11-1 has a syntax error: An asterisk is not allowed in a variable name.

Listing 11-1. Syntax Error: Bad Character in a Variable Name

```
$*monkeys += 12;
```

When given the code in Listing 11-1, PHP reports a parse error. PHP 4 prints the following:

```
Parse error: parse error, expecting 'T_VARIABLE' or "$"
```

PHP 5 is a little more helpful, telling you what character was inappropriate:

```
Parse error: parse error, unexpected '*', expecting T_VARIABLE or '$'
```

What the error message means is that after the `$`, the parser was looking for either a variable name to indicate a variable such as `$monkeys` or another `$` to indicate a variable variable such as `$$animal`.

As soon as the tokenizer encounters a parse error, it quits. When handed a program with multiple syntax errors, PHP prints an error message and exits after seeing the first syntax error. If you fix that error and run the program again, PHP quits after seeing the next syntax error. And so on. If the parser can't tokenize the entire program successfully, it doesn't hand off control to the next stage in the process.

You can examine the tokenized representations of PHP source files with the functions in the tokenizer extension. The `token_get_all()` function returns an array of the tokens that correspond to the PHP code passed into the function. Each element in that array is either a string or an array. The string elements are simple tokens such as `;` or `=`. These tokens are "simple" because they have no additional information associated with them. The array elements are for tokens such as `T_VARIABLE`. These tokens do have additional information. With a `T_VARIABLE` token, for example, the additional information is the variable name.

Each token has an ID number assigned to it by the Zend Engine. The first element of the array is this number, and the second element of the array is the

---

2. The PHP Manual lists all of the possible tokens at `http://www.php.net/tokens`.

associated content. For example, $monkeys is a T_VARIABLE token. Because T_VARIABLE's token number is 306, the token array for $monkeys is (306,"monkeys"). The Zend Engine deals internally with tokens just by their assigned number. The text representations, such as T_VARIABLE, are for human convenience. The token_name() function translates from token numbers such as 306 to their string equivalents such as T_VARIABLE. Listing 11-2 is a program that prints the tokenized representation of a PHP script.

Listing 11-2. Printing Tokens

```
// Load the PHP source code
$s = file_get_contents($argv[1]);
// Compute all of the tokens in the code
$tokens = token_get_all($s);
// Initialize token count
$i = 1;
foreach ($tokens as $token) {
    printf('%3d: ',$i);
    if (is_array($token)) {
        // $token[1] is the token content, we'll replace whitespace
        // to make it more readable
        $t_content = str_replace(array("\n",' ',),array('{NL}','{SP}'),
                                $token[1]);
        // Print the symbolic token name and the content
        printf("%12s %s\n",token_name($token[0]), $t_content);
    } else {
        // Print the simple token string
        print "simple token $token\n";
    }
    $i++;
}
```

Listing 11-3 is a one-line program, and Listing 11-4 is the output of the token printing program in Listing 11-2 when operating on that one-line program.

Listing 11-3. More Monkeys, Please

```
<?php
$monkeys += 12;
?>
```

Listing 11-4. Tokenized Monkey Incrementing

```
1:   T_OPEN_TAG <?php{NL}
2:   T_VARIABLE $monkeys
```

```
3: T_WHITESPACE {SP}
4: T_PLUS_EQUAL +=
5: T_WHITESPACE {SP}
6:     T_LNUMBER 12
7: simple token ;
8: T_WHITESPACE {NL}
9:  T_CLOSE_TAG ?>{NL}
```

As you can see, every character in the source file is accounted for in the token list. Even the whitespace between operators and at the end of the lines corresponds to `T_WHITESPACE` tokens.

After a file has been successfully tokenized, the compiler goes to work, turning the sequence of tokens into opcodes. As tokens formalize the text of a source file, opcodes formalize tokens into a list of instructions. The opcodes are instructions for a PHP virtual machine, just like Java bytecodes are instructions for the Java virtual machine. (Although a language such as C is compiled to low-level assembly language instructions handled directly by the CPU, each PHP opcode is handled by a function, written in C, inside the PHP virtual machine.)

Each function and class method in a PHP program is compiled into an opcode list, and the code at the global scope in the program is compiled into an opcode list as well. The compiler also creates tables of all of the functions and classes that are defined in the program.

The VLD extension prints the opcode list that the compiler generates for a particular input.[3] Listing 11-5 shows what VLD prints for the code in Listing 11-3.

Listing 11-5. More Monkeys, Please: Opcodes

```
line     # op                           fetch          ext  operands
-------------------------------------------------------------------------------
   2     0 FETCH_RW                     local               $0, 'monkeys'
         1 ASSIGN_ADD                                        $0, 12
   4     2 RETURN                                            1
```

The one-line program in Listing 11-3, which is parsed into the nine tokens in Listing 11-4, becomes the three opcodes in Listing 11-5. Each opcode takes one or two operands as arguments and returns a result. Opcodes are listed in the `op` column. Results and operands are listed in the `operands` column.

The first opcode, `FETCH_RW`, associates the register `$0` with the variable `$monkeys`. Reading the register yields the value of the variable, and changing the register changes the value of the variable. The Zend Engine uses registers as scratch space during computations. The next operand, `ASSIGN_ADD`, adds its second operand to its first and assigns the result to the first operand. In this case, it adds `12` to register

---

3. VLD is available for download at `http://www.derickrethans.nl/vld.php`.

$0 and assigns the result to register $0. The last opcode, RETURN, is the last instruction in every PHP program. The RETURN opcode signals the end of the program.

Let's look at another example. Listing 11-6 contains a more complicated PHP program, and Listing 11-7 shows the corresponding opcodes.

Listing 11-6. Another PHP Program

```
$now = time();
if (($now % 2) == 0) {
    print "Even seconds";
} else {
    print "Odd Seconds";
}
```

Listing 11-7. Opcodes for Listing 11-6

```
line     #  op                           fetch          ext  operands
-------------------------------------------------------------------------------
   1     0  DO_FCALL                                      0  $1, 'time', 0
         1  FETCH_W                                          $0, 'now'
         2  ASSIGN                                           $0, $1
   2     3  FETCH_R                                          $3, 'now'
         4  MOD                                              ~4, $3, 2
         5  IS_EQUAL                                         ~5, ~4, 0
         6  JMPZ                                             ~5, ->10
   3     7  PRINT                                            ~6, 'Even+seconds'
         8  FREE                                             ~6
   4     9  JMP                                              ->12
   5    10  PRINT                                            ~7, 'Odd+Seconds'
        11  FREE                                             ~7
   8    12  RETURN                                           1
```

Listing 11-6 calls the time() function and then prints a message that depends on whether the value returned from time() is odd or even. How is that task represented in the opcodes of Listing 11-7?

Instruction 0, DO_FCALL, calls a function. Its operands indicate that the function being called is named time, the function is passed zero arguments, and the result of the function should be put in register $1.

Instruction 1, FETCH_W, associates register $0 with the variable $now for writing. The FETCH_RW opcode in Listing 11-5 allows reading the value of a variable or writing a new value. FETCH_W is just for writing a new value.

Instruction 2, ASSIGN, assigns the value of register $1 to register $0. This puts the result of time() into $now.

Instruction 3, FETCH_R, associates register $3 with $now for reading.

Instruction 4, MOD, computes the value of register $3 mod 2 and stores the value in the temporary variable ~4. In VLD output, $ is used to indicate registers, and ~ is used to indicate temporary variables.

Instruction 5, IS_EQUAL, tests if temporary variable ~4 is equal to 0. If it is, then temporary variable ~5 is set to 1; otherwise, ~5 is set to 0.

Instruction 6, JMPZ, means "jump if zero." If temporary variable ~5 is 0, then control jumps to opcode 10. Temporary variable ~5 is 0 if temporary variable ~4 (the result of `$now % 2`) is not zero. This means that the jump happens if $now is odd.

Instruction 7, PRINT, prints the string `Even seconds`. VLD URL-encodes strings before displaying them, which is why Listing 11-6 shows this string as Even+seconds. The return value of the `print` statement (which is always 1) is stored in the temporary variable ~6.

Instruction 8, FREE, frees the resources used for the temporary variable ~6. The compiler recognizes that ~6 isn't used in the program anymore, so it inserts the FREE opcode to clean up the space used by the temporary variable.

Instruction 9, JMP, jumps to instruction 12. This has the effect of skipping over the `else` clause because the `if` test expression was `true`.

Instruction 10, PRINT, prints the string `Odd seconds`. This instruction is the target of the jump in instruction 6. The return value of the `print` statement is stored in ~7.

Instruction 11, FREE, frees temporary variable ~7.

Instruction 12, RETURN, signals the end of the script. It provides a jump target for instruction 9 so that the `else` clause of the `if` statement can be skipped.

After the compiler is finished building the opcode lists, control passes to the executor, which starts at the top of the opcode list for the code in the global scope and executes each opcode. At this point, your PHP program is finally doing something familiar, such as printing a form or talking to a database. Each opcode triggers the executor to call a C function particular to that opcode. These C functions are called *opcode handlers*. The opcode handler for the MOD opcode does the modulus division operation specified by the operands. The opcode handler for the PRINT opcode calls another Zend Engine function that in turn calls a printing function. There are about 150 opcodes in the Zend Engine virtual machine, and each has their own opcode handler.

Beyond those shown in the examples in this chapter, there are lots more opcodes to handle arrays, classes, loops, and all of the other language features of PHP. No matter how complicated, every PHP program is boiled down to a set of opcode lists that run in the Zend Engine virtual machine.

The tokenize/compile/execute process happens for the main PHP script being executed as well as for any included files.[4] The tokenizing and compiling

---

4. Included or required files are handled identically except that if there is a problem with a required file, script execution halts.

of an included file happens at runtime, when the command to include the file (the opcode INCLUDE_OR_EVAL) is encountered by the executor. So, any parse errors or other problems in included files aren't discovered until after the main script starts running.

Seeing How a Code Cache Works

All of the steps described in the previous section occur on every request for a PHP page. The page is loaded from disk by the Zend Engine, tokenized, and compiled into opcodes. Then the opcode list is executed. Every include file referenced by the main page also has to be loaded, tokenized, compiled, and executed.

A code cache prevents this tremendous repetition of effort by storing the opcode lists that correspond to a particular file, as well as lists of the functions and classes defined in the file. The first time that file is needed in response to a request or an include command, it is tokenized, compiled, and executed in the usual way. However, the opcode, function, and class lists aren't discarded when the request is over. The code cache keeps them around (on disk or in shared memory, depending on how the cache is configured).

The next time PHP needs to execute the same file, the code cache steps in and provides the already-compiled opcode list. PHP doesn't have to retokenize and recompile the file. Figure 11-2 shows how the code cache can skip the tokenization and compilation steps for a file it has already seen.

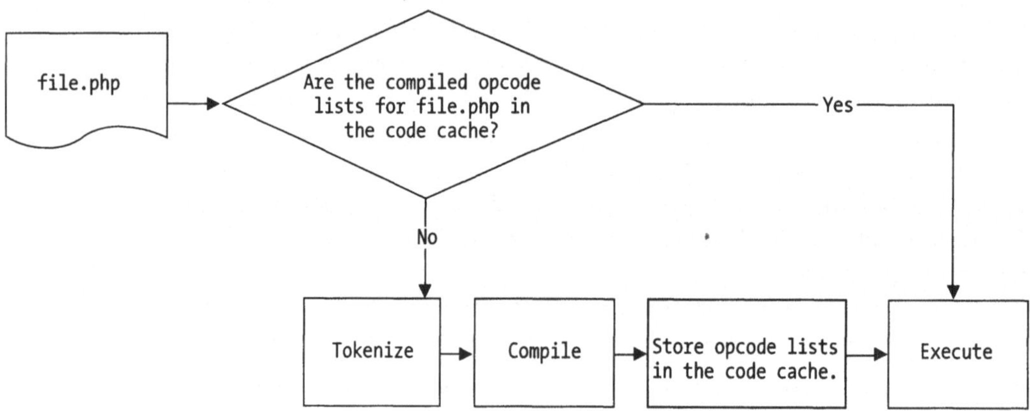

Figure 11-2. Running a PHP script with a code cache

Seeing How a Debugger Works

A debugger replaces the C-level compilation and executor functions in the Zend Engine with its own functions. These new functions call the built-in compilation and executor functions for the actual compilation and execution of the PHP script, but they also keep track of timing information, function calls, and other program execution data. The debugger's functions act like a secretary to the high-powered CEO that is the Zend Engine. You can't call the CEO on the phone directly. Instead, you have to call the CEO's office and talk to the secretary. The assistant then passes your call on and keeps track of who is calling and how long you talk.

When you run a PHP script with a debugger installed, the actual opcodes of your script still run, but the debugger sits on top of the Zend Engine making notes as the program runs.

With the information it gathers, the debugger can do many things:

- **Profiling**: Computing how long functions take to compile and execute. Where does the program spend its time when running?

- **Function call tracing**: Listing which functions call which other functions. What is the path taken through your code when it runs?

- **Code coverage tracing**: Tracking which lines of code are actually executed. Are there lines in your program that never run?

- **Breakpoint management**: Stopping execution at a particular place so you can inspect the environment. When a certain line of code is reached, what are the values of local variables?

Examining Some Differences Between the Internals of PHP 4 and PHP 5

The big difference between PHP 4 and PHP 5 is that they use different versions of the Zend Engine. PHP 4 uses Zend Engine 1, and PHP 5 uses Zend Engine 2. Zend Engine 2 has new capabilities and opcodes that enable PHP 5 features such as exceptions and revamped object handling.

Because of the separation between the Zend Engine and PHP, PHP built-in functions continue to work in PHP 5 as they did in PHP 4. However, the new engine functionality has been used in some PHP 5–specific extensions such as SimpleXML. PHP 5's object model allows for extensions to take control over every aspect of object usage. Instead of a generic handler for all objects that must retrieve a object property from an internal list of property names and values, objects in PHP 5 can have a handler that does just about anything when a property access is attempted. For example, when you access a property of a SimpleXML document object, the SimpleXML extension is able to intercept that property access, find the appropriate XML tag in its internal representation of an XML document, and return that tag as a string or another SimpleXML document object.

The organization of the executor is also different in PHP 5. In PHP 4, the executor function contains a giant `switch` statement whose cases check the value of the current opcode and call appropriate functions for the opcode. In PHP 5, as mentioned in the "Going from Source File to Output" section of this chapter, the executor maintains a table of opcode handler functions and calls the function pointed to in the table for a particular opcode. The opcode handler function table makes it easy in PHP 5 to change the handler function for an opcode. For example, you could use this functionality if you wanted to write an extension that timed how long each opcode took to execute. You would override each opcode handler with a new function, written in C. This function would record the time, call the original opcode handler, and then record the time again. The difference in time values is how long the original opcode handler takes to run.

CHAPTER 12

Profiling and Debugging with Xdebug

LEARN HOW TO EFFICIENTLY optimize your PHP programs with the Xdebug extension. With it, you can examine the flow of function calls in your programs and get detailed statistics about how long it takes for each function to execute. By focusing your efforts on the slowest parts of your program, you get the most out of the time spent optimizing and debugging.

Xdebug also supports remote debugging and includes a remote debugging client for you to use. In remote debugging mode, your running PHP script connects with the remote debugging client. From this client, you can inspect variables in the running script, stop execution at particular lines in the script, and look under the covers of a running PHP program.

This chapter covers Xdebug version 1.3.0.

Installing Xdebug

The easiest way to install Xdebug is with the `pear install` command:

```
% pear install xdebug
```

This installs the Xdebug module into your PHP installation. Because Xdebug is a PHP extension written in C, `pear install` needs to know the location of your C compiler and some other configuration settings. If installation via PEAR doesn't work (because, for example, your C compiler is in a nonstandard location), you have two other choices: You can download a binary Xdebug module from `http://www.xdebug.org`, or you can download the source code and build Xdebug yourself.

The front page of `http://www.xdebug.org/` contains links to available Xdebug binary downloads. Copy the downloaded file (ending in `.so` for Linux and Mac OS X or ending in `.dll` for Windows) to the appropriate extension directory.[1]

To build Xdebug on Unix, download the `.tar.gz` source code archive from `http://www.xdebug.org/` and unpack it. Change into the `xdebug-1.3.0/` directory, and

1. The extension directory is the value of the `extension_dir` configuration setting.

run phpize to create the necessary configuration scripts.[2] Then, run ./configure and make to build the xdebug.so file. Last, run make install to copy the xdebug.so file into PHP's extension directory. You may have to run make install as the superuser for proper file access permissions.

Whether you install Xdebug with pear install, use a binary module, or build from the source code, you must adjust your PHP configuration to make it Xdebug-aware. Add a zend_extension line that specifies the location of the xdebug.so file to the php.ini file. For example:

```
zend_extension=/usr/local/lib/php/extensions/no-debug-non-zts-20020429/xdebug.so
```

If you're using the CGI or CLI version of PHP, the PHP binary reads the .ini file each time it runs, so PHP is immediately Xdebug-aware. If you're using a Web server–embedded version of PHP, you need to restart the Web server to signal PHP about the configuration change.

Tracing Functions

Xdebug's tracing feature keeps track of function calls in your PHP programs. To see a list of all function calls in your program, call xdebug_start_trace() to tell Xdebug to start tracking function calls and then call xdebug_dump_function_trace() to print a list of all the functions called since xdebug_start_trace(). The short program in Listing 12-1 counts the number of letters and nonletters in the value of $phrase. The output of xdebug_dump_function_trace(), shown in Figure 12-1, illustrates how various functions are called in Listing 12-1.

Listing 12-1. Counting Letters and Tracing Functions

```
xdebug_start_trace();
function letter() { $GLOBALS['letter']++; }
function something_else() { $GLOBALS['something_else']++; }
$phrase = "Is 5 OK?";
for ($i = 0, $j = strlen($phrase); $i < $j; $i++) {
    if (preg_match('/[[:alpha:]]/', $phrase{$i})) {
        letter();
    } else {
        something_else();
    }
}
print "Letters: $letter, Other: $something_else";
xdebug_dump_function_trace();
```

2. The phpize program is installed when PHP is installed. It should be in the same directory as the php binary.

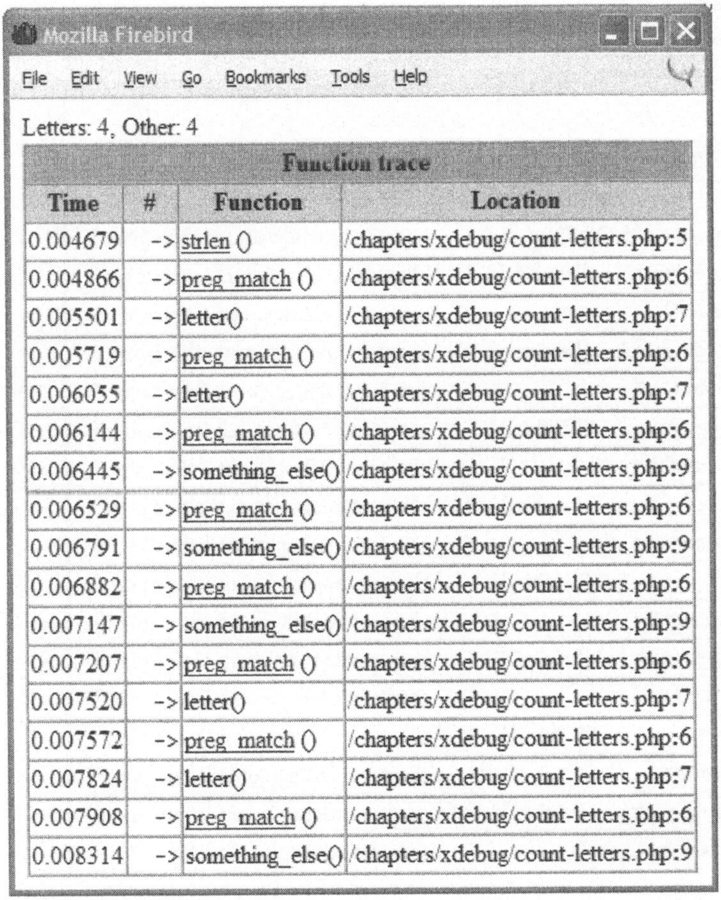

Mozilla Firebird

File Edit View Go Bookmarks Tools Help

Letters: 4, Other: 4

Function trace			
Time	**#**	**Function**	**Location**
0.004679	->	strlen ()	/chapters/xdebug/count-letters.php:5
0.004866	->	preg_match ()	/chapters/xdebug/count-letters.php:6
0.005501	->	letter()	/chapters/xdebug/count-letters.php:7
0.005719	->	preg_match ()	/chapters/xdebug/count-letters.php:6
0.006055	->	letter()	/chapters/xdebug/count-letters.php:7
0.006144	->	preg_match ()	/chapters/xdebug/count-letters.php:6
0.006445	->	something_else()	/chapters/xdebug/count-letters.php:9
0.006529	->	preg_match ()	/chapters/xdebug/count-letters.php:6
0.006791	->	something_else()	/chapters/xdebug/count-letters.php:9
0.006882	->	preg_match ()	/chapters/xdebug/count-letters.php:6
0.007147	->	something_else()	/chapters/xdebug/count-letters.php:9
0.007207	->	preg_match ()	/chapters/xdebug/count-letters.php:6
0.007520	->	letter()	/chapters/xdebug/count-letters.php:7
0.007572	->	preg_match ()	/chapters/xdebug/count-letters.php:6
0.007824	->	letter()	/chapters/xdebug/count-letters.php:7
0.007908	->	preg_match ()	/chapters/xdebug/count-letters.php:6
0.008314	->	something_else()	/chapters/xdebug/count-letters.php:9

Figure 12-1. The output of Listing 12-1 includes a function trace.

As you can see in Figure 12-1, the output of `xdebug_dump_function_trace()` is an HTML table with one row for each function call. The table shows the elapsed time into the program when the function was called, the nesting level of the function call (all of the function calls in Listing 12-1 happen at the top level), the function name, and the filename and line number of the function call. The function trace shows that `preg_match()` is called once for each character in `$phrase` and then either `letter()` or `something_else()` is called depending on what that character is.

You can tell Xdebug to also keep track of function parameters by turning on the `xdebug.collect_params` configuration setting. Figure 12-2 shows the output of Listing 12-1 with `xdebug.collect_params` activated.

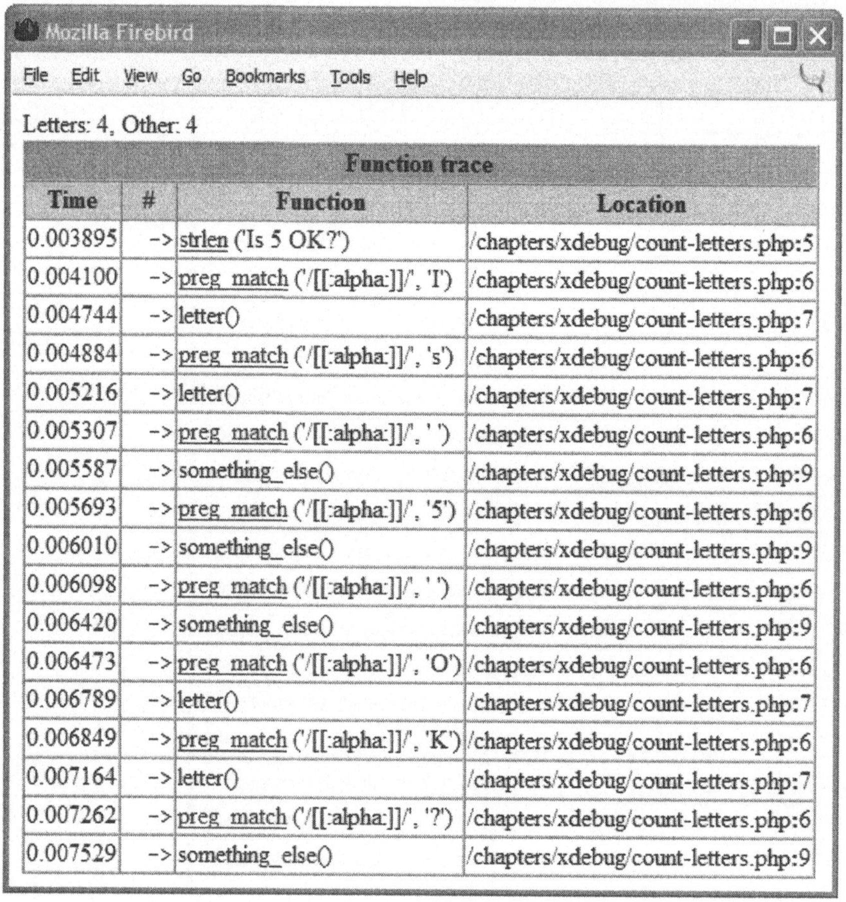

Mozilla Firebird

File Edit View Go Bookmarks Tools Help

Letters: 4, Other: 4

Function trace			
Time	#	Function	Location
0.003895	->	strlen ('Is 5 OK?')	/chapters/xdebug/count-letters.php:5
0.004100	->	preg_match ('/[[:alpha:]]/', 'I')	/chapters/xdebug/count-letters.php:6
0.004744	->	letter()	/chapters/xdebug/count-letters.php:7
0.004884	->	preg_match ('/[[:alpha:]]/', 's')	/chapters/xdebug/count-letters.php:6
0.005216	->	letter()	/chapters/xdebug/count-letters.php:7
0.005307	->	preg_match ('/[[:alpha:]]/', ' ')	/chapters/xdebug/count-letters.php:6
0.005587	->	something_else()	/chapters/xdebug/count-letters.php:9
0.005693	->	preg_match ('/[[:alpha:]]/', '5')	/chapters/xdebug/count-letters.php:6
0.006010	->	something_else()	/chapters/xdebug/count-letters.php:9
0.006098	->	preg_match ('/[[:alpha:]]/', ' ')	/chapters/xdebug/count-letters.php:6
0.006420	->	something_else()	/chapters/xdebug/count-letters.php:9
0.006473	->	preg_match ('/[[:alpha:]]/', 'O')	/chapters/xdebug/count-letters.php:6
0.006789	->	letter()	/chapters/xdebug/count-letters.php:7
0.006849	->	preg_match ('/[[:alpha:]]/', 'K')	/chapters/xdebug/count-letters.php:6
0.007164	->	letter()	/chapters/xdebug/count-letters.php:7
0.007262	->	preg_match ('/[[:alpha:]]/', '?')	/chapters/xdebug/count-letters.php:6
0.007529	->	something_else()	/chapters/xdebug/count-letters.php:9

Figure 12-2. A function trace with parameters

Xdebug can also log function calls to a file. Pass a filename to `xdebug_start_trace()`, and the function trace is written to that file. If the file already exists, then Xdebug appends trace information to the end of the file.

Additionally, `xdebug_get_function_trace()` returns an array holding the current function trace information. While `xdebug_dump_function_trace()` prints the trace information, `xdebug_get_function_trace()` provides the data in a format you can manipulate. Each element of the array that `xdebug_get_function_trace()` returns is an associative array. Table 12-1 describes the elements in these associative arrays.

Table 12-1. Information Returned by `xdebug_get_function_trace()`

Key	Value	Always Present?
`function`	Name of function	Yes
`file`	Full pathname of file the function was called from	Yes
`line`	Line in `file` that the function was called from	Yes
`time_index`	Time (in seconds) since the beginning of script execution when the function was called	Yes
`params`	Array of arguments to the function	Only if `xdebug.collect_params` is on
`memory_usage`	Amount of memory (in bytes) in use by the script when the function was called	Only if PHP is compiled with `--enable-memory-limit`

Listing 12-2 uses `xdebug_get_function_trace()` to produce a report of how many times each function is called.

Listing 12-2. Counting Function Calls

```
xdebug_start_trace();
function letter() { $GLOBALS['letter']++; }
function something_else() { $GLOBALS['something_else']++; }
$phrase = "Is 5 OK?";
for ($i = 0, $j = strlen($phrase); $i < $j; $i++) {
    if (preg_match('/[[:alpha:]]/', $phrase{$i})) {
        letter();
    } else {
        something_else();
    }
}
print "Letters: $letter, Other: $something_else\n";
$trace = xdebug_get_function_trace();
$functions_called = array();
// Count up each function call
foreach ($trace as $function_call) {
    $functions_called[$function_call['function']]++;
}
```

```
// Display the results
foreach ($functions_called as $function => $count) {
    print "Function $function() called $count time(s).\n";
}
```

Listing 12-2 prints the following:

```
Letters: 4, Other: 4
Function strlen() called 1 time(s).
Function preg_match() called 8 time(s).
Function letter() called 4 time(s).
Function something_else() called 4 time(s).
```

The function trace displayed by `xdebug_dump_function_trace()` or returned by `xdebug_get_function_trace()` is a listing of all function calls in a script up to that point. Xdebug can also produce a function stack trace, which is the list of functions called that have not yet finished. Listing 12-3 calls `xdebug_get_function_stack()` to produce a function stack trace inside its `show_output()` function.[3]

Listing 12-3. Displaying a Function Stack Trace

```
function check_input($var_name) {
    $len = strlen($GLOBALS[$var_name]);
    if (($len > 0) && ($len < 13)) {
        return true;
    } else {
        return false;
    }
}
function show_output($var_name) {
    print "$var_name --> " . $GLOBALS[$var_name] . "\n";
    $stack = xdebug_get_function_stack();
    print_r($stack);
}
function process_vars() {
    $vars = array('name');
    foreach ($vars as $var) {
        if (check_input($var)) {
            show_output($var);
        }
```

3. The `xdebug_get_function_stack()` function behaves like the PHP built-in function `debug_backtrace()`, which is available in PHP versions 4.3.0 and later. If you're using an earlier version of PHP, then you can rely on Xdebug for this functionality.

```
    }
}
$name = 'Ireneo Funes';
process_vars();
```

Listing 12-3 prints the following:

```
name --> Ireneo Funes
Array
(
    [0] => Array
        (
            [function] => {main}
            [file] => /books/php-gems/listing-12-3.php
            [line] => 0
            [params] => Array
                (
                )
        )
    [1] => Array
        (
            [function] => process_vars
            [file] => /books/php-gems/listing-12-3.php
            [line] => 23
            [params] => Array
                (
                )
        )
    [2] => Array
        (
            [function] => show_output
            [file] => /books/php-gems/listing-12-3.php
            [line] => 18
            [params] => Array
                (
                )
        )
```

Each element of the array returned by `xdebug_get_function_stack()` represents one level of the function stack. The first element, with `function` set to `{main}`, is for the top level of the program, outside of any function. Each subsequent array element corresponds to a function call. The second element of the array says that `process_vars()` was called on line 23 of the file, and the third element of the array says that `show_output()` was called on line 18 of the file. The `params` subarrays are empty if the xdebug.collect_params configuration setting is off. The function_stack() function obeys the collect_params setting just as xdebug_get_function_trace() does.

When your program has an error, it's helpful to look at the function stack trace. Instead of just a message containing the line number on which the error happened, you can see which functions called which other functions during the program execution before the error occurred. By default, Xdebug displays a function stack trace when an error occurs.[4] For example, consider Listing 12-4, which contains almost the same code as Listing 12-3. In Listing 12-4, however, the show_output() function doesn't call xdebug_get_function_stack() but incorrectly uses strcmp(). Figure 12-3 shows what the Xdebug function stack trace looks like in this error context.

Listing 12-4. Incorrect Use of strcmp() *in* show_output()

```
function check_input($var_name) {
    $len = strlen($GLOBALS[$var_name]);
    if (($len > 0) && ($len < 13)) {
        return true;
    } else {
        return false;
    }
}
function show_output($var_name) {
    print "$var_name --> " . $GLOBALS[$var_name] . "\n";
    if (strcmp($var_name)) {
        print "Good name.";
    }

}
function process_vars() {
    $vars = array('name');
    foreach ($vars as $var) {
        if (check_input($var)) {
            show_output($var);
        }
    }
}
$name = 'Ireneo Funes';
process_vars();
```

4. The function stack trace is displayed as long as the error_reporting configuration setting indicates that the error should be flagged. Xdebug doesn't display or log an error when PHP without Xdebug would display one—it just changes what is displayed or logged when an error happens.

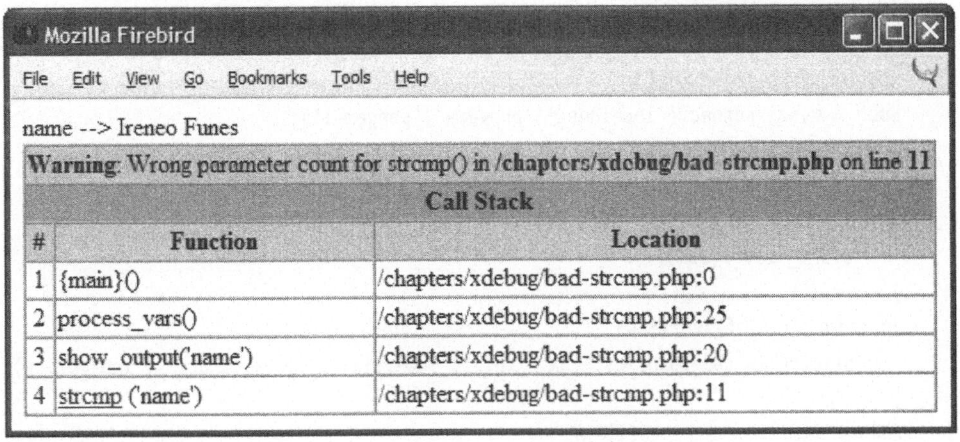

Mozilla Firebird

File Edit View Go Bookmarks Tools Help

name --> Ireneo Funes

Warning: Wrong parameter count for strcmp() in **/chapters/xdebug/bad strcmp.php** on line **11**

Call Stack		
#	Function	Location
1	{main}()	/chapters/xdebug/bad-strcmp.php:0
2	process_vars()	/chapters/xdebug/bad-strcmp.php:25
3	show_output('name')	/chapters/xdebug/bad-strcmp.php:20
4	strcmp ('name')	/chapters/xdebug/bad-strcmp.php:11

Figure 12-3. Displaying a function stack trace on error

If you don't want Xdebug to display function stack traces on error, set the `xdebug.default_enable` configuration setting to `off` or call `xdebug_disable()` in your code. Either of these actions restores PHP's standard error display formatting.

Profiling

The profiling capabilities of Xdebug provide reports on where your PHP programs spend their time while running. This lets you find code that is slow and directs you to what needs improvement. A profiler not only tells you how long a function call takes but how many times a function is called. Consider a program that calls a `match_strings()` function (which takes 0.1 seconds to run) 30 times and calls a `parse_input()` function (which takes 2 seconds to run) just once. If you make `match_strings()` twice as fast, cutting its running time to 0.05 seconds, the program is 1.5 seconds faster. If you make `parse_input()` twice as fast, you trim only 1 second from the program's runtime. Using a profiler wisely means focusing on improvements that produce the biggest decrease in total program runtime, taking into account the frequency that each function is called.

To start profiling, call `xdebug_start_profiling()`. This tells Xdebug to begin gathering statistics about your program.

To view profiling information, call `xdebug_dump_function_profile()` at the end of your program. Listing 12-5 prints data from a database table and then displays a function profile. Figure 12-4 shows the output of the program in Listing 12-5.

Listing 12-5. Printing Data from the Database and a Profile Report

```
xdebug_start_profiling();
$dbh = mysql_connect('localhost','phpgems','phpgems1');
mysql_select_db('phpgems');
$res = mysql_query('SELECT * FROM ice_cream');
while ($ob = mysql_fetch_object($res)) {
    print_flavor($ob);
}
function print_flavor($ob) {
    printf("%s (%d calories): $%.2f<br>", $ob->flavor, $ob->calories, $ob->price);
}
xdebug_dump_function_profile();
```

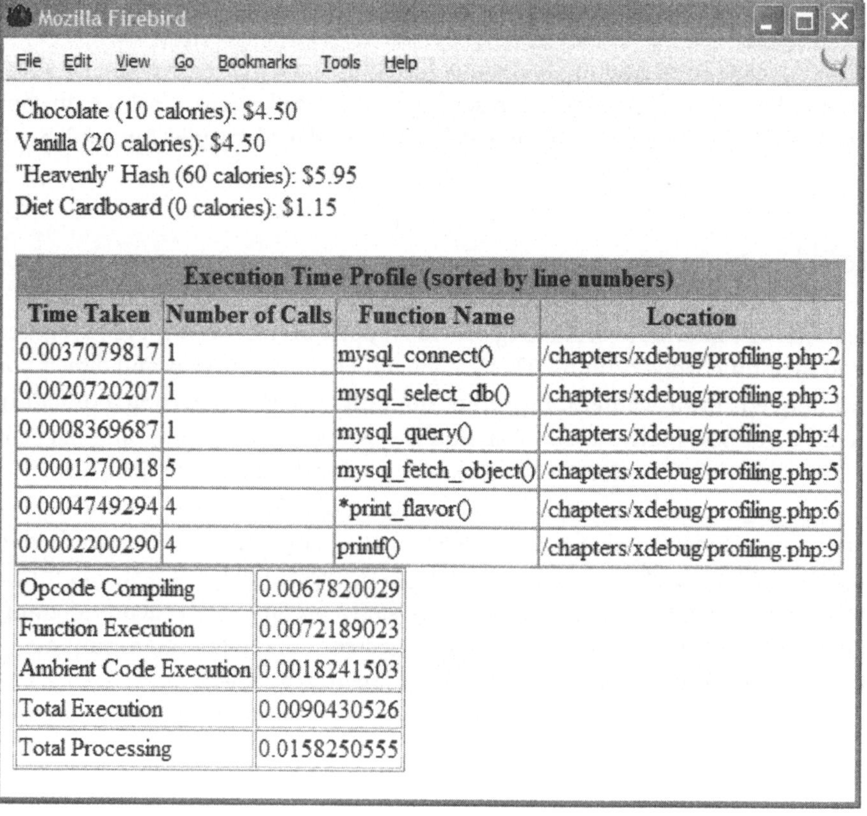

Execution Time Profile (sorted by line numbers)			
Time Taken	Number of Calls	Function Name	Location
0.0037079817	1	mysql_connect()	/chapters/xdebug/profiling.php:2
0.0020720207	1	mysql_select_db()	/chapters/xdebug/profiling.php:3
0.0008369687	1	mysql_query()	/chapters/xdebug/profiling.php:4
0.0001270018	5	mysql_fetch_object()	/chapters/xdebug/profiling.php:5
0.0004749294	4	*print_flavor()	/chapters/xdebug/profiling.php:6
0.0002200290	4	printf()	/chapters/xdebug/profiling.php:9

Opcode Compiling	0.0067820029
Function Execution	0.0072189023
Ambient Code Execution	0.0018241503
Total Execution	0.0090430526
Total Processing	0.0158250555

Figure 12-4. A profile report

The profile report in Figure 12-4 lists each function that was called, how much time was spent in the function, how many times the function was called, and the source file and line number from which the function was called. The asterisk next to `print_flavor()` indicates it is a user-defined function. After the list of function calls, the profile report includes some timing information for the whole script. The Opcode Compiling entry is the time spent compiling the script source into Zend Engine opcodes. This is time you could have saved if you had used a code cache. (See Chapter 13 for more information about code caches.) The Function Execution entry is the time spent executing functions in the main PHP script or any code in an included file. The Ambient Code Execution entry is the time spent executing code in the main PHP script outside of any function calls. The Total Execution entry is the sum of Function Execution and Ambient Code Execution, and the Total Processing entry is the sum of Opcode Compiling and Total Execution.

By default, `xdebug_dump_function_profile()` displays information sorted by script line number, but you can pass it an argument to organize the output differently. Table 12-2 lists the mode arguments that `xdebug_dump_function_profile()` accepts.

Table 12-2. Profiling Output Modes

Constant	Mode Type	Data Sorted By
XDEBUG_PROFILER_LBL	Execution Time Profile	Line numbers
XDEBUG_PROFILER_CPU	Execution Time Profile	Execution time
XDEBUG_PROFILER_NC	Execution Time Profile	Number of calls to each function
XDEBUG_PROFILER_FS_AV	Function Summary Profile	Average execution time
XDEBUG_PROFILER_FS_SUM	Function Summary Profile	Total execution time
XDEBUG_PROFILER_FS_NC	Function Summary Profile	Number of function calls
XDEBUG_PROFILER_SD_LBL	Stack Dump Profile	Line numbers
XDEBUG_PROFILER_SD_CPU	Stack Dump Profile	Execution time
XDEBUG_PROFILER_SD_NC	Stack Dump Profile	Number of calls to each function

You can also dump profiling information to a file. Pass the filename you want the information stored in to `xdebug_start_profiling()`, and make sure that the configuration setting `html_errors` is `off`. Then `xdebug_dump_function_profile()` writes the profile data to the file instead of displaying it on the screen.

A few other configuration settings tell Xdebug to automatically save profile data on all of your scripts to files. You don't even have to modify your scripts. Set `xdebug.auto_profile` to `1` and `xdebug.output_dir` to the directory in which you want the profiling information saved.[5] With these settings, each script execution is profiled and the script execution's profiling information is saved to a distinct file. By default, these profiling reports are in XDEBUG_PROFILER_LBL format. You can change that with the xdebug.auto_profile_mode configuration setting. For example, to have the automatic profiling reports in XDEBUG_PROFILER_FS_AV format, set xdebug.auto_profile_mode to XDEBUG_PROFILER_FS_AV.

Using Remote Debugging

Xdebug works with a remote debugging client to allow you to set breakpoints in your programs and examine variables while the program is running. You can engage in this kind of debugging activity for regular executable programs with a tool such as gdb or Microsoft Visual Studio. With Xdebug, you can do it for a PHP script. You access the script in the usual way through your Web browser with any submitted form variables and cookies, and Xdebug lets you peek inside while the script is running.

The remote debugging client, called debugclient, is not included if you install Xdebug using pear install. You can download a binary executable of debugclient from http://www.xdebug.org/ or build it from source. If you're using the source distribution of Xdebug, debugclient is in the debugclient subdirectory of the code. Change into that directory, run ./configure, and then run make. The debugclient file in that directory is the debugclient program.

To activate remote debugging with debugclient, set the xdebug.remote_enable configuration setting to 1. This can be in a php.ini file for CGI or CLI versions of PHP or in a Web server configuration file or .htaccess file for Web server–embedded versions of PHP.

When you start debugclient, it waits for a network connection from Xdebug inside a running PHP script. By default, Xdebug tries to connect to debugclient on the same machine on which the script is running. If you're running debugclient on a different host, set the xdebug.remote_host configuration setting to the name of that host.

If you do PHP development with a Web server on your desktop computer, then the default setting is fine. Run both the Web server and debugclient on your computer, and they will find each other. If you use a separate computer as a Web server, run debugclient on your desktop computer but set xdebug.remote_host on the Web server to the name of your desktop computer. When you run a PHP script while xdebug.remote_enable is turned on, Xdebug pauses the script before it

---

5. Make sure the user that PHP or your Web server is running as has write access to this directory.

starts executing and connects to debugclient. Once debugclient receives a connection, it displays a prompt, shown in Figure 12-5.

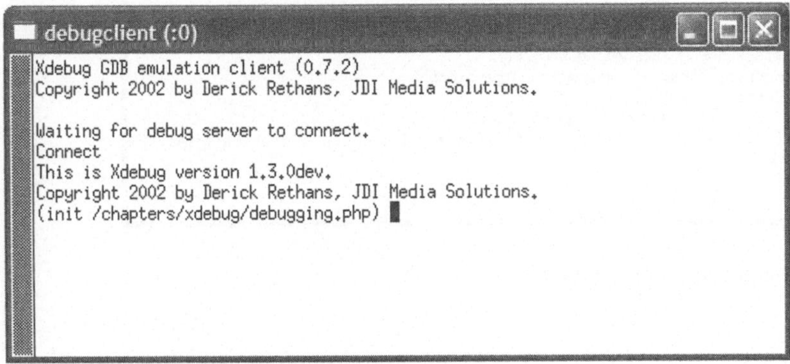

Figure 12-5. The initial debugclient *prompt*

At this prompt, you can set a breakpoint for later in the program with the break command. Entering break {main} stops execution at the first line of PHP encountered. Or, you can specify a function name or filename and line number. Figure 12-6 shows setting a breakpoint on the print_flavor() function. To specify a file and line number, separate them with a colon. For example, break debugging.php:56 sets a breakpoint on line 56 of the file debugging.php.

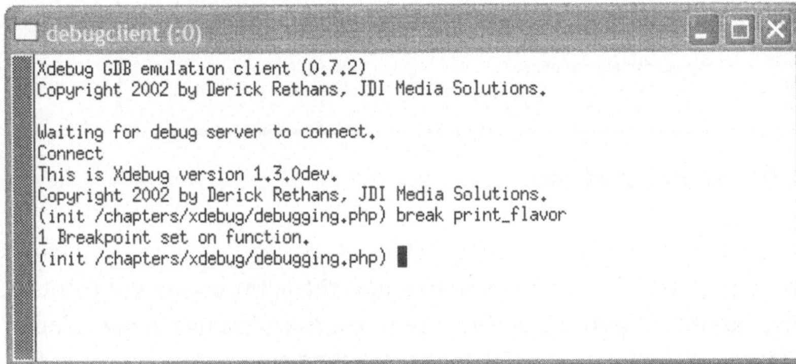

Figure 12-6. Setting a breakpoint in debugclient

Next, entering run executes the program up to the breakpoint. At this prompt, you can examine variables or a stack trace. Figure 12-7 shows execution stopped at the print_flavor() breakpoint.

```
debugclient (:0)
Waiting for debug server to connect.
Connect
This is Xdebug version 1.3.0dev.
Copyright 2002 by Derick Rethans, JDI Media Solutions.
(init /chapters/xdebug/debugging.php) break print_flavor
1 Breakpoint set on function.
(init /chapters/xdebug/debugging.php) run
Starting program: /chapters/xdebug/debugging.php
Breakpoint, print_flavor()
        at /chapters/xdebug/debugging.php:5
8           printf("%s (%d calories): $%.2f<br>", $ob->flavor, $ob->calories, $o
b->price);

(cmd)
```

Figure 12-7. Stopping at a breakpoint

The bt command shows a backtrace, which lists the functions called leading up to the point at which execution is stopped. Figure 12-8 shows the backtrace at the `print_flavor()` breakpoint.

```
debugclient (:0)
(init /chapters/xdebug/debugging.php) run
Starting program: /chapters/xdebug/debugging.php
Breakpoint, print_flavor()
        at /chapters/xdebug/debugging.php:5
8           printf("%s (%d calories): $%.2f<br>", $ob->flavor, $ob->calories, $o
b->price);

(cmd) bt
#1  print_flavor ()
    at /chapters/xdebug/debugging.php:5
#2  {main} ()
    at /chapters/xdebug/debugging.php:0

(cmd)
```

Figure 12-8. Displaying a backtrace

The `show` command lists variables in use, and the `print` command prints the value of a variable. Figure 12-9 uses `show` to list the variables in use inside the `print_flavor()` function and `print` to display the value of the `$ob` variable. Note that variable names must be passed to `print` without their leading `$`. In other words, use `print ob`, not `print $ob`.

```
debugclient (:0)
(cmd) bt
#1  print_flavor ()
    at /chapters/xdebug/debugging.php:5
#2  {main} ()
    at /chapters/xdebug/debugging.php:0

(cmd) show
$ob
(cmd) print ob
$ob = class stdClass {var $flavor = 'Chocolate'; var $price = '4.50'; var $calor
ies = '10'; var $id = '1'}

(cmd)
```

Figure 12-9. Displaying a variable and its value

The `show-local` command displays all the variables in use and their values. If you just want to see the value of one variable, use `print`. To see the values of all variables, use `show-local`.

Use `eval` to evaluate some PHP code. The code can contain variable names. For example, Figure 12-10 shows `eval` with code that finds the length of the current flavor.

```
debugclient (:0)
    at /chapters/xdebug/debugging.php:5
#2  {main} ()
    at /chapters/xdebug/debugging.php:0

(cmd) show
$ob
(cmd) print ob
$ob = class stdClass {var $flavor = 'Chocolate'; var $price = '4.50'; var $calor
ies = '10'; var $id = '1'}

(cmd) eval strlen($ob->flavor);
9

(cmd)
```

Figure 12-10. Evaluating PHP code in the debugging client

Listing 12-6 is a postfix calculator that supports addition, subtraction, multiplication, and division. Postfix is a way of writing math operations where the operator comes after the operands. In postfix format, you write `5 8 +` instead of `5 + 8`. Postfix is handy because it's much simpler for a computer to parse, and you don't have to worry about operator precedence. In regular notation, `5 + 8 * 9` could be `(5 + 8) * 9 = 117` or `5 + (8 * 9) = 77`. You have to rely on parentheses or on rules such as "do multiplication before addition" to come up with the same answer each time. In postfix, however, the expression `5 8 + 9 *` unambiguously means "add five plus eight and then multiply the result by nine."

Unfortunately, the calculator in Listing 12-6 doesn't work. Entering the expression `5 8 + 9 *` produces the result `22`, when it should produce `117: (5 + 8) * 9`. Use Xdebug's remote debugging capabilities to figure out what's broken.

Listing 12-6. Broken Postfix Calculator

```
<form method="POST" action="<?php echo $_SERVER['PHP_SELF']; ?>">
<textarea name="exp"><?php echo htmlspecialchars($_REQUEST['exp']); ?>
</textarea>
<br>
<input type="submit" value="Compute">
</form>
<?php
if (strlen($_REQUEST['exp'])) {
    $ops = preg_split('@([\s-+*/^])@',$_REQUEST['exp'],-1,
                          PREG_SPLIT_DELIM_CAPTURE|PREG_SPLIT_NO_EMPTY);
    $stack = array();
    foreach ($ops as $op) {
        if (is_numeric($op)) {
            array_push($stack,$op);
        } elseif (strlen(trim($op)) > 0) {
            $operand_1 = array_pop($stack);
            $operand_2 = array_pop($stack);
            switch ($op) {
            case '+':
                $result = $operand_1 + $operand_2;
                array_push($stack,$result);
                break;
            case '-':
                $result = $operand_1 - $operand_2;
                array_push($stack,$result);
                break;
            case '*':
                $result = $operand_1 + $operand_2;
                array_push($stack,$result);
                break;
            case '/':
                $result = $operand_1 / $operand_2;
                array_push($stack,$result);
                break;
            default:
                array_push($stack,$operand_1);
                array_push($stack,$operand_2);
```

```
                    print "Unknown operator: $op <br>";
                    break;
                }
            }
        }
        echo "Result: <b>$stack[0]</b>";
    }
```

Request the page once without remote debugging turned on to bring up the empty form. Run the `debugclient` binary, turn on `xdebug.remote_enable`, and submit the form with `5 8 + 9 *` in the text area. You need to inspect what happens each time the program processes one operation in the expression. A good way to do that is to set a breakpoint inside the `foreach($ops as $op)` loop, such as on line 12. To set a breakpoint on line 12 of `calc.php`, enter `break calc.php:12` at the debugclient prompt, as shown in Figure 12-11.

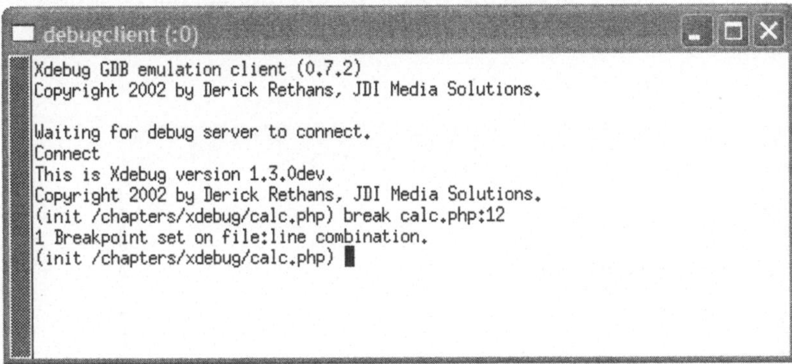

Figure 12-11. Setting a breakpoint at line 12 of `calc.php`

With the breakpoint set, start the program by typing `run` at the debugclient prompt. The program starts and runs until it reaches the breakpoint at line 12. Figure 12-12 shows what that looks like in `debugclient`. It also shows what the `$ops` array looks like at the breakpoint, using the `print` command.

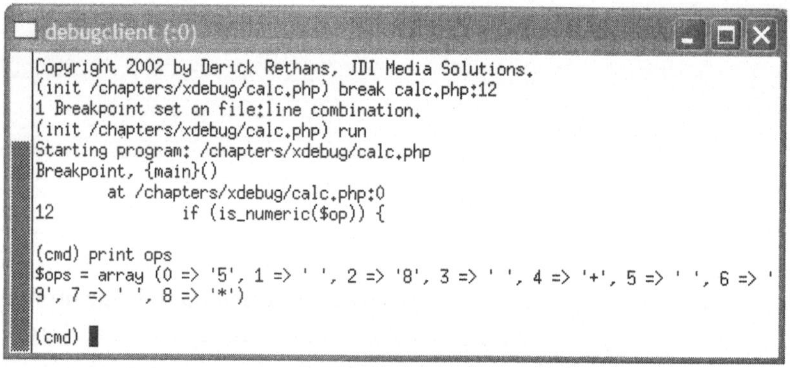

```
debugclient (:0)
Copyright 2002 by Derick Rethans, JDI Media Solutions.
(init /chapters/xdebug/calc.php) break calc.php:12
1 Breakpoint set on file:line combination.
(init /chapters/xdebug/calc.php) run
Starting program: /chapters/xdebug/calc.php
Breakpoint, {main}()
        at /chapters/xdebug/calc.php:0
12              if (is_numeric($op)) {

(cmd) print ops
$ops = array (0 => '5', 1 => ' ', 2 => '8', 3 => ' ', 4 => '+', 5 => ' ', 6 => '
9', 7 => ' ', 8 => '*')

(cmd)
```

Figure 12-12. Inspecting the value of `$ops`

To resume execution, type `continue` at the `debugclient` prompt. Because the breakpoint at line 12 is inside a loop, the program stops again when it returns to line 12. In Figure 12-13, the program has taken one trip through the `foreach` loop and has pushed the first number in the expression, `5`, onto the stack.

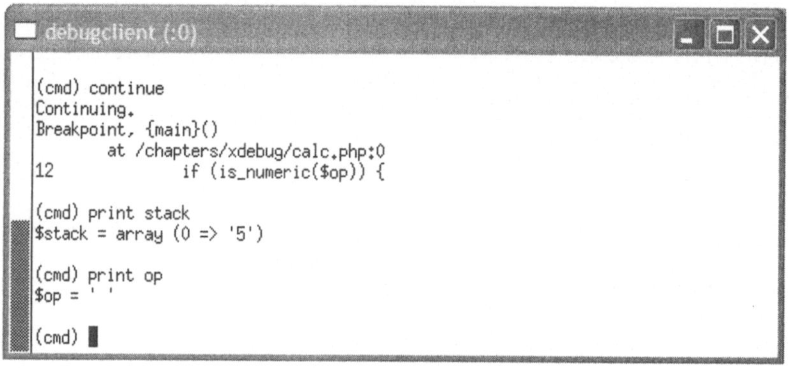

```
debugclient (:0)

(cmd) continue
Continuing.
Breakpoint, {main}()
        at /chapters/xdebug/calc.php:0
12              if (is_numeric($op)) {

(cmd) print stack
$stack = array (0 => '5')

(cmd) print op
$op = ' '

(cmd)
```

Figure 12-13. The `$stack` *variable after one loop iteration*

Figures 12-14, 12-15, and 12-16 show the values of `$stack` and `$op` at subsequent breakpoints: `8` is pushed onto the stack, then `5` and `8` are removed from the stack, and their sum, `13`, is pushed onto the stack.[6]

---

6. Intermediate steps where `$op` is " " are not shown.

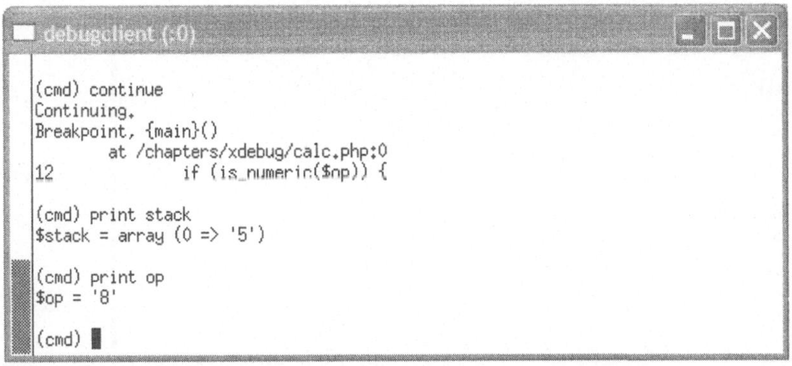

```
debugclient (:0)

(cmd) continue
Continuing.
Breakpoint, {main}()
        at /chapters/xdebug/calc.php:0
12              if (is_numeric($op)) {

(cmd) print stack
$stack = array (0 => '5')

(cmd) print op
$op = '8'

(cmd)
```

Figure 12-14. The `$stack` *variable as the program progresses*

```
debugclient (:0)

(cmd) continue
Continuing.
Breakpoint, {main}()
        at /chapters/xdebug/calc.php:0
12              if (is_numeric($op)) {

(cmd) print stack
$stack = array (0 => '5', 1 => '8')

(cmd) print op
$op = '+'

(cmd)
```

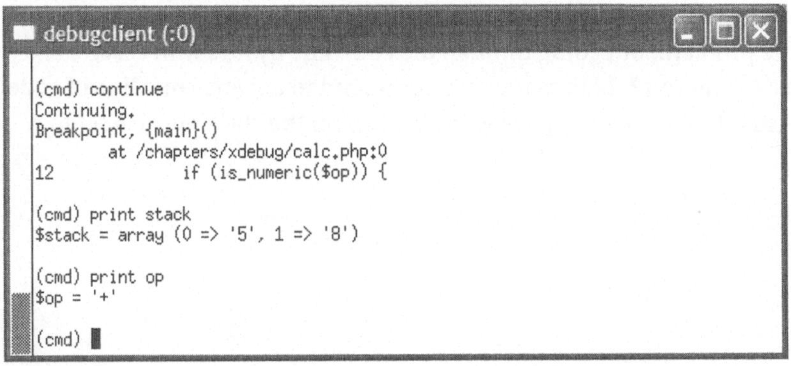

Figure 12-15. The `$stack` *variable as the program progresses further*

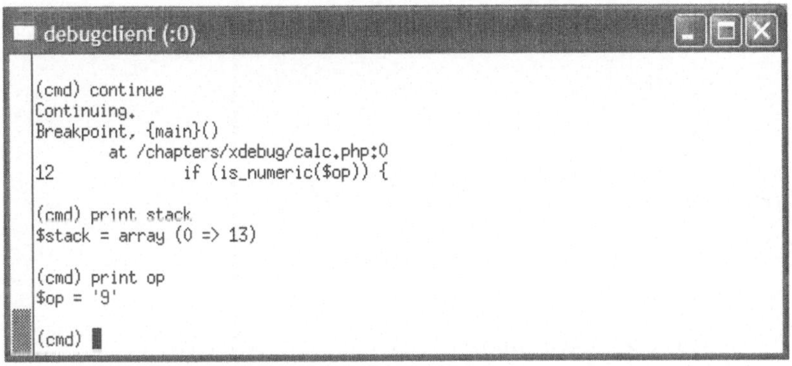

```
debugclient (:0)

(cmd) continue
Continuing.
Breakpoint, {main}()
        at /chapters/xdebug/calc.php:0
12              if (is_numeric($op)) {

(cmd) print stack
$stack = array (0 => 13)

(cmd) print op
$op = '9'

(cmd)
```

Figure 12-16. The `$stack` *variable as the program progresses even further*

So far, the calculator is running properly: Five plus eight is thirteen. So you haven't found the error yet. Figure 12-17 shows `debugclient` after another stop at the breakpoint: `9` is pushed onto the stack, joining `13`, and the current value of `$op` is `*`, for multiplication.

```
debugclient (:0)
(cmd) continue
Continuing.
Breakpoint, {main}()
        at /chapters/xdebug/calc.php:0
12              if (is_numeric($op)) {

(cmd) print stack
$stack = array (0 => 13, 1 => '9')

(cmd) print op
$op = '*'

(cmd)
```

Figure 12-17. The `$stack` *variable before the last operation*

If you're handy with multiplication and addition, you may have already figured out the problem, but going through the code line by line with `debugclient` makes it clear. Figure 12-18 uses the `step` command to advance one line of code at a time. This shows what happens with `13` and `9` on the stack and `$op` set to *.

```
debugclient (:0)
Breakpoint, {main}()
        at /chapters/xdebug/calc.php:0
12              if (is_numeric($op)) {

(cmd) print stack
$stack = array (0 => 13, 1 => '9')

(cmd) print op
$op = '*'

(cmd) step
15                  $operand_1 = array_pop($stack);

(cmd) step
16                  $operand_2 = array_pop($stack);

(cmd) step
17                  switch ($op) {

(cmd) step
18                  case '+':

(cmd) step
22                  case '-':

(cmd) step
26                  case '*':

(cmd) step
27                      $result = $operand_1 + $operand_2;

(cmd) step
28                      array_push($stack,$result);

(cmd) print operand_1
$operand_1 = '9'

(cmd) print operand_2
$operand_2 = 13

(cmd) print result
$result = 22

(cmd)
```

Figure 12-18. Stepping through the code

First, the two operands are popped off the stack and stored in `$operand_1` and `$operand_2`. Second, you move through the `switch` statement until you come to the `case` statement for *. Line 27 and line 28 operate on the operands and put the result on the stack. But as the `print` commands show, `$result` is `22`, not `113`. Line 27 mistakenly adds the two operands instead of multiplying them. Changing + to * in line 27 fixes the problem and makes the calculator work properly. At the end of a debugging session, press Ctrl+C to quit `debugclient`.

The remote debugging client gives you the opportunity to zero in on a code section that may be causing trouble and step through it, inspecting variables as you go. This technique is useful for finding bugs that may be hidden deep within your program. Because you can use the remote debugging client without modifying your programs, it's an attractive alternative to scattering `echo` statements in your code or using other haphazard methods.

CHAPTER 13

Accelerating with Code Caches

INSTALLING A CODE cache is quick and provides your Web site with an instantaneous speed increase. Code caches store compiled PHP pages, allowing PHP to avoid recompiling a page every time it is requested. If you're not currently using a code cache, read this chapter to learn the easiest way to boost performance with the smallest amount of effort. If you're already using a code cache, this chapter helps you optimize your setup.

The three code caches discussed in this chapter are the Alternative PHP Cache (APC), ionCube PHP Accelerator (PHPA), and Turck MMCache.[1] At their cores, they all perform the same task. Beyond that common core, however, they differ in speed, compatibility, ease of use, and design philosophy.

The speed differences, as illustrated in the benchmarks at the end of the chapter, are not tremendous. Your decision of which code cache to choose should be based on how much you value an easy-to-use administration tool, what operating system you use, and whether you want an open-source product. If speed is crucial for you, test each code cache against your particular mix of PHP scripts.

Tables 13-1, 13-2, and 13-3 list the advantages and disadvantages of the three code caches.

Table 13-1. APC

Advantages	**Disadvantages**
Easy to install from PECL.	No Windows support.
Source code is well-written and easy to read, which makes it excellent for learning.	No PHP 5 support yet.
Storage backend and locking mechanisms are very tweakable.	

1. Although there are also commercial code caches, such as the Zend Accelerator, this chapter focuses on freely available alternatives.

Table 13-2. PHPA

Advantages	Disadvantages
Binary-only distribution means installation is just copying a file.	No source code available.
Active support forum (`http://phpa.phorum.org/`).	Mediocre administrative interface.
	No PHP 5 support yet. No Windows or Mac OS X support.

Table 13-3. Turck MMCache

Advantages	Disadvantages
Windows support.	Erratic release schedule can be hard to keep up with.
PHP 5 support.	Code is harder to understand than APC.
Goes beyond code cache with additional functionality.	Big module (with all that additional functionality).
Easy-to-use Web interface.	Online documentation and support is sparse.
Compatible with Zend Optimizer.	

Working with APC: The Alternative PHP Cache

APC is an open-source code cache and optimizer. This section discusses APC 2.0b, which works with PHP 4 but not PHP 5. APC 2.0 runs on Linux, Mac OS X, FreeBSD, and OpenBSD. It is not available on Windows. APC does not work with PHP in CGI or CLI mode.

Installing APC

APC is a PECL module, so on Unix systems with PEAR configured properly, you can download, build, and install APC with this command:

```
% pear install apc
```

After the `pear` command completes, you must modify your `php.ini` file and restart your Web server, as described shortly. You can also build APC without PEAR. Download APC from `http://pecl.php.net/get/APC-2.0.tgz`, and unpack the `APC-2.0.tgz` file with `tar` and `gunzip`:

```
% gunzip -c APC-2.0.tgz | tar xf -
```

Next, change into the APC-2.0 directory, and run phpize to create the necessary configuration scripts:

```
% cd APC-2.0
% phpize
```

Now run ./configure and make to build APC:

```
% ./configure --enable-apc=shared
% make
```

Last, run make install to install APC. You may have to do this as the superuser so that you have appropriate permissions to copy the APC module into the PHP extension directory:

```
# make install
```

You can pass two arguments to ./configure that affect what APC is able to do. The --enable-mmap argument makes APC use memory-mapped files for its cache instead of shared memory. The --enable-sem argument makes APC use SystemV semaphores for locking instead of fcntl(2)-based file locks.

The combination of memory-mapped files and file locks is the safest because it avoids creating any semaphores or shared-memory segments that may not be destroyed properly after a Web server crash. Unless you're experiencing problems, though, stick with the default configuration for simplicity.

The default settings on Mac OS X may prevent you from using a shared memory cache larger than 4MB. You can either use sysctl to alter the system shared memory settings or compile with --enable-mmap to have a larger cache. As root, run these sysctl commands to increase the allowable size of shared memory segments:

```
# sysctl -w kern.sysv.shmmax=41943040
# sysctl -w kern.sysv.shmmin=1
# sysctl -w kern.sysv.shmmni=32
# sysctl -w kern.sysv.shmseg=8
# sysctl -w kern.sysv.shmall=8192
```

After make install copies the apc.so module file into the PHP extension directory, you must modify your php.ini file to make PHP APC-aware. Add an extension line such as this:

```
extension=apc.so
```

Next, restart your Web server so that PHP notices the change in `php.ini` and loads the APC extension. If APC is installed successfully, you'll see a message in your Web server error log that looks like this:

```
[apc-notice] APC version 2.0b -- startup complete
```

Configuring APC

Once you've added the extension line to `php.ini` and restarted your Web server, APC is active. It stores compiled opcode trees, function tables, and class tables in its cache and retrieves them when necessary. For basic APC usage, you don't need to do anything else. If you want more control over how APC operates, however, you can tweak configuration variables to tune your setup (see Table 13-4). You can set these variables only in `php.ini` or the Web server's configuration file, not inside scripts with `ini_set()` or in per-directory configuration files such as `.htaccess`.

Table 13-4. APC Configuration Variables

Configuration Variable	Default Value	Description
`apc.enabled`	1	Should APC be turned on?
`apc.optimization`	0	Should APC optimize compiled PHP code? If optimization is turned on, APC looks through the compiled code before it caches it and attempts to make it more efficient.
`apc.shm_size`	30	This is how large, in megabytes, the shared memory segments that APC uses for storage should be. On Mac OS X and other BSD-derived systems, you may have to set this to a much smaller value, such as 4.
`apc.shm_segments`	1	This is how many shared memory segments APC should use. If APC needs more shared memory for its cache and you can't increase `apc.shm_size` past a system maximum, increase this setting.
`apc.num_files_hint`	1000	APC creates two times `num_files_hint` slots in its cache. If you expect to cache more than 2,000 files with APC, increase this value.

Table 13-4. APC Configuration Variables (continued)

Configuration Variable	Default Value	Description
apc.gc_ttl	3600	When a file that is already in the cache is modified and then requested again, APC adds the new version of the file to the cache and marks the old version in the cache to be deleted. That old version isn't deleted until it has spent at least `apc.gc_ttl` seconds on the "to be deleted" list. This is to prevent problems if a Web server process crashes while it's executing a cached file. You usually don't need to modify this setting, but if you want more space in your cache, set `apc.gc_ttl` to `0` and APC won't wait at all to delete old file versions from the cache.
apc.mmap_file_mask		If APC is compiled with mmap support, this variable controls whether the mapped memory is backed by a file or by shared memory. To use a file, set `mmap_file_mask` to a pathname that ends with six X's in it, such as `/var/tmp/apc/cache.XXXXXX`. APC creates files whose names are the `mmap_file_mask` value with the X's replaced by unique identifiers. The `apc.shm_segments` variable controls how many files are created. To use shared memory–backed mmap, include the string `.shm` in the value (for example, `/apc-cache-XXXXXX.shm`). To use shared memory–backed mmap on Linux, you must have the `shmfs` file system mounted, and your `mmap_file_mask` value must start with a `/` and have no other `/` characters in it.
apc.filters		By default, APC caches every PHP file requested, included, or required. To exclude files from caching, set `apc.filters` to a comma-separated list of POSIX-extended regular expressions. If a filename matches one of the regular expressions, it isn't cached. For regular requests, the regexes are matched against the pathname of the PHP file requested (for example, `/www/docroot/catalog/buy.php`). For included or required files, the regexes are matched against the string passed to `include()` or `require()` (for example, `Auth/Auth.php` or `DB.php`), not the pathname of the included/required file.

This is an example of specifying apc.filters:

```
apc.filters = "user[0-9],/nocache/"
```

This prevents caching of files whose path contains /nocache/ or whose name contains user followed by a digit. Table 13-5 lists files that are and are not cached by this set of filters.[2]

Table 13-5. Cached and Filtered Files

Cached Requests	Filtered Requests	Cached Include /Require	Filtered Include /Require
/user.php	/user5.php	Auth/Auth.php	Auth/user9.php
/icecream.php	/luser627.php	DB.php	user/95.php
/useR9.php	/user9/pick.php	user.php	include/nocache/user.php
/user/all/list.php	/user/user95/ list/all.php	nocache/user.php	/nocache/user.php

When figuring out whether to filter a requested file, APC resolves any symbolic links and tests the filter against a file's true path. For example, with the previous filters, if you create a symbolic link called nocache in your document root directory that points to the document root directory itself, a request such as /nocache/user.php is resolved to /user.php and is not filtered. However, if you create an actual subdirectory called nocache, then a request to a file in that directory, such as /nocache/user.php, is filtered.

There is no symbolic link resolution for included/required files. The argument to include() or require() is compared to the filters. If it matches a filter, then the included/required file is not cached, no matter what the full pathname of the file is.

Files that change frequently are good candidates for exclusion from caching. Also, if the total compiled size of all your PHP files is larger than the amount of memory you can devote to the cache, then filters provide a way to select files for caching that provide the maximum benefit for your site: You can cache the large, complicated, or frequently accessed files.

Using APC

APC provides three user-level functions for you to interact with its cache. The apc_clear_cache() function removes everything from the cache, and the

2. If the path of the Web server's document root matches either filter, then no requests are cached; however, some included or required files may be.

apc_cache_info() and apc_sma_info() functions provide usage statistics on the cache and shared memory.

The apc_clear_cache() function is straightforward. Call it, and the cache is wiped out. Because APC automatically replaces old versions of files with new ones in the cache when the files change, you shouldn't need to clear the entire cache in regular practice. However, if you change a large number of files all at once, it can be more efficient to clear the entire cache rather than have APC compare modification times on each file as it is requested.

The apc_cache_info() function returns an associative array of information about the cache size and the files in the cache. Listing 13-1 is a program that formats the cache information for display. It tells you how many requests have been served out of the cache and which files are in the cache.

Listing 13-1. Displaying Information About APC's Cache

```
$cache = apc_cache_info();
echo '<h2>APC Cache Information</h2>';
echo '<ul>';
echo '<li>Allocated Cache Slots: ' . $cache['num_slots'] . '</li>';
echo '<li>Cache Hits: '             . $cache['num_hits'] . '</li>';
echo '<li>Cache Misses: '           . $cache['num_misses'] . '</li>';
printf("<li>Cache Hit Rate: %.2f%%</li>",
       $cache['num_hits']/($cache['num_hits'] + $cache['num_misses'])*100);
echo '</ul>';
echo '<h2>Cache Slot Information</h2>';
echo '<ul>';
if (count($cache['cache_list'])) {
    foreach ($cache['cache_list'] as $file) {
        print_file_info($file);
    }
} else {
    echo '<li>No files cached</li>';
}
echo '</ul>';
echo '<h2>Deleted List Information</h2>';
echo '<ul>';
if (count($cache['deleted_list'])) {
    foreach ($cache['deleted_list'] as $file) {
        print_file_info($file);
    }
} else {
    echo '<li>No files on deleted list</li>';
}
echo '</ul>';
```

```
function print_file_info($file) {
    echo '<li> File: ' . $file[filename] . '</li>';
    echo '<ul>';
    echo '<li> Hits: ' . $file['num_hits'] . '</li>';
    echo '<li> Created On: ' . strftime('%c',$file['creation_time']) . '</li>';
    echo '<li> Last Modified: ' . strftime('%c',$file['mtime']) . '</li>';
    if ($file['deletion_time']) {
        echo '<li> Marked for Deletion At: ' .
            strftime('%c',$file['deletion_time']) . '</li>';
    }
    if ($file['ref_count']) {
        echo '<li>Processes Currently Using This File: ' .
            $file['ref_count'] . '</li>';
    }
    echo "<li>Device/Inode: $file[device]/$file[inode] </li>";
    echo '</ul>';
}
```

The associative array returned by `apc_cache_info()` has five elements. The `num_slots`, `num_hits`, and `num_misses` elements are integers representing, respectively, the number of total cache slots, the number of times a request has been served from the cache, and the number of times the cache wasn't able to satisfy a nonfiltered request. The `cache_list` and `deleted_list` elements are arrays of files in the cache and files scheduled to be removed from the cache. Each element in the `cache_list` and `deleted_list` arrays is an associative array of information about a particular file.

Figure 13-1 shows the output of the program in Listing 13-1.

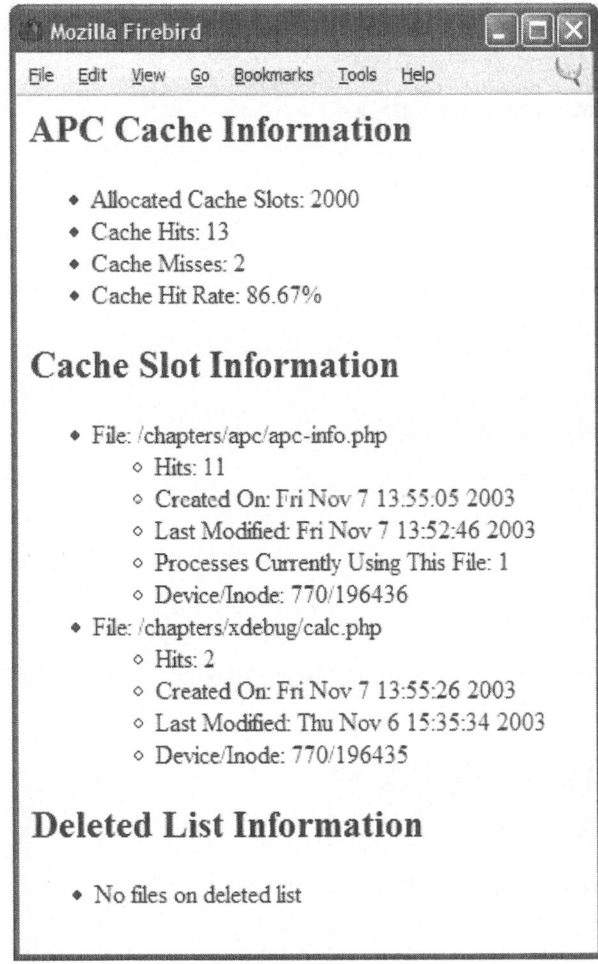

Figure 13-1. Cache information

The `apc_sma_info()` function returns an associative array with details of APC's shared memory usage. Listing 13-2 is a program that formats this information for display. It tells you how much of the allocated shared memory is used and how that memory is organized.

Listing 13-2. Displaying Information About APC's Shared Memory Usage

```
$sma = apc_sma_info();
echo '<h2>APC Shared Memory Information</h2>';
echo '<ul>';
echo '<li>Number of Segments: '          . $sma['num_seg'] . '</li>';
echo '<li>Segment Size: '                . $sma['seg_size'] . '</li>';
echo '<li>Available Memory (bytes): '    . $sma['avail_mem'] . '</li>';
```

```
printf('<li>Available Memory (%%): %.2f%%</li>',
       $sma['avail_mem'] / ($sma['num_seg'] * $sma['seg_size']) * 100);
echo '</ul>';
echo '<h2>Shared Memory Segment Information</h2>';
echo '<ul>';
foreach ($sma['block_lists'] as $i => $block_list) {
    echo "<li> Segment #$i </li>";
    echo '<ul>';
    foreach ($block_list as $j => $block) {
        echo "<li> Block $j </li>";
        echo '<ul>';
        echo "<li> Size: $block[size] </li>";
        echo "<li> Offset: $block[offset] </li>";
        echo '</ul>';
    }
    echo '</ul>';
}
echo '</ul>';
```

Figure 13-2 shows the output of the program in Listing 13-2.

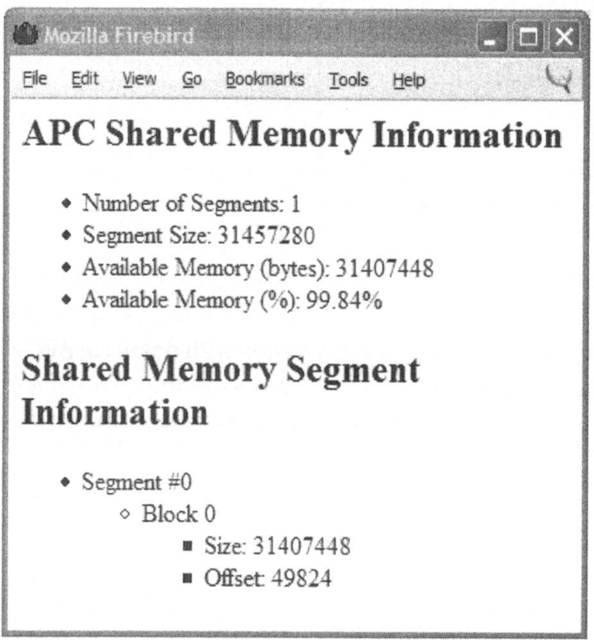

Figure 13-2. Shared memory information

The associative array returned by `apc_sma_info()` has four elements. The `num_seg`, `seg_size`, and `avail_mem` elements are integers representing, respectively, the number of shared memory segments in use by APC, the size of each segment, and the total amount of available memory in all segments. The `block_list` array element is itself an array with one element per shared memory segment. These elements describe the size of each segment and how much of the segment is in use.

Use the available memory calculation from Listing 13-2 to determine the appropriate size of your shared memory cache. The cache should be large enough to hold the compiled files for your Web site but not too much larger. Space that the shared memory cache reserves but doesn't use isn't available to other processes, so make sure you don't have excess memory devoted to APC.

Working with ionCube PHP Accelerator

PHPA is a free, closed-source code cache and optimizer. This chapter discusses PHPA 1.3.3r2, which works with PHP 4.*x*. PHPA runs on BSDI, FreeBSD, Linux, OpenBSD, and Solaris. It is not available on Windows or Mac OS X. PHPA does not work with PHP in CGI or CLI mode.

Installing PHPA

Download PHPA from `http://www.php-accelerator.co.uk/download.php`. Choose the right version of PHPA for your operating system and version of PHP. Unpack the `.tgz` file you've downloaded with `tar` and `gunzip`:

```
% gunzip -c php_accelerator-1.3.3r2_php-4.3.0_linux_i686-glibc2.1.3.tgz | \
  tar xf -
```

You need to copy the PHPA shared library file into your PHP extensions directory and the `phpa_cache_admin` program into a directory in your path. These commands should be executed as root. For example, if your PHP extensions directory is `/usr/local/lib/php/extensions/no-debug-non-zts-20020429`,[3] use this:

```
# cp php_accelerator_1.3.3r2.so \
  /usr/local/lib/php/extensions/no-debug-non-zts-20020429
# cp phpa_cache_admin /usr/local/bin
```

3. If you don't know what your PHP extensions directory is, find out by running `php-config --extension-dir`.

Next, add a zend_extension line to your php.ini file that makes PHP aware of PHPA:

```
zend_extension=/usr/local/lib/php/extensions/no-debug-non-zts-20020429/➥
php_accelerator_1.3.3r2.so
```

After php.ini is modified, restart your Web server so that PHPA is loaded. When PHPA is correctly installed, it creates a global variable called $_PHPA. Check for the presence of this variable to verify that PHPA is set up properly.

A var_dump($_PHPA) should produce the following:

```
array(3) {
  ["ENABLED"]=>
  bool(true)
  ["iVERSION"]=>
  int(10303)
  ["VERSION"]=>
  string(7) "1.3.3r2"
}
```

Configuring PHPA

PHPA uses both shared memory and the file system as the backing store for its cache. When a request comes in for a page that's not in the cache, PHPA stores the compiled page in a file and loads it into shared memory. On future requests for that page, the compiled page is retrieved from shared memory. The page may get purged from the shared memory cache if it hasn't been accessed for a while and PHPA needs the space for another page. If it's requested again after it was removed from memory, the compiled version is copied from the file cache back into shared memory. Before a compiled page is retrieved from the cache, PHPA checks to see whether the original file has changed since it was compiled. If it has changed, it is recompiled, and the new version is put into the cache.

Many configuration variables affect PHPA's behavior (see Table 13-6). In most circumstances, you don't need to adjust any of these variables—the default values work fine.

Table 13-6. PHPA Configuration Variables

Configuration Variable	Default Value	Description
phpa	on	Set this to off to disable PHPA.
phpa.tweaks	on	This controls PHPA's code optimizer. It should generally be left on.
phpa.enable_php_memory_bug_workaround	0	If PHP is configured with the --enable-memory-limit flag and you encounter a bug that causes PHP to report that a script has run out of memory when it hasn't, set this configuration variable to 1 to work around the bug.
File Cache Variables		
phpa.cache_dir	/tmp	Directory in which PHPA stores its cache files, one file per cached page or include. This path should be on a local, disk-based file system—no NFS or in-memory file systems.
phpa.file_perms	400	Octal cache file permissions. The default setting makes it so that only the Web server user can read the cache files. On a shared host, changing this variable to let the Web server group or other users read the cache files may make it possible for users to snoop on each other's Web site code.
phpa.ignore_files		A comma-separated list of strings. If the end of a file path matches one of these strings, the file is not cached on disk or in shared memory. For example, setting this variable to dog.php,cat.php prevents caching of files, in any directory, named dog.php, scat.php, and catdog.php. A file's full path with any symbolic links resolved is used in this comparison. Included/required files are not treated differently than requested files.
phpa.ignore_dirs		A comma-separated list of strings. If the beginning of a file path matches one of these strings, the file is not cached on disk or in shared memory. For example, setting this variable to /home prevents caching any files whose path begins with /home: /home/info.php, /home/user/public_html/index.php, and /homework/test.php. A file's full path with any symbolic links resolved is used in this comparison. Included/required files are not treated differently than requested files.

Table 13-6. PHPA Configuration Variables (continued)

Configuration Variable	Default Value	Description
phpa.cache_file_➥ prune_period	1h	The interval between scans of the file cache for pruning old files. The value 1h sets the interval to one hour. Similarly, s, m, and d in the value mean seconds, minutes, and days. For example, 3d is three days, 90s is 90 seconds, and 5m is five minutes. Scanning happens after a page request has completed, so if the prune period is set to one hour and your Web server goes 90 minutes between requests, the pruning happens after the second request, 90 minutes after the first request. To disable file pruning, set this variable to 0.
phpa.cache_file_ttl	1d	The age of a cached file that triggers its removal during a prune scan. If this value is 1d, a file is removed from the cache during a prune scan if the file was created more than a day before the prune scan and not recopied into shared memory in more than a day. If you restart your Web server on a regular schedule, set this value to a larger amount than the time between server restarts so that the files in the cache can be recopied to the shared memory cache when the server restarts.
Shared Memory Cache Variables		
phpa.shm_size	8	Size, in megabytes, of the shared memory cache. Only integer values are allowed for this setting. The PHPA documentation recommends setting this to 2MB larger than the maximum amount of memory usage that phpa_cache_admin reports. (The next section of this chapter explains how to use phpa_cache_admin.)
phpa.shm_key	0xc0deb00	Shared memory key. This can be specified as a decimal or hexadecimal number. You need to change this setting only if you want to run multiple independent copies of PHPA on the same machine or you have an existing application that is already using PHPA's default shared memory key.
phpa.shm_perms	666	Octal shared memory permissions. The default value lets any user read and write the shared memory segment. If you are on a shared server, this should be set to 600 (so only the Web server user can read and write the shared memory) or 660 (so only the Web server user and members of the Web server's group can read and write the shared memory).

Table 13-6. PHPA Configuration Variables (continued)

Configuration Variable	Default Value	Description
phpa.shm_user		User that owns the shared memory segment. This defaults to the user that Apache runs as, specified in the Apache configuration file. You may need to explicitly set this value and phpa.shm_group if you see errors in your Web server error log about problems creating the shared memory cache.
phpa.shm_group		Group that owns the shared memory segment. This defaults to the group that Apache runs as, specified in the Apache configuration file.
php.shm_release_➥ at_exit	on	Should the shared memory segment and semaphores in use be released when the Web server shuts down and deleted if found when the Web server starts? If you turn this off, the shared memory cache persists across Web server restarts.
phpa.shm_stats_➥ check_period	5m	The interval between scans of the shared memory cache to remove old entries.
phpa.shm_ttl	12h	The age of a cached file in shared memory that triggers its removal by the scan that removes old entries. If this value is 12h, the scan removes all files from shared memory that haven't been accessed via a page request or an include in 12 hours. The process of removing old entries from shared memory is separate from removing old files from the file cache. A file can be removed from shared memory but remain in the file cache. When a request for a page that is not in shared memory but in the file cache comes in, the compiled page is copied from the file cache into shared memory and used.
phpa.shm_ignore_files		A comma-separated list of strings. If the end of a file path matches one of these strings, the file is not cached in shared memory. This variable works just like phpa.ignore_files except that a matching file is still cached in the file cache.
phpa.shm_ignore_dirs		A comma-separated list of strings. If the beginning of a file path matches one of these strings, the file is not cached in shared memory. This variable works just like phpa_ignore_dirs except that a matching file is still cached in the file cache.

Table 13-6. PHPA Configuration Variables (continued)

Configuration Variable	Default Value	Description
phpa.shm_max_processes	512	The number of Apache processes that can connect to the shared memory cache. The PHPA documentation recommends this be set to one more than the Apache `MaxClients` parameter. If you have more Apache processes than the value of this setting, the extra processes still use the file cache.
phpa.lock_threshold0	10	An Apache process waiting to get a lock on the shared memory cache waits this many seconds before writing a warning to the log.
phpa.lock_threshold1	10	An Apache process waiting to get a lock on the shared memory cache waits this many seconds before breaking the cache lock and accessing the cache.

Using PHPA

The `phpa_cache_admin` tool is the only way to interact with PHPA. Aside from the `$_PHPA` variable, PHPA doesn't change anything in user-space PHP. There are no new PHP functions available to manipulate PHPA settings or get information about PHPA's behavior. Table 13-7 lists the arguments that `phpa_cache_admin` understands.

Table 13-7. Arguments to `phpa_cache_admin`

Argument (Short)	Argument (Long)	Description
-m	--mem-info	Display information about shared memory usage.
-f	--file-info	Display information about files in the memory cache.
-p	--process-info	Display information about Apache processes using the cache.
-v	--verbose	When combined with `-m`, `-f`, or `-p`, this argument causes `phpa_cache_admin` to display more detailed information.
-d	--disable-cache	Turn off the shared memory cache, but leave the file cache active.

Table 13-7. Arguments to phpa_cache_admin *(continued)*

Argument (Short)	Argument (Long)	Description
-e	--enable-cache	Turn on the shared memory cache.
-r	--reinitialise-cache*	Clear the cache. If you try to reinitialize the cache when there are requests in progress, the cache is disabled, reinitialized when the requests finish, and then enabled.
-D	--delete-cache	Delete the shared memory cache. This should be done only if a Web server crash has left PHPA's shared memory cache active. Deleting the cache while PHPA is running causes PHPA to break.
-k	--shm-key	With this argument, you can pass php_cache_admin a different shared memory key. Put the new key on the command line after the argument (for example, -k 0x1234abcd or --shm-key 328242).
-V	--version	Print PHPA's version number.
-h, -?	--help	Get a list of allowable arguments to phpa_cache_admin.

* This isn't a typo—it's the British spelling of *reinitialize.*

The -m argument provides information about the size and structure of the memory cache. By itself, it produces a cryptic blast of numbers:

```
% phpa_cache_admin -m
8388608:8372136:591936:606240:7758236:21964:0:0:m
```

With the -v option, it prints the same information, but it's formatted and annotated for easier human consumption:

```
% phpa_cache_admin -mv
shm size 8.0MB bytes
mempool size 8.0MB
mempool bytes allocated 578.1KB
mempool max bytes allocated 592.0KB
mempool bytes free 7.4MB
mempool overhead 21.4KB
cache enabled
```

The first six colon-delimited fields in the output of `phpa_cache_admin -m` correspond to the first six lines of output from `phpa_cache_admin -mv`. The first field/line is the size of the shared memory segment. Not all of this can be used for cache storage, so the second field/line (`mempool size`) gives the size of the shared memory cache. The next two fields/lines are the number of bytes in the cache currently in use and the maximum number of cache bytes ever in use since PHPA was started. The memory cache can shrink as old entries are removed. The fifth and sixth fields/lines report the amount of space left in the cache and the amount of cache storage used for file metadata and other housekeeping details.

The seventh field in the short output corresponds to the `cache enabled` line in the verbose output. If the cache was disabled, the verbose output would say `cache disabled`, and instead of a zero, the seventh field in the short output would be an epoch timestamp of when the cache was disabled.

Similarly, the eighth field in the short output relates to cache reinitialization. If PHPA is waiting for a request to complete before it can reinitialize the cache, the field contains an epoch time stamp of when the reinitialization request was made, and the verbose output gets a `cache set to reinitialise` line at its end. In the previous example, the eighth field is zero, and there is no `cache set to reinitialise` line, which means that the cache is humming along just fine and isn't waiting to reinitialize itself.

The trailing `m` in the short output indicates that the line contains memory information. This sets it apart from the file information lines, which end with `f`, and the process information lines, which end with `p`. If you write a program to parse the output of `phpa_cache_admin`, use these line-ending characters to interpret the information properly.

The `-f` argument to `phpa_cache_admin` reports on the compiled files in the memory cache. The output of `-fv` is as follows. The `-v` option applies formatting to time stamps, expiration times, and file sizes. Without `-v` these values are displayed as integers.

```
% phpa_cache_admin -fv
11h59m56s:12h:/chapters/phpa/qf-intro-example.php:5.5KB:770:48227:➥
2003-11-10 12.50.16:2003-11-10 12.54.20:f
11h59m56s:12h:/usr/local/lib/php/HTML_QuickForm/QuickForm.php:241.6KB:➥
833:49446:2003-09-18 16.39.14:2003-11-10 12.50.21:f
11h59m56s:12h:/usr/local/lib/php/PEAR.php:93.1KB:833:312785:2003-09-19➥
16.36.12:2003-11-10 12.50.21:f
11h59m56s:12h:/usr/local/lib/php/HTML_QuickForm/QuickForm/select.php:➥
58.5KB:833:49650:2003-08-12 10.13.02:2003-11-10 12.50.21:f
11h59m56s:12h:/usr/local/lib/php/HTML_QuickForm/QuickForm/element.php:➥
28.6KB:833:49670:2003-07-17 16.37.59:2003-11-10 12.50.21:f
11h59m56s:12h:/usr/local/lib/php/HTML_QuickForm/QuickForm/input.php:➥
13.8KB:833:49677:2003-07-17 16.37.59:2003-11-10 12.50.21:f
```

```
11h59m56s:12h:/usr/local/lib/php/HTML/Common.php:29.8KB:833:199181:➥
2003-08-13 09.50.54:2003-11-10 12.50.21:f
11h59m56s:12h:/usr/local/lib/php/HTML_QuickForm/QuickForm/submit.php:➥
4.6KB:833:49689:2003-07-17 16.37.59:2003-11-10 12.50.21:f
11h59m56s:12h:/usr/local/lib/php/HTML_QuickForm/QuickForm/text.php:➥
4.0KB:833:49690:2003-07-17 16.37.59:2003-11-10 12.50.21:f
11h59m56s:12h:/usr/local/lib/php/HTML_QuickForm/QuickForm/Renderer/Default.php➥
:47.9KB:833:49697:2003-07-17 16.37.59:2003-11-10 12.50.21:f
11h59m56s:12h:/usr/local/lib/php/HTML_QuickForm/QuickForm/Validate.php:➥
19.5KB:833:49702:2003-09-18 16.39.14:2003-11-10 12.50.21:f
11h59m56s:12h:/usr/local/lib/php/HTML_QuickForm/QuickForm/Renderer.php:➥
4.2KB:833:49783:2003-04-18 23.09.38:2003-11-10 12.50.21:f
```

The first file in the list, `/chapters/phpa/qf-intro-example.php`, requires `HTML/QuickForm.php`, which in turn requires all of the other files that have been compiled and put into the memory cache. Table 13-8 lists the meaning of each colon-delimited field in the lines of the file report.

Table 13-8. Fields in `phpa_cache_admin -f` *Output*

Field Number	Description
1	Time until the file is removed from the memory cache
2	Time-to-live setting in effect for the file
3	Source filename
4	Size of the compiled file in the file cache
5	Device number of the source file
6	Inode number of the source file
7	Last modification time of the source file
8	Time the source file was cached

The `-p` option to `phpa_cache_admin` displays details about the Web server processes that are using the cache. If no requests are being processed when you run `phpa_cache_admin`, you get information only about the number of processes that are using the cache:

```
% phpa_cache_admin -pv
cache in use by 3 procs (max 3)
0 active requests (max 2)
% phpa_cache_admin -p
3:3:0:2:p
```

The previous output means that three Web server processes are attached to the shared memory cache, which is the maximum number that have done so since PHPA was started. There are no active requests, and at most there have been two simultaneously active requests. The nonverbose output contains the same information in colon-delimited fields: number of processes using the cache, maximum number of processes to use the cache, number of active requests, and maximum number of simultaneously active requests.

If any requests are active when `phpa_cache_admin` runs, it also prints information about the active requests. With the `-v` flag, you are told the IDs of active Web server processes, how long ago the request started, and the pathnames of the files involved with the request:

```
% phpa_cache_admin -pv
cache in use by 3 procs (max 3)
1 active request (max 2)
Process 11093. Request started 2 seconds ago.
  Using /chapters/phpa/qf-intro-example.php
  Using /usr/local/lib/php/HTML_QuickForm/QuickForm.php
  Using /usr/local/lib/php/PEAR.php
  Using /usr/local/lib/php/HTML/Common.php
  Using /usr/local/lib/php/HTML_QuickForm/QuickForm/text.php
  Using /usr/local/lib/php/HTML_QuickForm/QuickForm/input.php
  Using /usr/local/lib/php/HTML_QuickForm/QuickForm/element.php
  Using /usr/local/lib/php/HTML_QuickForm/QuickForm/select.php
  Using /usr/local/lib/php/HTML_QuickForm/QuickForm/submit.php
  Using /usr/local/lib/php/HTML_QuickForm/QuickForm/Validate.php
  Using /usr/local/lib/php/HTML_QuickForm/QuickForm/Rule/Required.php
  Using /usr/local/lib/php/HTML_QuickForm/QuickForm/Rule.php
```

Without the `-v` flag, you actually get more information about each file used by the request. The colon-delimited fields in each line of output after the first contain the Web server process ID, epoch time stamp of request start, device number of the file, inode number of the file, and filename. Each line also ends with a `p` to indicate it's part of the process report output. This is what a nonverbose process report looks like:

```
% phpa_cache_admin -p
3:3:1:2:p
11093:1068492698:770:52665:/chapters/phpa/qf-intro-example.php:p
11093:1068492698:833:49446:/usr/local/lib/php /HTML_QuickForm/QuickForm.php:p
11093:1068492698:833:312785:/usr/local/lib/php/PEAR.php:p
11093:1068492698:833:199181:/usr/local/lib/php/HTML/Common.php:p
11093:1068492698:833:49690:/usr/local/lib/php/HTML_QuickForm/QuickForm/text.php:p
11093:1068492698:833:49677:/usr/local/lib/php/HTML_QuickForm/QuickForm/input.php:p
```

```
11093:1068492698:833:49670:/usr/local/lib/php/HTML_QuickForm/QuickForm/➥
element.php:p
11093:1068492698:833:49650:/usr/local/lib/php/HTML_QuickForm/QuickForm/select.php:p
11093:1068492698:833:49689:/usr/local/lib/php/HTML_QuickForm/QuickForm/submit.php:p
11093:1068492698:833:49702:/usr/local/lib/php/HTML_QuickForm/QuickForm/➥
Validate.php:p
11093:1068492698:833:297601:/usr/local/lib/php/HTML_QuickForm/QuickForm/➥
Rule/Required.php:p
11093:1068492698:833:51574:/usr/local/lib/php/HTML_QuickForm/QuickForm/Rule.php:p
```

Working with Turck MMCache

Turck MMCache is a free, open-source code cache and optimizer. This chapter discusses version 2.4.6, which works with PHP 4 and PHP 5. MMCache runs on Linux, Windows, and Mac OS X, but not with PHP in CGI or CLI mode. It also offers a cache API available from your PHP scripts, which you can use to store and retrieve arbitrary information in its cache. MMCache also has a session handler so that your PHP sessions can use its shared memory cache for storage.

Installing MMCache

Download MMCache from `http://sourceforge.net/project/showfiles.php?group_id=69426`. That page contains links to binary downloads for Windows and source code downloads for other operating systems.

To build MMCache from source, download `turck-mmcache-2.4.6.tar.gz` from the SourceForge download page listed previously and unpack it with `tar` and `gunzip`:

```
% gunzip -c turck-mmcache-2.4.6.tar.gz | tar xf -
```

Next, change into the `turck-mmcache-2.4.6` directory and run `phpize` to create the necessary configuration scripts:

```
% cd turck-mmcache-2.4.6
% phpize
```

Now, run `./configure` and `make` to build MMCache:

```
% ./configure --enable-mmcache=shared
% make
```

Last, run `make install` to install MMCache. You may have to do this as the superuser so that you have appropriate permissions to copy the MMCache module into the PHP extension directory:

```
# make install
```

If you're using a binary distribution for Windows, make sure to select the correct binary download that corresponds to the version of PHP you use. Unzip the downloaded archive, and copy the `mmcache.dll` file to your PHP extensions directory.

The next step is the same whether you are building from source or using a binary distribution. You must modify your `php.ini` file to make PHP MMCache-aware. On Unix, add an `extension` line like this:

```
extension=mmcache.so
```

On Windows, use this `extension` line:

```
extension=mmcache.dll
```

By default, MMCache uses both shared memory and disk for cache storage. On Windows, the default directory for disk storage is `c:\tmp\mmcache`. On Unix, it's `/tmp/mmcache`. Create this directory, and make sure the user your Web server runs as has write permission to it. If you don't want MMCache to store cache files on disk or you want MMCache to use a different directory, you can find the configuration variables that control those settings in the next section of this chapter.

Last, restart your Web server so that PHP notices the change in `php.ini` and loads the MMCache extension.

Configuring MMCache

MMCache gets to work after you've added the extension line to `php.ini` and restarted your Web server. However, MMCache offers a number of configuration variables you can use to adjust its performance and setup. Table 13-9 lists these variables.

Table 13-9. MMCache Configuration Variables

Configuration Variable	Default Value	Description	Settable Context*
`mmcache.enable`	1	Should MMCache be turned on?	`PHP_INI_ALL`
`mmcache.optimizer`	1	Should MMCache optimize compiled PHP code? If the optimizer is turned on, MMCache looks through the compiled code before it caches it and attempts to make it more efficient.	`PHP_INI_ALL`

Table 13-9. MMCache Configuration Variables (continued)

Configuration Variable	Default Value	Description	Settable Context*
mmcache.debug	0	Should MMCache log debugging information?	PHP_INI_SYSTEM
mmcache.check_mtime	1	Should MMCache automatically recompile PHP files if they've been modified?	PHP_INI_SYSTEM
mmcache.filter		A space- or tab-separated list of patterns that specifies files to include or exclude from caching. Some filter examples are listed after this table.	PHP_INI_ALL
mmcache.shm_size	0	How many megabytes of shared memory MMCache uses. When set to 0, MMCache uses the system default value.	PHP_INI_SYSTEM
mmcache.shm_max	0	The maximum size (in bytes) of a value that can be put into shared memory with mmcache_put(). You can specify an integer or an integer with k at the end to indicate kilobytes or an m to indicate megabytes. The values 1048576, 1024k, and 1M are treated as the same value. A value of 0 means there is no maximum.	PHP_INI_SYSTEM
mmcache.shm_ttl	0	If there is no space in shared memory for a new file, MMCache removes scripts that haven't been accessed for at least mmcache.shm_ttl seconds. A value of 0 means that files aren't removed from shared memory.	PHP_INI_SYSTEM
mmcache.shm_➥ prune_period	0	If MMCache can't allocate space in shared memory, it removes old scripts from memory if the previous attempt at script removal happened more than mmcache.shm_prune_period seconds ago. A value of 0 means that MMCache doesn't remove scripts from shared memory.	PHP_INI_SYSTEM

Table 13-9. MMCache Configuration Variables (continued)

Configuration Variable	Default Value	Description	Settable Context*
mmcache.shm_only	0	Should MMCache store compiled scripts on disk and shared memory? A value of 0 means yes. A value of 1 means that compiled scripts are stored only in shared memory. The value of this variable does not affect where other data such as sessions are stored.	PHP_INI_SYSTEM
mmcache.keys	shm_➥ and_disk	Where should keys be cached? Allowable values are shm_and_disk (cache in shared memory and disk), shm_only (shared memory), disk_only (disk), shm (shared memory but use disk if shared memory is full or the data is larger than mmcache.shm_max bytes), and none (no caching).	PHP_INI_SYSTEM
mmcache.sessions	shm_➥ and_disk	Where should session data be cached? Allowable values are the same as for mmcache.keys.	PHP_INI_SYSTEM
mmcache.content	shm_➥ and_disk	Where should content be cached? Allowable values are the same as for mmcache.keys.	PHP_INI_SYSTEM
mmcache.compress	1	Should MMCache compress cached content? When this is turned on, MMCache uses a content encoding such as gzip or deflate to deliver cached page output when it can.	PHP_INI_ALL
mmcache.cache_dir	/tmp/mmcache (Unix), c:\ tmp\mmcache (Windows)	Disk cache directory.	PHP_INI_SYSTEM
mmcache.admin.name		Required username to use the mmcache() function. If this variable or mmcache.admin.password isn't set, then MMCache doesn't require login to access mmcache().	PHP_INI_SYSTEM

Table 13-9. MMCache Configuration Variables (continued)

Configuration Variable	Default Value	Description	Settable Context*
mmcache.admin➥ .password		Required password to access the mmcache() function. The value of this variable should be the result of calling crypt() on the plain-text password. If this variable or mmcache.admin.name isn't set, then MMCache doesn't require login to access mmcache().	PHP_INI_SYSTEM

* PHP_INI_SYSTEM means that the variable can be set in php.ini or in the Web server configuration file. PHP_INI_ALL means that the variable can be set in php.ini, in the Web server configuration file, in a per-directory configuration file such as .htaccess, or inside a script.

The mmcache.filter variable controls what files MMCache caches. When mmcache.filter is empty, MMCache caches all PHP files. This is the default and the simplest mode of operation. To exclude files from being cached, set mmcache.filter to one or more patterns that each begin with !. These exclusion patterns can contain the shell wildcard * to match any number of characters and ? to match one character. You can also match a range of characters with square-bracket syntax: [a-z] matches any lowercase letter. The patterns are matched against the full pathname of a file with any symbolic links resolved. Requested files and included/required files are treated the same way. For example, the following filter excludes any files underneath the /opt/www/www.example.com directory from being cached:

```
mmcache.filter="!/opt/www/www.example.com/*"
```

Because filters are matched against full pathnames, you must account for directories in your patterns. If you want to exclude all files with a particular name in any directory, put */ before the filename. This filter excludes a file named nocache.php, whatever its directory, from being cached:

```
mmcache.filter="!*/nocache.php"
```

To use more than one pattern, separate each pattern with a space or a tab. These filters exclude any file named nocache.php and everything underneath the /opt/www/www.example.com directory:

```
mmcache.filter="!*/nocache.php !/opt/www/www.example.com/*"
```

Because spaces are used as a pattern delimiter, you can't use them in patterns, even if you backslash-escape them.

If all of the patterns in the filter list begin with `!`, then MMCache doesn't cache any file that matches any of the patterns but caches everything else. You can also instruct MMCache to cache *only* certain files with inclusion patterns. These use the same syntax as the exclusion patterns, but they don't begin with `!`. For example, this pattern tells MMCache to cache only files that are under the `/opt/www/cache.example.com` directory:

```
mmcache.filter="/opt/www/cache.example.com"
```

This pattern tells MMCache to cache only files either that are under the `/opt/www/cache.example.com` directory or that begin with a numeral and end with `.php`:

```
mmcache.filter="/opt/www.cache.example.com [0-9]*.php"
```

If you specify any inclusion patterns, then only files that match at least one of the inclusion patterns are cached. All other files are not cached.

You can specify both inclusion and exclusion patterns at the same time. This filter list caches everything under `/opt/www/cache.example.com` but doesn't cache any files that begin with `tmp` and end with `.php`, whatever their directory:

```
mmcache.filter="/opt/www/cache.example.com !*/tmp*.php"
```

If you specify both inclusion and exclusion patterns, the exclusion patterns take precedence. If a file matches both an inclusion pattern and an exclusion pattern, the exclusion pattern wins—the file is not cached even though it matches an inclusion pattern.

Using MMCache

MMCache provides an administrative interface for monitoring its cache via the `mmcache()` function. The `mmcache.php` script that comes with MMCache just calls the `mmcache()` function. If you've set `mmcache.admin.name` and `mmcache.admin.password`, then `mmcache()` outputs appropriate authentication headers to make sure that the correct username and password are provided before it displays information. You can use the `mmcache_password.php` script that comes with MMCache to help generate the appropriate values for `mmcache.admin.name` and `mmcache.admin.password`.

Figure 13-3 shows the page that `mmcache()` generates.

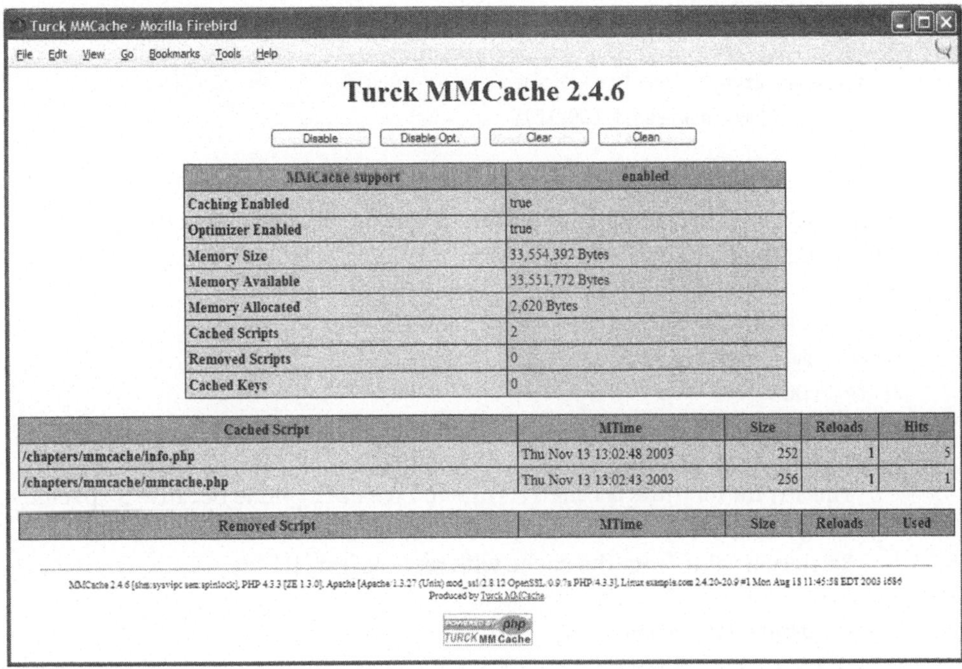

Figure 13-3. MMCache administrative interface

The MMCache administrative interface provides information about used and available memory, what files are in the cache, and what files have been removed from the cache. You can disable the cache by clicking the Disable button at the top of the page. When the cache is disabled, this button becomes an Enable button that you can click to re-enable the cache. Similarly, the Disable Opt button disables the optimizer and can be used to re-enable it.

The Clear button removes everything from the cache. The Clean button removes all expired data from the cache.

Storing Data in the Cache

In addition to automatically caching compiled PHP scripts, MMCache provides functions for you to store arbitrary data in the cache. Because this data is stored in shared memory, it's faster than a disk-based session store. Plus, the MMCache cache is not user-specific like `$_SESSION`. Use the MMCache cache for data that users should share. Also, MMCache provides a much easier interface than PHP's `shmop` or `shm_*` functions.

Each piece of data you store in the cache must be identified by a unique string key. The `mmcache_put()` function stores a value in the cache:

```
// store a scalar value
mmcache_put('flavor','Chocolate');
// store an array
mmcache_put('my cookies',$_COOKIE);
```

By default, keys are put into the cache with no expiration time. To have a key expire after a certain number of seconds, pass the number to `mmcache_put()` as a third argument:

```
// this lasts fifteen seconds
mmcache_put('flavor','Chocolate',15);
// this lasts one hour
mmcache_put('second flavor','Vanilla',3600);
```

This expiration time is called a Time to Live (TTL) value because it specifies how long the key stays alive in the cache.

Retrieve a value from the cache with `mmcache_get()`:

```
// This prints "Chocolate"
print mmcache_get('flavor');
// This makes $some_cookies an array
$some_cookies = mmcache_get('my cookies');
```

If you try to retrieve a value that has already expired, `mmcache_get()` returns `NULL`.

You can store scalars, arrays, and objects in the cache. You can't store resources such as database connection handles. If you store an object in the cache, make sure the object's class is defined before you retrieve the object from the cache.

Remove a key and value from the cache entirely with `mmcache_rm()`:

```
// Remove key "flavor" and its value
mmcache_rm('flavor');
// Remove key "my cookies" and its value
mmcache_rm('my cookies');
```

MMCache removes expired keys from the cache when it allocates new cache space, but you can also force all expired keys to be deleted by calling `mmcache_gc()`:

```
// Clean up expired keys
mmcache_gc();
```

Creating Locks

MMCache uses locks internally to serialize access to the cache. It also provides two functions so that you can use its locking facilities in your scripts. The mmcache_lock() function creates a lock, and the mmcache_unlock() function releases a lock. Any locks a request creates are also released automatically when the request finishes. Use locks to prevent multiple requests from accessing the same resource at the same time. For example, this code uses a lock to ensure exclusive access to a file:

```
mmcache_lock('guestbook');
$fh = fopen('/tmp/guestbook.txt','a') or die("Can't open guestbook");
fwrite($fh,$_REQUEST['guestbook_entry']);
fwrite($fh,"\n--\n");
fclose($fh);
mmcache_unlock('guestbook');
```

If one request is holding a lock and another request tries to create a lock of the same name, the second request waits for a tenth of a second and tries to create the lock again. The second request continues to wait and retry until the first request releases the lock.[4] Once the first request finishes, its lock is released, and the second lock can finally get it.

Storing Sessions in the Cache

When MMCache is loaded, it registers itself as an additional session handler back end. To use its cache for session storage, put this line in your php.ini or .htaccess file:

```
session.save_handler=mmcache
```

Content Caching

The code cache stores compiled pages so that when they are rerequested, they don't have to be compiled again. Instead, the compiled page is executed and the results are displayed. MMCache's content cache does a similar thing with page output. It stores the output of a PHP script in the cache and subsequently retrieves that output from the cache instead of rerunning the code in the page.

The mmcache_cache_page() function stores page output in content cache and retrieves it. If mmcache_cache_page() doesn't find anything in the cache corresponding to the key it's passed, it captures the output of the current page,

4. As of MMCache 2.4.6, if a request is waiting for a lock and is cancelled by the browser or reaches its time limit (from the max_execution_time configuration variable or set_time_limit() function), it doesn't end but keeps waiting for the lock.

displays it, and then stores it in the cache. Call mmcache_cache_page() with a key that uniquely identifies the page being called:

```
mmcache_cache_page($_SERVER['PHP_SELF']);
require 'DB.php';
$dbh = DB::connect('mysql://phpgems:phpgems1@david-vm.home/phpgems');
print '<table>';
print '<tr><th>Flavor</th><th>Price</th><th>Calories</th>';
$rows = $dbh->getAll('SELECT flavor,price,calories FROM ice_cream');
foreach ($rows as $row) {
    printf('<tr><td>%s</td><td>$%.02f</td><td>%d</td></tr>',
           $row[0], $row[1], $row[2]);
}
print '</table>';
```

The first time the page is requested, the code runs as usual: It opens a connection to the database, retrieves rows, and prints an HTML table. However, MMCache also stores the output of the page in the content cache, using the value of $_SERVER['PHP_SELF'] as a key. On a subsequent request for the same page, mmcache_cache_page() checks the content cache, finds an entry whose key is the value of $_SERVER['PHP_SELF'], prints the content stored in the cache, and exits. The remaining code on the page is not executed.

To remove a page from the content cache, call mmcache_rm_page() with the key of the page to remove:

```
mmcache_rm_page($_SERVER['PHP_SELF']);
mmcache_rm_page('/catalog/specials.php');
```

By default, mmcache_cache_page() caches the output of a page until it is removed by mmcache_rm_page(). You can give a cached page a TTL value in seconds by passing the value as the second argument to mmcache_cache_page(). For example, this caches output for 15 seconds:

```
mmcache_cache_page($_SERVER['PHP_SELF'], 15);
require 'DB.php';
$dbh = DB::connect('mysql://phpgems:phpgems1@david-vm.home/phpgems');
print '<table>';
print '<tr><th>Flavor</th><th>Price</th><th>Calories</th>';
$rows = $dbh->getAll('SELECT flavor,price,calories FROM ice_cream');
foreach ($rows as $row) {
    printf('<tr><td>%s</td><td>$%.02f</td><td>%d</td></tr>',
           $row[0], $row[1], $row[2]);
}
print '</table>';
```

The first time this page is requested, the code in it is executed and the output is stored in the content cache, the same as if no TTL value is specified. During a subsequent request for the page that happens in the following 15 seconds, `mmcache_cache_page()` retrieves the output from the content cache, prints it, and exits. After 15 seconds, however, `mmcache_cache_page()` behaves as if there is nothing stored in the cache under the specified key—it lets the code in the page run as usual, grabs the output, and puts it in the cache.

This feature is especially useful for pages that contain frequently updated dynamic data that may be too expensive to compute on every request. Instead of the database queries that grab a list of signed-in users or the ten most recent headlines executing every time your home page is requested, they can run only once every few minutes. This strikes a balance between providing up-to-date information and reducing server load.

Take care, however, to ensure that the key you pass to `mmcache_cache_page()` uniquely identifies the page being requested. If no form variables are submitted to the page, then `$_SERVER['PHP_SELF']` should suffice. However, if the page code takes different decisions based on form variables, user agent, or other information, you must include that information in the cache key. Otherwise, the output retrieved from the cache is not appropriate for the request. Use `serialize()` to make string representations of arrays of relevant data:

```
// use $_REQUEST in the cache key
mmcache_cache_page($_SERVER['PHP_SELF'] . serialize($_REQUEST));

// use $_GET, a cookie value, and the user_agent string
$cache_key_info = array($_GET, $_COOKIE['user_id'],
                        $_SERVER['HTTP_USER_AGENT']);
mmcache_cache_page($_SERVER['PHP_SELF'] . serialize($cache_key_info);
```

Only output generated after `mmcache_cache_page()` is called gets put into the cache. Code in the page before the call to `mmcache_cache_page()` runs each time the page is requested. For example, this page prints two time stamps:

```
print strftime('%c <br>');
mmcache_cache_page($_SERVER['PHP_SELF'], 10);
print strftime('%c');
```

The first time the page runs, the two timestamps are equal. Over the next ten seconds, as the page is rerequested, the first time stamp is updated and displays the current time while the second time stamp stays at its initial value. After ten seconds, when the page output expires from the content cache, the second time stamp is updated. Because the first `strftime()` is before `mmcache_cache_page()`, it runs each time the page is requested. The second `strftime()` is after `mmcache_cache_page()`, so its output is stored in the content cache and then subsequently retrieved. To cache an entire page, be sure that mmcache_cache_page() is at the top of the page.

Two other content cache functions cache smaller chunks of information than an entire page. The mmcache_cache_output() function caches the output of a specific piece of PHP code, and the mmcache_cache_result() function caches the return value of a piece of PHP code. Pass each of these functions a cache key, code to evaluate, and an optional TTL:

```
// Cache the current time for sixty seconds.
mmcache_cache_output('current_time',"print strftime('%H:%M');", 60);

// Do the same thing with mmcache_cache_result(). Since mmcache_cache_result()
// returns the cached value instead of printing it, you must print it yourself.
print mmcache_cache_result('current_time',"strftime('%H:%M');", 60);

// Make sure to pass variable names in single-quoted strings
// (or backslash-escape the dollar signs)
mmcache_cache_output('user_list','get_logged_in_users($dbh)', 120);
mmcache_cache_output('user_list',"get_logged_in_users(\$dbh)", 120);
```

Information put into the content cache with mmcache_cache_output() or mmcache_cache_result() is removed when its TTL expires. To explicitly remove the information, use mmcache_rm():

```
mmcache_rm('user_list');
mmcache_rm('current_time');
```

When paired with MMCache's core code caching abilities, the content cache functions let you operate extremely efficiently. Not only are your scripts compiled only once, but they are run only once. Using content caching for computationally expensive parts of your site can provide a huge performance boost.

Benchmarking Cache Performance

Table 13-6 displays the relative performance of PHPA, APC, and MMCache. The request used for the benchmark was retrieving the front page (/index.php) of a clean installation of XOOPS 2.0.5.[5] The only modification made to the XOOPS setup after installation was removing the three default ad banners from the XOOPS banners module so that each request would return an identical response with no banner rotation.

---

5. This is available for download from http://www.xoops.org/general/download.php.

The XOOPS front page was chosen for the benchmark because it involves many files. In addition to the `index.php` page requested, 38 other files are included or required to complete the request.

The tests were performed using Apachebench v1.3d (Revision 1.70) on a 1GHz Pentium III server with a MAXTOR 6L020J1 20GB IDE disk running Linux 2.4.18. The configuration tested is Apache 1.3.29 with PHP 4.3.4 and MySQL 4.0.15. Apachebench was run on the same server as Apache and MySQL and made Web requests via `localhost`.

The data in Table 13-10 reflect runs of 200 requests each. For each code cache, Apachebench was run five times for each concurrency value. The table includes the data for the best-performing run for each code cache and concurrency value. Each response body of each request was 3,724 bytes. Figure 13-4 shows the requests per second processed with each code cache.

Table 13-10. Code Cache Benchmark Results

	No Cache	PHPA 1.3.3r2	APC 2.0b (shm/fcntl)	APC 2.0b (shm/sem)	APC 2.0b (mmap/fcntl)	APC 2.0b (mmap/sem)	MMCache 2.4.6
1 Concurrent Request							
Total time (secs)	36.78	13.18	13.25	13.25	13.63	13.32	12.70
Requests/second	5.44	15.17	15.09	15.09	14.67	15.02	15.75
Performance relative to no cache	100%	279%	278%	278%	270%	276%	290%
5 Concurrent Requests							
Total time (secs)	37.50	13.37	13.42	13.55	13.42	13.63	12.79
Requests/second	5.33	14.96	14.90	14.76	14.90	14.68	15.64
Performance relative to no cache	100%	280%	279%	277%	279%	275%	293%
10 Concurrent Requests							
Total time (secs)	38.18	13.85	13.82	14.06	14.18	13.87	13.26
Requests/second	5.24	14.45	14.47	14.23	14.11	14.42	15.09
Performance relative to no cache	100%	276%	276%	272%	269%	275%	288%
20 Concurrent Requests							
Total time (secs)	40.03	14.87	14.46	14.81	15.20	14.90	13.88
Requests/second	5.00	13.45	13.83	13.51	13.16	13.43	14.41
Performance relative to no cache	100%	269%	277%	270%	263%	269%	288%

Table 13-10. Code Cache Benchmark Results (continued)

	No Cache	PHPA 1.3.3r2	APC 2.0b (shm/ fcntl)	APC 2.0b (shm/sem)	APC 2.0b (mmap/ fcntl)	APC 2.0b (mmap/sem)	MMCache 2.4.6
40 Concurrent Requests							
Total time (secs)	42.86	15.62	15.38	15.65	15.80	16.10	14.66
Requests/second	4.67	12.80	13.00	12.78	12.66	12.42	13.65
Performance relative to no cache	100%	274%	279%	274%	271%	266%	292%

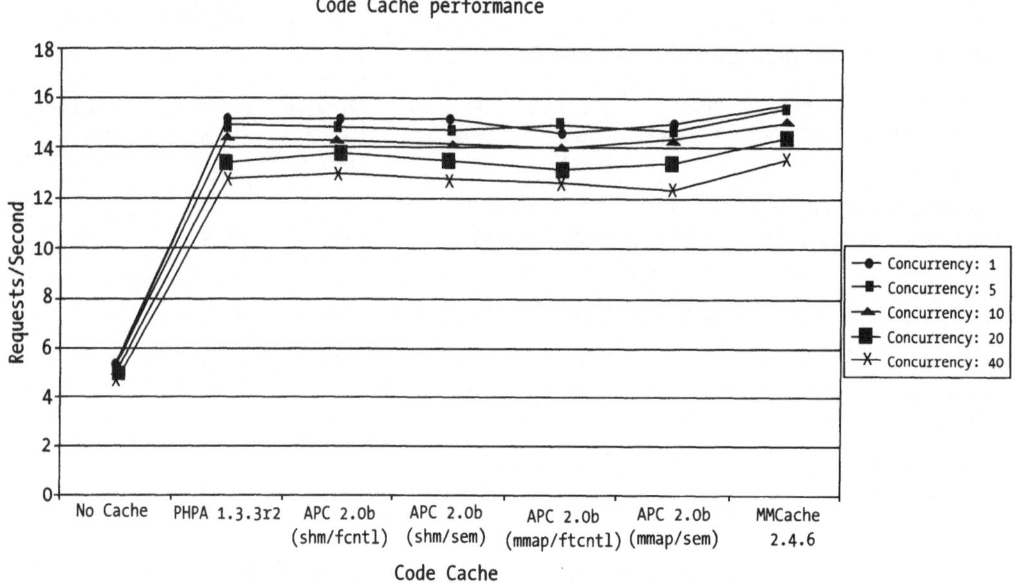

Figure 13-4. Requests/second performance for each code cache

Although MMCache demonstrates the best performance in the tests, it is only slightly better than PHPA or APC. Remember, if speed is such a critical factor in your choice of code cache, test each against your specific collection of PHP scripts.

Index

Symbols

A

B

C

D

G

H

I

J

K

L

M

N

O

P

Q

R

S

T

U

Z